FOUNDATIONS IN URBAN PLANNING

EBENEZER HOWARD

Including:

GARDEN CITIES OF TO-MORROW
by Ebenezer Howard, 1902

&

THE GARDEN CITY MOVEMENT UP-TO-DATE
by Ewart G. Culpin, 1913

Edited and with an introduction by
Thomas C. Myers, Jr.

De Facto Publishing • 2010

Published by De Facto Publishing
www.defactopublish.com

For information on volume purchases, licensing, or educational adoption, please visit the publisher's web site or email info@defactopublish.com.

"Garden Cities of To-Morrow" originally published in 1902 by Swan Sonnenschein & Co., Ltd., London. Supplemental information from "To-Morrow: A Peaceful Path to Real Reform" originally published in 1898 by Swan Sonnenschein & Co., Ltd., London.

"The Garden City Movement Up-To-Date," Second Edition, originally published in 1913 by The Garden Cities and Town Planning Association, London.

ISBN: 1453831452
EAN-13: 9781453831458

EDITOR'S INTRODUCTION

It is easy to understand why many readers of Ebenezer Howard's classic work "Garden Cities of To-Morrow" believe it to be a purely Utopian treatise, a sort of wishful-thinking manifesto from a century ago. To do so, however, is to grossly underestimate the impact of Howard's work on the field of urban planning and the importance of the ideas contained in this small volume.

While "Garden Cities" does contain elaborate rhetoric promoting reform and elevation of the working class, it also features a thoughtful, deliberate assessment of the criteria necessary for a well-functioning town. Howard goes to great lengths to propose specific arrangements of residential, commercial, and municipal resources and rightly identifies the necessary interdependencies between them. The conclusions drawn from his analysis are as insightful today as they were in the early twentieth century. They form the backbone of contemporary planning movements such as New Urbanism and Smart Growth and enlighten other planning theories regarding green spaces, transportation, and sustainability.

To properly understand Howard's work, one must first recognize the perspective upon which it was written—namely that of the deplorable conditions of working-class London around 1900, with its soot-choked slums and almost helpless working conditions. The average Londoner lived a miserable life: miniscule pay, terrible housing, poor health, tedious commutes, food and water shortages, and so on. It is understandable that Howard's basis for proposing a new town and a new means of urban development, realigned with country living, is a rational outcome of the existing conditions of that era.

First and foremost, Howard advocated the creation of limited-population, fixed-size (pedestrian-scale), self-sufficient and sustainable towns centered around well-planned transportation systems. Specifically, Howard's prototypical Garden City was 6,000 acres (including agricultural, commercial, residential, and municipal uses), of which 1,000 acres were for the city itself; featured a population of 32,000; and contained all of the features necessary for self-sufficient city and country life—town hall, schools, shops, farms, parks, residences, industry, etc. The town was sized so a resident could walk from one point to another in at most 600 yards; however, it also featured wide, well-landscaped streets, avenues, and boulevards interconnected in a radial grid, in addition to being connected to other towns via modern railways and roads.

In considering town extensions, Howard recognized the importance of maintaining physical constraints on the size of Garden City. He envisioned a "green belt" extending around the town, and as population demands warranted, a new Garden City would be established beyond this green belt, again connected via rail and road. By constraining Garden City's growth, Howard hoped to avert the sprawl of London's slums and maintain the proper scale of town-country living that he felt necessary for healthy living.

Howard approaches his reforms squarely from a capitalistic perspective, arguing that the path forward necessarily relies upon free enterprise—on the parts of the project's sponsors as well as its participants, the working class—in order to succeed. Where many Utopian writings rely upon socialistic principles of government and community-owned enterprise, Howard argues the exact opposite. He directly contrasts his "scheme" (to use his terminology) with those of socialism and communism, identifying the key differences and shortcomings of both. Detailed financial estimates accompanying the work illustrate the sources from which the venture could be funded as well as the municipal uses of such funds.

As further credibility to Howard's idea, a number of Garden Cities were actually realized in the early twentieth century, a true international movement, and many are still in existence today. An update to Howard's proposal is included in this volume—"The Garden City Movement Up-To-Date," published by the Garden City and Town Planning Association in 1913, inventorying and describing the progress of the movement's first decade. The results are impressive and give life to some of Howard's more esoteric ideas.

In terms of editing the two works included in this volume, several points are worth mentioning. First, Howard's "Garden Cities" has been repaginated to make it better fit this volume's trim size. In doing so, original page numbers have been maintained in its table of contents and index as well as throughout the text in the form of superscript notations indicating the start of each page. Thus, the reader can benefit from the improved flow but still rely on original page numbering where necessary. Additionally, an "editor's postscript" has been included after Howard's work and prior to the "Movement Up-To-Date" text. This brief summary provides examples of several illustrations and diagrams included in the 1898 edition of Howard's work ("To-Morrow: A Peaceful Path to Real Reform") but excluded from the 1902 version. In several cases, the missing diagrams actually help the readability of the later text. Also included in the postscript are present-day estimates of key financial figures included in Howard's work, to assist the reader in better understanding the scale of his proposal. Finally, the supplemental work, "The Garden City Movement Up-To-Date" by Ewart Culpin is included in facsimile copy, maintaining all original formatting and page numbering.

It is the editor's sincere hope that the modern practitioner or student of urban planning will find inspiration in this volume. This work is one in a series of "Foundations in Urban Planning" that aim to make available hard-to-find editions in an affordable, high quality format. —T. M.

VOLUME CONTENTS

GARDEN CITIES

OF

TO-MORROW

(BEING THE SECOND EDITION OF "TO-MORROW: A PEACEFUL
PATH TO REAL REFORM")

BY

EBENEZER HOWARD

"New occasions teach new duties;
Time makes ancient good uncouth;
They must upward still, and onward,
Who would keep abreast of Truth.
Lo, before us, gleam her camp-fires!
We ourselves must Pilgrims be,
Launch our 'Mayflower,' and steer boldly
Through the desperate winter sea,
Nor attempt the Future's portal
With the Past's blood-rusted key."
—"The Present Crisis."—J. R. Lowell.

LONDON
SWAN SONNENSCHEIN & CO., Ltd.
PATERNOSTER SQUARE
1902

CONTENTS

LIST OF ILLUSTRATIONS

GARDEN CITIES OF TO-MORROW.

INTRODUCTION.

"New forces, new cravings, new aims, which had been silently gathering beneath the crust of re-action, burst suddenly into view."—Green's "Short History of the English People," Chap. x.

"Change is consummated in many cases after much argument and agitation, and men do not observe that almost everything has been silently effected by causes to which few people paid any heed. In one generation an institution is unassailable, in the next bold men may assail it, and in the third bold men defend it. At one time the most conclusive arguments are advanced against it in vain, if indeed they are allowed utterance at all. At another time the most childish sophistry is enough to secure its condemnation. In the first place, the institution, though probably indefensible by pure reason, was congruous with the conscious habits and modes of thought of the community. In the second, these had changed from influences which the acutest analysis would probably fail to explain, and a breath sufficed to topple over the sapped structure."—*The Times*, 27th November, 1891.

In these days of strong party feeling and of keenly-contested social and religious issues, it might perhaps be thought difficult to find a single question having a vital bearing upon national life and well-being on which all persons, no matter of what political party, or of what [p. 10] shade of sociological opinion, would be found to be fully and entirely agreed. Discuss the temperance cause, and you will hear from Mr. John Morley that it is "the greatest moral movement since the movement for the abolition of slavery"; but Lord Bruce will remind you that "every year the trade contributes £40,000,000 to the revenue of the country, so that practically it maintains the Army and Navy, besides which it affords employment to many thousands of persons"—that "even the teetotalers owe much to the licensed victuallers, for if it were not for them the refreshment bars at the Crystal Palace would have been closed long ago." Discuss the opium traffic, and, on the one hand, you will hear that opium is rapidly destroying the *morale* of the people of China, and, on the other, that this is quite a delusion, and that the Chinese are capable, thanks to opium, of doing work which to a European is quite impossible, and that on food at which the least squeamish of English people would turn up their noses in disgust.

Religious and political questions too often divide us into hostile camps; and so, in the very realms where calm, dispassionate thought and pure emotions are the essentials of all advance towards right beliefs and sound principles of action, the din of battle and the struggles of contending hosts are more forcibly suggested to the onlooker than the really sincere love of truth and love of country which, one may yet be sure, animate nearly all breasts.

There is, however, a question in regard to which one can scarcely find any difference of opinion. It is well-nigh universally agreed by men of all parties, not only in England, but all over Europe and America and our [p. 11] colonies, that it is deeply to be deplored that the people should continue to stream into the already over-crowded cities, and should thus further deplete the country districts.

Lord Rosebery, speaking some years ago as Chairman of the London County Council, dwelt with very special emphasis on this point: —

"There is no thought of pride associated in my mind with the idea of London. I am always haunted by the awfulness of London: by the great appalling fact of these millions cast down, as it would appear by hazard, on the banks of this noble stream, working each in their own groove and their own cell, without regard or knowledge of each other, without heeding each other, without having the slightest idea how the other lives—the heedless casualty of unnumbered thousands of men. Sixty years ago a great Englishman, Cobbett, called it a wen. If it was a wen then, what is it now? A tumour, an elephantiasis sucking into its gorged system half the life and the blood and the bone of the rural districts."—March, 1891.

Sir John Gorst points out the evil, and suggests the remedy:

"If they wanted a permanent remedy of the evil they must remove the cause; they must back the tide, and stop the migration of the people into the towns, and get the people back to the land. The interest and the safety of the towns themselves were involved in the solution of the problem."—*Daily Chronicle*, 6th November, 1891.

Dean Farrar says:

"We are becoming a land of great cities. Villages are stationary or receding; cities are enormously increasing. And if it be true that great cities tend more and more to become the graves of the physique of our race, can we wonder at it when we see the houses so foul, so squalid, so ill-drained, so vitiated by neglect and dirt?" [p. 12]

Dr. Rhodes, at the Demographic Congress, called attention to

"the migration which was going on from the English agricultural districts. In Lancashire and other manufacturing districts 35 per cent. of the population were over 60 years of age, but in agricultural districts they would have over 60 per cent. Many of the cottages were so abominable that they could not call them houses, and the people so deteriorated in physique that they were not able to do the amount of work which able-bodied persons should do. Unless something was done to make the lot of the agricultural labourer better, the exodus would go on, with what results in the future he dared not say."—*Times*, 15th August, 1891.

The Press, Liberal, Radical, and Conservative, views this grave symptom of the time with the same alarm. *The St. James's Gazette*, on June 6, 1892, remarks:

"How best to provide the proper antidote against the greatest danger of modern existence is a question of no mean significance."

The Star, 9th October, 1891, says:

"How to stem the drift from the country is one of the main problems of the day. The labourer may perhaps be restored to the land, but how will the country industries be restored to rural England?"

The Daily News, a few years ago, published a series of articles, "Life in our Villages," dealing with the same problem.

Trade Unionist leaders utter the same note of warning. Mr. Ben Tillet says:

"Hands are hungry for toil, and lands are starving for labour." [p. 13]

Mr. Tom Mann observes:

"The congestion of labour in the metropolis is caused mainly by the influx from the country districts of those who were needed there to cultivate the land."

All, then, are agreed on the pressing nature of this problem, all are bent on its solution, and though it would doubtless be quite Utopian to expect a similar agreement as to the value of any remedy that may be proposed, it is at least of immense importance that, on a subject thus universally regarded as of supreme importance, we have such a consensus of opinion at the outset. This will be the more remarkable and the more hopeful sign when it is shown, as I believe will be conclusively shown in this work, that the answer to this, one of the most pressing questions of the day, makes of comparatively easy solution many other problems which have hitherto taxed the ingenuity of the greatest thinkers and reformers of our time. Yes, the key to the problem how to restore the people to the land—that beautiful land of ours, with its canopy of sky, the air that blows upon it, the sun that warms it, the rain and dew that moisten it—the very embodiment of Divine love for man—is indeed a *Master-Key*, for it is the key to a portal through which, even when scarce ajar, will be seen to pour a flood of light on the problems of intemperance, of excessive toil, of restless anxiety, of grinding poverty—the true limits of Governmental interference, ay, and even the relations of man to the Supreme Power.

It may perhaps be thought that the first step to be taken towards the solution of this question—how to restore the people to the land—would involve a careful [p. 14] consideration of the very numerous causes which have hitherto led to their aggregation in large cities. Were this the case, a very prolonged enquiry would be necessary at the outset. Fortunately, alike for writer and for reader, such an analysis is not, however, here requisite, and for a very simple reason, which may be stated thus: —Whatever may have been the causes which have operated in the past, and are operating now, to draw the people into the cities, those causes may all be summed up as "attractions"; and it is obvious, therefore, that no remedy can possibly be effective which will not present to the people, or at least to considerable portions of them, greater "attractions" than our cities now possess, so that the force of the old "attractions" shall be overcome by the force of new "attractions" which are to be created. Each city may be regarded as a magnet, each person as a needle; and, so viewed, it is at once seen that nothing short of the discovery of a method for constructing magnets of yet greater power than our cities possess can be effective for re-distributing the population in a spontaneous and healthy manner.

So presented, the problem may appear at first sight to be difficult, if not impossible, of solution. "What," some may be disposed to ask, "can possibly be done to make the country more attractive to a work-a-day people than the town—to make wages, or at least the standard of physical comfort, higher in the country than in the town; to secure in the country equal possibilities of social intercourse, and to make the prospects of advancement for the average man or woman equal, not to say superior, to those enjoyed in our large cities?" The issue one constantly finds presented in a form very similar to that. The [p. 15] subject is treated continually in the public press, and in all forms of discussion, as though men, or at least working-men, had not now, and never could have, any choice or alternative, but either, on the one hand, to stifle their love for human society—at least in wider relations than can be found in a strangling village—or, on the other hand, to forego almost entirely all the keen and pure delights of the country. The question is universally considered as though it were now, and for ever must remain, quite impossible for working people to live in the country and yet be engaged in pursuits other than agricultural; as though crowded, unhealthy cities were the last word of economic science; and as if our present form of industry, in which sharp lines divide agricultural from industrial pursuits, were necessarily an enduring one. This fallacy is the very common one of ignoring altogether the possibility of alternatives other than those presented to the mind. There are in reality not only, as is so constantly assumed, two alternatives—town life and country life—but a third alternative, in which all the advantages of the most energetic and active town life, with all the beauty and delight of the country, may be secured in perfect combination; and the certainty of being able to live this life will be the magnet which will produce the effect for which we are all striving—the spontaneous movement of the people from our crowded cities to the bosom of our kindly mother earth, at once the source of life, of happiness, of wealth, and of power. The town and the country may, therefore, be regarded as two magnets, each striving to draw the people to itself—a rivalry which a new form of life, partaking of the nature of both, comes to take part in. This may be illustrated [p. 16] by a diagram of "The Three Magnets," in which the chief advantages of the Town and of the Country are set forth with their corresponding drawbacks, while the advantages of the Town-Country are seen to be free from the disadvantages of either.

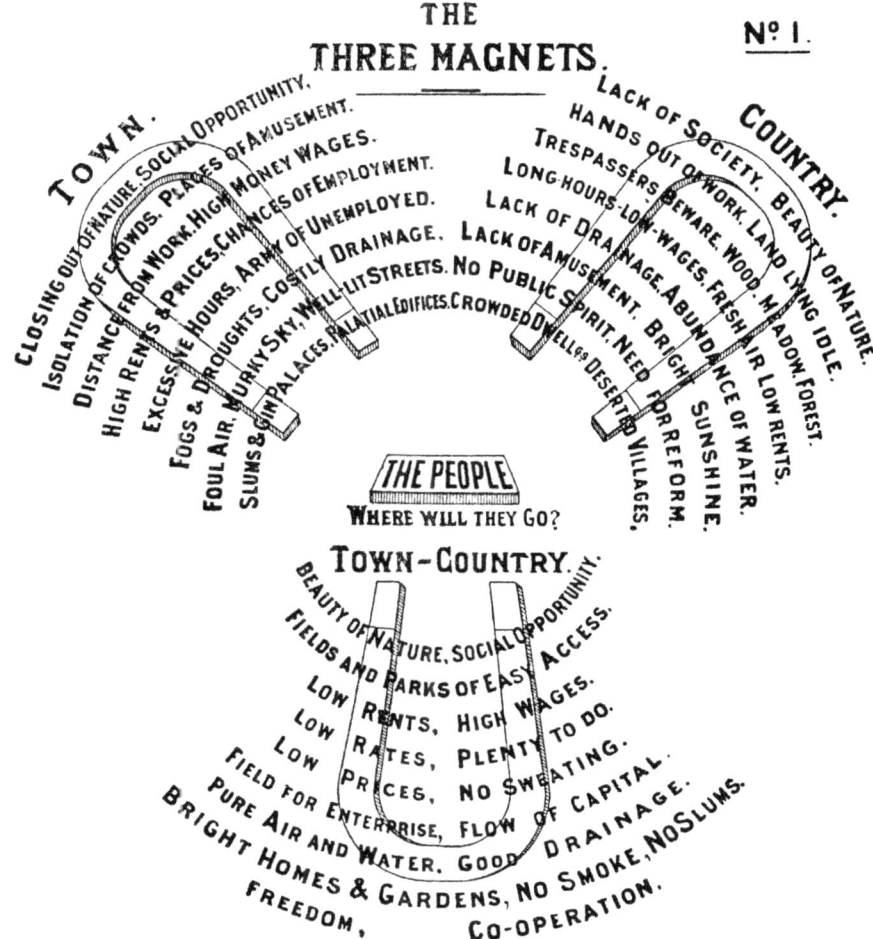

The Town magnet, it will be seen, offers, as compared with the Country magnet, the advantages of high wages, opportunities for employment, tempting prospects of advancement, but these are largely counterbalanced by high rents and prices. Its social opportunities and its places of amusement are very alluring, but excessive hours of toil, distance from work, and the "isolation of crowds" tend greatly to reduce the value of these good things. The well-lit streets are a great attraction, especially in winter, but the sunlight is being more and more shut out, while the air is so vitiated that the fine public buildings, like the sparrows, rapidly become covered with soot, and the very statues are in despair. Palatial edifices and fearful slums are the strange, complementary features of modern cities.

The Country magnet declares herself to be the source of all beauty and wealth; but the Town magnet mockingly reminds her that she is very dull for lack of society, and very sparing of her gifts for lack of capital. There are in the country beautiful vistas, lordly parks, violet-scented woods, fresh air, sounds of rippling water; but too often one sees those threatening words, "Trespassers will be prosecuted." Rents, if estimated by the acre, are certainly low, but such low rents are the natural fruit of low wages rather than a cause of substantial comfort; while long hours and lack of amusements forbid the bright sunshine and the pure air to gladden the hearts [p. 17] of the people. The one industry, agriculture, suffers frequently from excessive rainfalls; but this wondrous harvest of the clouds is seldom properly ingathered, so that, in times of drought, there is frequently, even for drinking purposes, a most insufficient supply.[1] Even the natural healthfulness of the country is largely lost for lack of proper drainage and other sanitary conditions, while, in parts almost deserted by the people, the few who remain are yet frequently huddled together as if in rivalry with the slums of our cities.

But neither the Town magnet nor the Country magnet represents the full plan and purpose of nature. Human society and the beauty of nature are meant to be enjoyed together. The two magnets must be made one. As man and woman by their varied gifts and faculties supplement each other, so should town and country. The town is the symbol of society—of mutual help and

---

[1] Dr. Barwise, Medical Officer of Health for the County Council of Derbyshire, giving evidence before a Select Committee of the House of Commons, on 25th April, 1894, on the Chesterfield Gas and Water Bill, said, in answer to Question 1873: "At Brimington Common School I saw some basins full of soapsuds, and it was all the water that the whole of the children had to wash in. They had to wash one after another in the same water. Of course, a child with ringworm or something of that kind might spread it through the whole of the children.... The schoolmistress told me that the children came in from the playground hot, and she had seen them actually drink this dirty water. In fact, when they were thirsty there was no other water for them to have."

friendly cooperation, of fatherhood, motherhood, brotherhood, sisterhood, of wide relations between man and man—of broad, expanding sympathies—of science, art, culture, religion. And the country! The country is the symbol of God's [p. 18] love and care for man. All that we are and all that we have comes from it. Our bodies are formed of it; to it they return. We are fed by it, clothed by it, and by it are we warmed and sheltered. On its bosom we rest. Its beauty is the inspiration of art, of music, of poetry. Its forces propel all the wheels of industry. It is the source of all health, all wealth, all knowledge. But its fulness of joy and wisdom has not revealed itself to man. Nor can it ever, so long as this unholy, unnatural separation of society and nature endures. Town and country *must be married*, and out of this joyous union will spring a new hope, a new life, a new civilisation. It is the purpose of this work to show how a first step can be taken in this direction by the construction of a Town-country magnet; and I hope to convince the reader that this is practicable, here and now, and that on principles which are the very soundest, whether viewed from the ethical or the economic standpoint.

I will undertake, then, to show how in "Town-country" equal, nay better, opportunities of social intercourse may be enjoyed than are enjoyed in any crowded city, while yet the beauties of nature may encompass and enfold each dweller therein; how higher wages are compatible with reduced rents and rates; how abundant opportunities for employment and bright prospects of advancement may be secured for all; how capital may be attracted and wealth created; how the most admirable sanitary conditions may be ensured; how beautiful homes and gardens may be seen on every hand; how the bounds of freedom may be widened, and yet all the best results of concert and co-operation gathered in by a happy people. [p. 19]

The construction of such a magnet, could it be effected, followed, as it would be, by the construction of many more, would certainly afford a solution of the burning question set before us by Sir John Gorst, "how to back the tide of migration of the people into the towns, and to get them back upon the land."

A fuller description of such a magnet and its mode of construction will form the theme of subsequent chapters. [p. 20]

CHAPTER I.

THE TOWN-COUNTRY MAGNET.

"I will not cease from mental strife,
Nor shall my sword sleep in my hand,
Till we have built Jerusalem
In England's green and pleasant land."
—Blake.

"Thorough sanitary and remedial action in the houses that we have; and then the building of more, strongly, beautifully, and in groups of limited extent, kept in proportion to their streams and walled round, so that there may be no festering and wretched suburb anywhere, but clean and busy street within and the open country without, with a belt of beautiful garden and orchard round the walls, so that from any part of the city perfectly fresh air and grass and sight of far horizon might be reachable in a few minutes' walk. This the final aim."—John Ruskin, "Sesame and Lilies."

THE reader is asked to imagine an estate embracing an area of 6,000 acres, which is at present purely agricultural, and has been obtained by purchase in the open market at a cost of £40[1] an acre, or £240,000. The purchase money is supposed to have been raised on mortgage debentures, bearing interest at an average rate not ex- [p. 21] ceeding £4 per cent.[2] The estate is legally vested in the names of four gentlemen of responsible position and of undoubted probity and honour, who hold it in trust, first, as a security for the debenture-holders, and, secondly, in trust for the people of Garden City, the Town-country magnet, which it is intended to build thereon. One essential feature of the plan is that all ground rents, which are to be based upon the annual value of the land, shall

---

[1] This was the average price paid for agricultural land in 1898: and, though this estimate may prove far more than sufficient, it is hardly likely to be much exceeded.

[2] The financial arrangements described in this book are likely to be departed from in form, but not in essential principle. And until a definite scheme has been agreed upon, I think it better to repeat them precisely as they appeared in "To-Morrow," the original title of this book—the book which led to the formation of the Garden City Association. See Appendix.

be paid to the trustees, who, after providing for interest and sinking fund, will hand the balance to the Central Council of the new municipality,[1] to be employed by such Council in the creation and maintenance of all necessary public works—roads, schools, parks, etc.

The objects of this land purchase may be stated in various ways, but it is sufficient here to say that some of the chief objects are these: To find for our industrial population work at wages of *higher purchasing power*, and to secure healthier surroundings and more regular employment. To enterprising manufacturers, co-operative societies, architects, engineers, builders, and mechanicians of all kinds, as well as to many engaged in various professions, it is intended to offer a means of securing new and better employment for their capital and talents, while to the agriculturists at present on the estate, as well as to those who may migrate [p. 22] thither, it is designed to open a new market for their produce close to their doors. Its object is, in short, to raise the standard of health and comfort of all true workers of whatever grade—the means by which these objects are to be achieved being a healthy, natural, and economic combination of town and country life, and this on land owned by the municipality.

Garden City, which is to be built near the centre of the 6,000 acres, covers an area of 1,000 acres, or a sixth part of the 6,000 acres, and might be of circular form, 1,240 yards (or nearly three-quarters of a mile) from centre to circumference. (Diagram 2 is a ground-plan of the whole municipal area, showing the town in the centre; and Diagram 3, which represents one section or ward of the town, will be useful in following the description of the town itself—a **description which is, however, merely suggestive, and will probably be much departed from.**)

Six magnificent boulevards—each 120 feet wide—traverse the city from centre to circumference, dividing it into six equal parts or wards. In the centre is a circular space containing about five and a half acres, laid out as a beautiful and well-watered garden; and, surrounding this garden, each standing in its own ample grounds, are the larger public buildings—town hall, principal concert and lecture hall, theatre, library, museum, picture-gallery, and hospital.

The rest of the large space encircled by the "Crystal Palace" is a public park, containing 145 acres, which includes ample recreation grounds within very easy access of all the people.

Running all round the Central Park (except where it [p. 23] is intersected by the boulevards) is a wide glass arcade called the "Crystal Palace," opening on

---

[1] This word, "municipality," is not used in a technical sense.

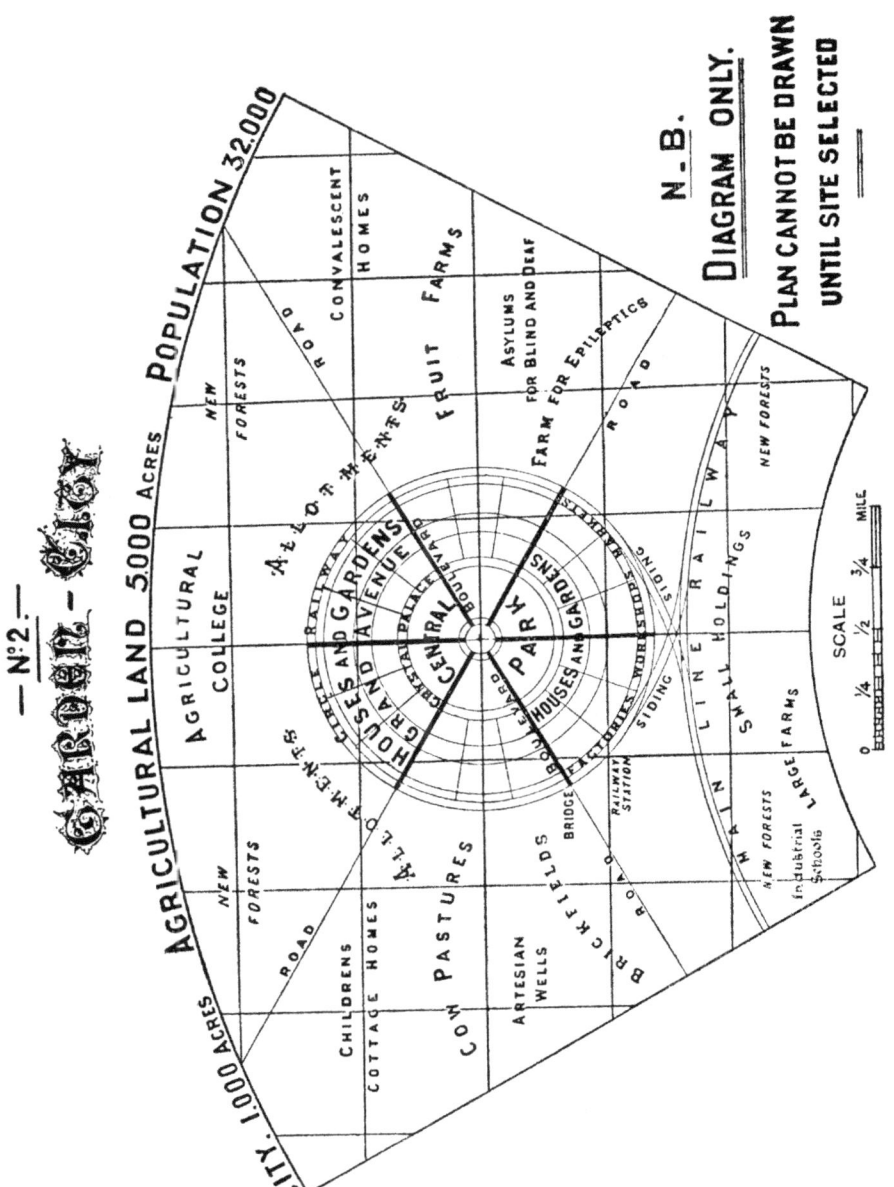

GARDEN CITY.

— Nº 2. —

POPULATION 32,000

AGRICULTURAL LAND 5,000 ACRES

CITY. 1,000 ACRES

N.-B.
DIAGRAM ONLY.
PLAN CANNOT BE DRAWN
UNTIL SITE SELECTED

SCALE
0 ¼ ½ ¾ MILE

to the park. This building is in wet weather one of the favourite resorts of the people, whilst the knowledge that its bright shelter is ever close at hand tempts people into Central Park, even in the most doubtful of weathers. Here manufactured goods are exposed for sale, and here most of that class of shopping which requires the joy of deliberation and selection is done. The space enclosed by the Crystal Palace is, however, a good deal larger than is required for these purposes, and a considerable part of it is used as a Winter Garden—the whole forming a permanent exhibition of a most attractive character, whilst its circular form brings it near to every dweller in the town—the furthest removed inhabitant being within 600 yards.

Passing out of the Crystal Palace on our way to the outer ring of the town, we cross Fifth Avenue—lined, as are all the roads of the town, with trees—fronting which, and looking on to the Crystal Palace, we find a ring of very excellently-built houses, each standing in its own ample grounds; and, as we continue our walk, we observe that the houses are for the most part built either in concentric rings, facing the various avenues (as the circular roads are termed), or fronting the boulevards and roads, which all converge to the centre of the town. Asking the friend who accompanies us on our journey what the population of this little city may be, we are told about 30,000 in the city itself, and about 2,000 in the agricultural estate, and that there are in the town 5,500 building lots of an *average* size of 20 feet x 130 feet—the minimum space allotted for the purpose being 20 x 100. [p. 24]

Noticing the very varied architecture and design which the houses and groups of houses display—some having common gardens and co-operative kitchens—we learn that general observance of street line or harmonious departure from it are the chief points as to house-building over which the municipal authorities exercise control, for, though proper sanitary arrangements are strictly enforced, the fullest measure of individual taste and preference is encouraged.

Walking still toward the outskirts of the town, we come upon "Grand Avenue." This avenue is fully entitled to the name it bears, for it is 420 feet wide,[1] and, forming a belt of green upwards of three miles long, divides that part of the town which lies outside Central Park into two belts. It really constitutes an additional park of 115 acres—a park which is within 240 yards of the furthest removed inhabitant. In this splendid avenue six sites, each of four acres, are occupied by public schools and their surrounding play-grounds and gardens, while other sites are reserved for churches, of such denominations as the reli-

---

[1] Portland Place, London, is only 100 feet wide.

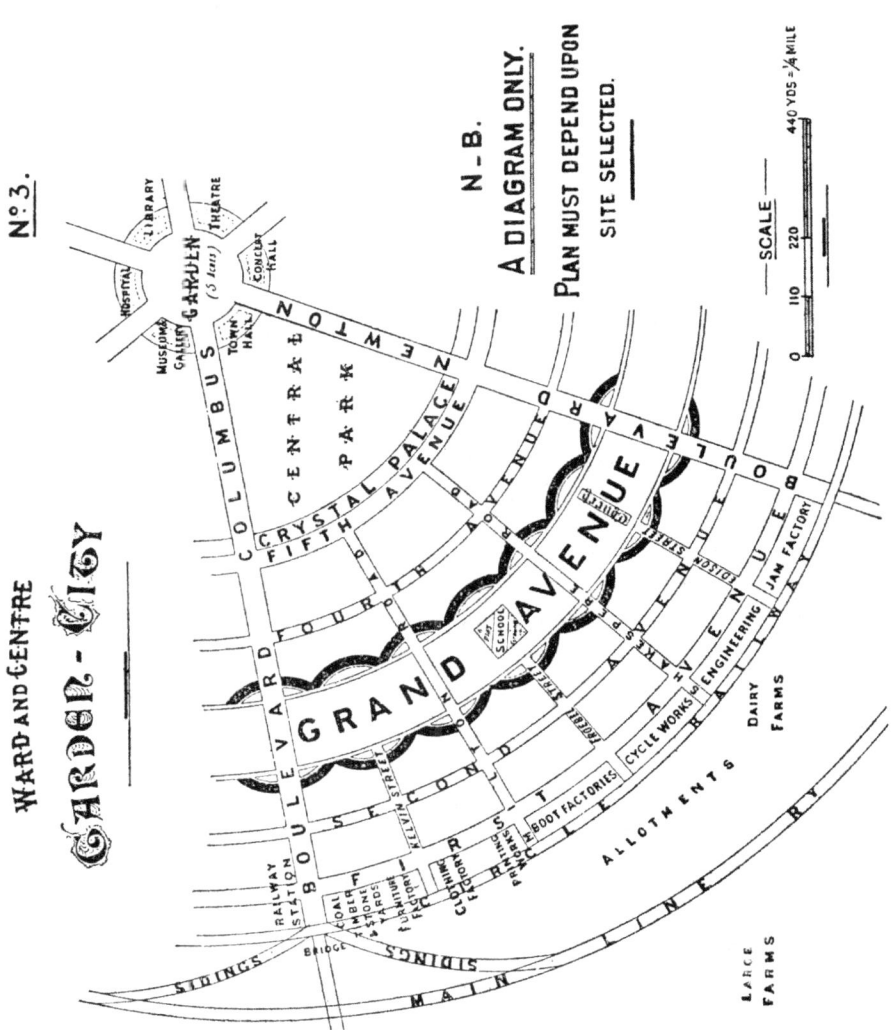

N°.3.

WARD and CENTRE GARDEN-CITY

N.B.
A DIAGRAM ONLY.
PLAN MUST DEPEND UPON
SITE SELECTED.

SCALE
0   110   220   440 YDS =¼ MILE

gious beliefs of the people may determine, to be erected and maintained out of the funds of the worshippers and their friends. We observe that the houses fronting on Grand Avenue have departed (at least in one of the wards—that of which Diagram 3 is a representation)—from the general plan of concentric rings, and, in order to ensure a longer line of frontage on Grand Avenue, are arranged in crescents—thus also to the eye yet further enlarging the already splendid width of Grand Avenue. [p. 25]

On the outer ring of the town are factories, warehouses, dairies, markets, coal yards, timber yards, etc., all fronting on the circle railway, which encompasses the whole town, and which has sidings connecting it with a main line of railway which passes through the estate. This arrangement enables goods to be loaded direct into trucks from the warehouses and workshops, and so sent by railway to distant markets, or to be taken direct from the trucks into the warehouses or factories; thus not only effecting a very great saving in regard to packing and cartage, and reducing to a minimum loss from breakage, but also, by reducing the traffic on the roads of the town, lessening to a very marked extent the cost of their maintenance. The smoke fiend is kept well within bounds in Garden City; for all machinery is driven by electric energy, with the result that the cost of electricity for lighting and other purposes is greatly reduced.

The refuse of the town is utilised on the agricultural portions of the estate, which are held by various individuals in large farms, small holdings, allotments, cow pastures, etc.; the natural competition of these various methods of agriculture, tested by the willingness of occupiers to offer the highest rent to the municipality, tending to bring about the best system of husbandry, or, what is more probable, the best *systems* adapted for various purposes. Thus it is easily conceivable that it may prove advantageous to grow wheat in very large fields, involving united action under a capitalist farmer, or by a body of co-operators; while the cultivation of vegetables, fruits, and flowers, which requires closer and more personal care, and more of the artistic and inventive faculty, may possibly be best dealt with by individuals, or [p. 26] by small groups of individuals having a common belief in the efficacy and value of certain dressings, methods of culture, or artificial and natural surroundings.

This plan, or, if the reader be pleased to so term it, this absence of plan, avoids the dangers of stagnation or dead level, and, though encouraging individual initiative, permits of the fullest co-operation, while the increased rents which follow from this form of competition are common or municipal property, and by far the larger part of them are expended in permanent improvements.

While the town proper, with its population engaged in various trades, callings, and professions, and with a store or depôt in each ward, offers the most natural market to the people engaged on the agricultural estate, inasmuch as to the extent to which the townspeople demand their produce they escape altogether any railway rates and charges; yet the farmers and others are not by any means limited to the town as their only market, but have the fullest right to dispose of their produce to whomsoever they please. Here, as in every feature of the experiment, it will be seen that it is not the area of rights which is contracted, but the area of choice which is enlarged.

This principle of freedom holds good with regard to manufacturers and others who have established themselves in the town. These manage their affairs in their own way, subject, of course, to the general law of the land, and subject to the provision of sufficient space for workmen and reasonable sanitary conditions. Even in regard to such matters as water, lighting, and telephonic communication—which a municipality, if efficient and honest, is certainly the best and most natural body to [p. 27] supply—no rigid or absolute monopoly is sought; and if any private corporation or any body of individuals proved itself capable of supplying on more advantageous terms, either the whole town or a section of it, with these or any commodities the supply of which was taken up by the corporation, this would be allowed. No really sound system of *action* is in more need of artificial support than is any sound system of *thought*. The area of municipal and corporate action is probably destined to become greatly enlarged; but, if it is to be so, it will be because the people possess faith in such action, and that faith can be best shown by a wide extension of the area of freedom.

Dotted about the estate are seen various charitable and philanthropic institutions. These are not under the control of the municipality, but are supported and managed by various public-spirited people who have been invited by the municipality to establish these institutions in an open healthy district, and on land let to them at a pepper-corn rent, it occurring to the authorities that they can the better afford to be thus generous, as the spending power of these institutions greatly benefits the whole community. Besides, as those persons who migrate to the town are among its most energetic and resourceful members, it is but just and right that their more helpless brethren should be able to enjoy the benefits of an experiment which is designed for humanity at large. [p. 28]

CHAPTER II.

THE REVENUE OF GARDEN CITY, AND HOW IT IS OBTAINED—THE AGRICULTURAL ESTATE.

AMONGST the essential differences between Garden City and other municipalities, one of the chief is its method of raising its revenue. Its entire revenue is derived from rents; and one of the purposes of this work is to show that the rents which may very reasonably be expected from the various tenants on the estate will be amply sufficient, if paid into the coffers of Garden City, (*a*) to pay the interest on the money with which the estate is purchased, (*b*) to provide a sinking-fund for the purpose of paying off the principal, (*c*) to construct and maintain all such works as are usually constructed and maintained by municipal and other local authorities out of rates compulsorily levied, and (*d*) (after redemption of debentures) to provide a large surplus for other purposes, such as old-age pensions or insurance against accident and sickness.

Perhaps no difference between town and country is more noticeable than the difference in the rent charged for the use of the soil. Thus, while in some parts of London the rent is equal to £30,000 an acre, £4 an acre is an extremely high rent for agricultural land. This enormous difference of rental value is, of course, almost entirely due to the presence in the one case and the absence in the other of a large population; and, as it [p. 29] cannot be attributed to the action of any particular individuals, it is frequently spoken of as the "unearned increment," *i.e.*, unearned by the landlord, though a more correct term would be "collectively-earned increment."

The presence of a considerable population thus giving a greatly additional value to the soil, it is obvious that a migration of population on any considerable scale to any particular area will be certainly attended with a corresponding rise in the value of the land so settled upon, and it is also obvious that such increment of value may, with some foresight and pre-arrangement, become the property of the migrating people.

Such foresight and pre-arrangement, never before exercised in an effective manner, are displayed conspicuously in the case of Garden City, where the land, as we have seen, is vested in trustees, who hold it in trust (after payment of the debentures) for the whole community, so that the entire increment of value gradually created becomes the property of the municipality, with the effect that though rents may rise, and even rise considerably, such rise in rent will not become the property of private individuals, but will be applied in relief of rates. It is this arrangement which will be seen to give Garden City much of its magnetic power.

The site of Garden City we have taken to be worth at the time of its purchase £40 an acre, or £240,000. The purchase money may be assumed to represent 30 years' purchase, and on this basis the annual rent paid by the former tenants was £8,000. If, therefore, there was a population of 1,000 persons upon the estate at the time of the purchase, then each man, woman, and child was contributing towards this rent-roll an average sum of £8 per [p. 30] annum. But the population of Garden City, including its agricultural land, is, when completed, 32,000, and the estate has cost them a sum on which they pay an annual charge by way of interest of £9,600. Thus, while before the experiment was initiated, 1,000 persons out of their united earnings contributed £8,000 a year, or *£8 a head*, on the completion of the town 32,000 persons out of their united earnings will contribute £9,600 a year, or an average of *6s. a head*.

This sum of 6s. per head per annum is all the rent, strictly speaking, which the inhabitants of Garden City will ever be called upon to pay; for it is all the rent which they *pay away*, any further sum they pay being a contribution towards their rates.

Let us now suppose that each person, besides contributing annually 6s. a head, contributes an average annual sum of £1 14s., or £2 in all. In that case two things may be noticed. First, each person will be paying for ground rent and rates only one-fourth of the sum which each person before the purchase paid in ground-rent alone; and, secondly, the Board of Management, after the payment of interest on the debentures, will receive an annual sum of £54,400, which, as will be presently shown, would, after providing a sinking fund (of £4,400), defray all those costs, charges, and expenses which are usually met by local taxation.

The average annual sum contributed by each man, woman, and child in England and Wales for local purposes is about £2 a head, and the average sum contributed for ground rent is, at a very low estimate, about £2 10s. The average yearly contribution for ground-rent and local rates is, therefore, about £4 10s. It might, [p. 31] therefore, be safely assumed that the people of Garden City would willingly pay £2 per head in complete discharge of ground-rent and local rates; but to make the case the clearer and stronger, we will test the supposed willingness of the tenants of Garden City to pay such a sum as £2 a year for rates and rents in another way.

For this purpose, let us deal first with the agricultural estate, leaving the town estate to be dealt with separately. Obviously the rent which can be secured will be considerably greater than before the town was built. Every farmer now has a market close to his doors. There are 30,000 townspeople to be fed. Those persons, of course, are perfectly free to get their food stuffs from any part of the world, and in the case of many products will doubtless continue to be supplied from abroad. These farmers are hardly likely to supply them with tea, with coffee, with spices, with tropical fruits or with sugar,[1] and their struggle to compete with America and Russia for the supply of wheat or flour to the town may be as keen as ever. But surely the struggle will not be so despairing. A ray—a beam of hope will gladden the heart of the despairing home-producer of wheat, for while the American has to pay railway charges to the sea-board, charges for Atlantic transit and railway charges to the consumer, the farmer of Garden City has a market at his very doors, and this a market which the rent he contributes will help to build up.[2] [p. 32]

Or, consider vegetables and fruits. Farmers, except near towns, do not often grow them now. Why? Chiefly because of the difficulty and uncertainty of a market, and the high charges for freights and commission. To quote the words of Dr. Farquharson, M.P., when they "try to dispose of these things they find themselves struggling so hopelessly in a spider's web of rings, and middlemen, and speculators, that they are more than half-inclined to give up the attempt in despair, and fall back on those things that stand up straight and square to their prices in the open market." A curious calculation may be interesting with regard to milk. Assuming each person in the town consumed only one-third of a pint a day, then 30,000 would consume 1,250 gallons a day, and might thus save, taking railway charges at a penny per gallon, upwards of £1,900 per

---

[1] The electric light, with cheap motive power for its generation, with glass-houses, may make even some of these things possible.

[2] See "Fields, Farms, and Workshops," by Prince Krapotkin, 1/-, and "The Coming Revolution," by Capt. Petavel, 1/-, both published by Swan Sonnenschein & Co.

annum in railway rates upon the one item of milk, a saving which must be multiplied by a large figure in order to realise the general saving to be effected by placing consumer and producer in such close association. In other words, the combination of town and country is not only healthful, but economic—a point which every step taken will serve to make yet more clear.

But the rents which the agricultural tenants of Garden City would be willing to pay would increase for another reason. The waste products of the town could, and this without heavy charges for railway transport or other expensive agencies, be readily brought back to the soil, thus increasing its fertility. The question of sewage disposal is naturally a difficult one to deal with, but its inherent difficulty is often much increased by artificial and imperfect conditions already in existence. Thus, Sir Benjamin Baker, in his joint report with Mr. (now Sir) [p. 33] Alexander Binnie to the London County Council, says: "In approaching the consideration of the vast question of the whole sewerage system of the Metropolis, and the state of the Thames, as a practical problem . . . we had clearly at once to recognise the fact that the general features of the main drainage system were unalterably settled, and must be accepted in the same way as the main lines of thoroughfares have to be accepted whether quite as we could wish them to be or not." But on Garden City site, given the skilful engineer, he would have comparatively little difficulty. He would have, as it were, a clean sheet on which to prepare his plans, and the whole estate being equally the property of the municipality, he would have a free course before him, and would doubtless succeed in adding greatly to the productiveness of the agricultural estate.

The great increase in the number of allotments, especially such favourably situated allotments as are shown in Diagram 2, would also tend to raise the total sum offered in rent.

There are yet other reasons why the rent which a farmer on the Garden City estate would be willing to pay for his farm, or a labourer for his allotment, would tend to increase. The productiveness of the agricultural part of the estate, besides being increased by a well-devised system of sewage disposal, and by a new and somewhat extensive market, with unique conveniences for transit to more distant markets, would also be increased because the tenure on which the land is held encourages maximum cultivation. It is a just tenure. The agricultural portion of the estate is let at fair rents, with a right to continue in occupation as long as the tenant is [p. 34] willing to pay a rent equal to that offered by any would-be occupier, less, say, 10 per cent. in favour of the occupying tenant—the incoming tenant having also to compensate the outgoing tenant for all unexhausted improvements. Under this system, while it would be impossible for the tenant to secure to himself any undue share of that natural increment of land-value which would be brought about by the general growth in well-being of the town, he would yet have, as all tenants in possession probably should have, a preference over any new-comer, and would know that he would not lose those fruits of his past industry which were not yet ingathered but were still adding their value to the soil. Surely no one can doubt that such a tenure would, of itself, tend greatly to increase at once the activity and industry of the tenant, the productivity of the soil, and the rent which the tenant would be willing to pay.

That there would be this increased offer of rent will become yet more obvious if we consider for a moment the *nature* of the rent paid by a tenant of Garden City. Part of what he pays would be in respect of interest on the debentures on which the money to purchase the estate was raised, or in the redemption of those debentures, and would thus, except so far as the debentures were held by residents on the estate, pass away from the community altogether; but the whole of the remaining sum paid would be expended locally, and the farmer would have a share equal to that of every adult in the administration of such money. The term "rent," therefore, has, in Garden City, acquired a new meaning, and, for the sake of clearness, it will be necessary in future to use terms which will not be ambiguous. That part of the rent [p. 35] which represents interest on debentures will be hereafter called "landlord's rent"; that part which represents repayment of purchase-money "sinking fund"; that part which is devoted to public purposes "rates"; while the total sum will be termed "rate-rent."

From these considerations, surely it is obvious that the "*rate-rent*" which the farmer will be willing to pay into the treasury of Garden City will be considerably higher than the rent he would be willing to pay to a private landlord, who, besides increasing his rent as the farmer makes his land more valuable, will also leave him with the full burden of local taxation resting upon him. In short the plan proposed embraces a system of sewage-disposal which will return to the soil in a transmuted form many of those products the growth of which, by exhausting its natural fertility, demand elsewhere the application of manures so expensive that the farmer becomes sometimes blinded to their necessity, and it also embraces a system of rate-rents by which many of the farmer's hard-earned sovereigns, hitherto lost to him by being paid away to his landlord, shall return to his exhausted exchequer, not indeed in the form in which they left it, but in a variety of useful forms, such as roads, schools, markets, which will assist him most materially, though indirectly, in his work, but which, under present conditions, entail so severe a burden as to make him naturally slow to see their inherent necessity, and even to look upon some of them with suspicion and dislike. Who can doubt that if the farm and the farmer can be placed under conditions so healthful and natural alike in a physical and moral sense, the willing soil and the hopeful farmer will alike respond to their new en- [p. 36] vironment—the soil becoming more fertile by every blade of grass it yields, the farmer richer by every penny of rate-rent he contributes?

We are now in a position to see that the rate-rent which will be readily paid by farmer, small occupier, and allotment holder, would be considerably greater than the rent he paid before (1) because of the presence of a new town population demanding new and more profitable farm products, in respect of which railway charges can be largely saved; (2) by the due return to the soil of its natural elements; (3) by the just, equitable, and natural conditions on which the land is held; and (4) by reason of the fact that the rent now paid is *rate and rent*, while the rent formerly paid left the rates to be paid by the tenant.

But certain as it is that the "*rate-rent*" would represent a very considerable increase over the bare *rent* formerly paid by the tenants on the estate, it is still very much a matter of conjecture what the "rate-rent" would be; and we shall, therefore, be acting prudently if we greatly under-estimate the "rate-rent" which would probably be offered. If, then, in view of all the circumstances, we estimate that the *farming population* of Garden City will be prepared to pay for rates and rent 50 per cent. more than they before paid for *rent alone*, we shall reach the following result: —

Estimated Gross Revenue from Agricultural Estate.

Original rent paid by tenants of 5,000 acres, say	£6,500
Add 50 per cent. for contributions to rates and sinking fund, – – – – – –	3,250
Total "rate-rent" from agricultural estate, – – – – –	£9,750 [p. 37]

We shall in the next chapter estimate the amount which may, on the most reasonable calculation, be expected from the town estate, and then proceed to consider the sufficiency of the total rate-rents for the municipal needs of the town. [p. 38]

CHAPTER III.

THE REVENUE OF GARDEN CITY—TOWN ESTATE.

"Whatever reforms be introduced into the dwellings of the London poor, it will still remain true that the whole area of London is insufficient to supply its population with fresh air and the free space that is wanted for wholesome recreation. A remedy for the overcrowding of London will still be wanted. . . . There are large classes of the population of London whose removal into the country would be in the long run economically advantageous; it would benefit alike those who moved and those who remained behind. . . . Of the 150,000 or more hired workers in the clothes-making trades, by far the greater part are very poorly paid, and do work which it is against all economic reason to have done where ground-rent is high."—Professor Marshall, "The Housing of the London Poor," *Contemporary Review*, 1884.

HAVING in the last chapter estimated, the gross revenue which may be anticipated from the agricultural part of the estate at £9,750, we will now turn to the town estate (where, obviously, the conversion of an agricultural area into a town will be attended with a very large rise in land values), and endeavour roughly to estimate—again taking care to keep well within the mark—the amount of "rate-rent" which will be freely offered by the tenants of the town estate.

The site of the town proper consists, it will be remembered, of 1,000 acres, and is assumed to have cost £40,000, the interest of which, at 4 per cent., is £1,600 per annum. This sum of £1,600 is, therefore, all the landlord's rent which the people of the town site will be called upon to pay, any additional "rate-rent" they may contribute being devoted either to the payment of the purchase- [p. 39] money as "sinking-fund," or applied as "rates" to the construction and maintenance of roads, schools, water-works, and to other municipal purposes. It will be interesting, therefore, to see what sort of a burden "landlord's rent" will represent per head, and what the community would secure by such contribution. Now, if the sum of £1,600, being the annual interest or "landlord's rent," be divided by 30,000 (the supposed population of the town), it will be found to equal an annual contribution by each man, woman, and child of *rather less than 1s. 1d. per head*. This is all the "landlord's rent" which will ever be levied, any additional sum collected as "rate-rent" being applied to sinking-fund or to local purposes.

And now let us notice what this fortunately-placed community obtains for this insignificant sum. It obtains for 1s. 1d. per head per annum, first, ample sites for homes, these averaging, as we have seen, 20 feet by 130 feet, and accommodating, on an average, 5½ persons to each lot. It obtains ample space for roads, some of which are of truly magnificent proportions, so wide and spacious that sunlight and air may freely circulate, and in which trees, shrubs, and grass give to the town a semi-rural appearance. It also obtains ample sites for town-hall, public library, museum and picture-gallery, theatre, concert-hall, hospital, schools, churches, swimming baths, public markets, etc. It also secures a central park of 145 acres, and a magnificent avenue 420 feet wide, extending in a circle of over three miles, unbroken save by spacious boulevards and by schools and churches, which, one may be sure, will not be the less beautiful because so little money has been expended on their sites. [p. 40]

It secures also all the land required for a railway 4¼ miles long, encompassing the town; 82 acres for warehouses, factories, markets, and a splendid site for a crystal palace devoted to shopping, and serving also as a winter garden.

The leases under which all building sites are let do not, therefore, contain the usual covenant by the tenant to pay all rates, taxes, and assessments levied in respect of such property, but, on the contrary, contain a covenant by the landlord to apply the whole sum received, first, in payment of debenture interest; secondly, towards the redemption of the debentures; and thirdly, as to the whole of the balance, into a public fund, to be applied to public purposes, among these being the rates levied by public authorities, other than the municipal authority, of the city.[1]

Let us now attempt to estimate the rate-rents which may be anticipated in respect of our town-estate.

First, we will deal with the home-building lots. All are excellently situated, but those fronting Grand Avenue (420 feet) and the magnificent boulevards (120 feet) would probably call forth the highest tenders. We can here deal only with averages, but we think anyone would admit that an average rate-rent of 6s. a foot frontage for home lots would be extremely moderate. *This would make the rate-rent of a building lot 20 feet wide in an average position £6 a year, and on this basis the 5,500 building lots would yield a gross revenue of £33,000.*

---

[1] The question of the form of Leases to be granted is one which is being carefully considered by the Land Tenure Section of the Garden City Association.

The rate-rents from the sites of factories, warehouses, [p. 41] markets, etc., cannot perhaps be so well estimated by the foot frontage, but we may perhaps safely assume that an average employer would willingly pay £2 in respect of each employee. It is, of course, not suggested that the rate-rent levied should be a poll-tax; it would, as has been said, be raised by competition among the tenants; but this way of estimating rate-rent to be paid will perhaps give a ready means by which manufacturers or other employers, co-operative societies, or individuals working on their own account, would be able to judge whether they would be lightly rated and rented as compared with their present position. It must be, however, distinctly borne in mind that we are dealing with *averages*; and if the figure should seem high to a large employer, it will seem ridiculously low to a small shopkeeper.

Now, in a town with a population of 30,000, there would be about twenty thousand persons between the ages of 16 and 65; and if it is assumed that 10,625 of these would be employed in factories, shops, warehouses, markets, etc., or in any way which involved the use of a site, other than a home-building site, to be leased from the municipality, there would be a revenue from this source of £21,250.

The gross revenue of the entire estate would therefore be: —

Rate-rent from agricultural estate (*see* p. 36),	–	£9,750
"	5,500 home building lots at £6 per lot, – – – – – –	33,000
"	from business premises 10,625 persons employed at an average of £2 a head,	21,250
		£64,000

Or £2 per head of population for rates and rent. [p. 42]

This sum would be available as follows: —

For landlord's rent or interest on purchase money £240,000 at 4 per cent., – – –	£9,600
For sinking fund (30 years), – – – –	4,400
For such purposes as are elsewhere defrayed out of rates, – – – – – –	50,000
	£64,000

It is now important to inquire whether £50,000 will suffice for the municipal needs of Garden City. [p. 43]

CHAPTER IV.

THE REVENUE OF GARDEN CITY—GENERAL OBSERVATIONS ON ITS EXPENDITURE.

BEFORE entering upon the question which presented itself at the conclusion of the last chapter—that of endeavouring to ascertain whether the estimated net available income of Garden City (£50,000 per annum) would be sufficient for its municipal needs, I will very shortly state how it is proposed to raise the money required for commencing operations. The money would be borrowed on "B" debentures,[1] and would be secured by a charge upon the "rate-rent," subject, of course, to the payment of interest and sinking fund in respect of the "A" debentures on which the purchase money of the estate is raised. It is, perhaps, superfluous to remark that, though in the case of the land purchase it might be requisite to raise the whole, or at least some very considerable part of the purchase money before possession would be given of the estate, or operations upon it commenced, yet in regard to public works to be carried out upon the estate, the case is quite different, and it would be by no means necessary or advisable to defer the commencement of operations until the whole sum which might be ultimately required should be raised. Probably no town was ever built on such onerous conditions as would be involved in the [p. 44] raising at the outset of such a very considerable sum as would defray the cost of all its public works; and though the circumstances under which Garden City is to be built may be unique, there is, as will by and by be seen, not only no need for making an exception of the town in respect of initial capital, but quite exceptional reasons will become more and more apparent which make the overlaying of the enterprise with superabundant capital altogether unnecessary, and therefore inexpedient; although, of course, there must be a sufficient sum to enable all real economies to be readily effected.

Perhaps it may be well in this connection to draw a distinction as to the

---

[1] *See* note on page 21.

amount of capital required between the case of the building of a town and the building, let us say, of a large iron bridge across an estuary. In the case of the bridge it is highly expedient to raise the entire sum required before commencing operations, for the simple reason that the bridge is not a bridge until the last rivet is driven home, nor, until its entire completion and its connection with the railways or roadways at either end, has it any revenue-earning power. Except, therefore, on the assumption that it is to be fully completed, it offers very little security for the capital sunk upon it. Hence it would be very natural for those who are asked to invest to say, "We will not put any money into this enterprise until you show us that you can get enough to complete it." But the money which it is proposed to raise for the development of Garden City site leads to speedy results. It is to be expended upon roads, schools, etc. These works will be carried out with due regard to the number of lots which have been let to tenants, who undertake to build as from a certain date; and, therefore, [p. 45] the money expended will very soon begin to yield a return in the shape of a rate-rent, representing, in reality, a greatly-improved ground-rent; when those who have advanced money on the "B" debentures will have a really first-class security, and further sums should be easily obtainable, and at a reduced rate of interest. Again, it is an important part of the project that each ward, or one-sixth part of the city, should be in some sense a complete town by itself, and thus the school buildings might serve, in the earlier stages, not only as schools, but as places for religious worship, for concerts, for libraries, and for meetings of various kinds, so that all outlay on expensive municipal and other buildings might be deferred until the later stages of the enterprise. Work, too, would be practically completed in one ward before commencing on another, and the operations in the various wards would be taken up in due and proper sequence, so that those portions of the town site on which building operations were not in progress would also be a source of revenue, either as allotments, cow-pastures, or, perhaps, as brickfields.

Let us now deal with the subject immediately before us. Will the principles on which Garden City is to be built have any bearing on the effectiveness of its municipal expenditure? In other words, will a given revenue yield greater results than under ordinary conditions? These questions will be answered in the affirmative. It will be shown that, pound for pound, money will be more effectively spent than elsewhere, and that there will be many great and obvious economies which cannot be expressed in figures with much accuracy, but which would certainly represent in the aggregate a very large sum. [p. 46]

The first great economy to be noticed is that the item of "landlord's rent," which, under ordinary conditions, largely enters into municipal expenditure, will, in Garden City, scarcely enter at all. Thus, all well-ordered towns require administrative buildings, schools, swimming baths, libraries, parks; and the sites which these and other corporate undertakings occupy are usually purchased. In such cases the money necessary for the purchase of the sites is generally borrowed on the security of the rates; and thus it is that a very considerable part of the total rates levied by a municipality are ordinarily applied, not to productive works, but either to what we have termed "landlord's rent," in the shape of interest on money borrowed to effect the purchase, or to the provision of a sinking fund in payment of the purchase money of the land so acquired, which is landlord's rent in a capitalised form.

Now, in Garden City, all such expenditure, with such exceptions as road sites on the agricultural estate, has been already provided for. Thus, the 250 acres for public parks, the sites for schools and other public buildings, will cost the ratepayers nothing whatever, or, to put it more correctly, their cost, which was really £40 per acre, has been covered, as we have seen, by the annual average contribution of 1s. 1d. per head, which each person is supposed to make in discharge of landlord's rent; and the revenue of the town, £50,000, is the *net* revenue after all interest and sinking fund in respect of the whole site has been deducted. In considering, therefore, the question whether £50,000 is a sufficient revenue, it must be remembered that in no case has any cost of municipal sites to be first deducted from that amount. [p. 47]

Another item in which a great economy will be effected will be found in a comparison between Garden City and any old city like London. London wishes to breathe a fuller municipal spirit, and so proceeds to construct schools, to pull down slums, to erect libraries, swimming baths, etc. In these cases, it has not only to purchase the freeholds of the sites, but also has usually to pay for the buildings which had been previously erected thereon, and which are purchased solely, of course, with a view to their demolition and to a clearing of the ground, and frequently it has also to meet claims for business-disturbance, together with heavy legal expenses in settling claims. In this connection it may be remarked that the inclusive cost of *sites* of schools purchased by the London School Board since its constitution, *i.e.*, the cost, including old buildings, business-disturbance, law charges, etc., has already reached the enormous sum of £3,516,072,[1] and the exclusive cost of the sites (370 acres in extent) ready for building by the Board is equal, on the average, to £9,500 per acre.

At this rate the cost of the 24 acres of school sites for Garden City would

[1] See Report, London School Board, 6th May, 1897, p. 1480.

be £228,000, so that another site for a model city could be purchased out of what would be saved in Garden City in respect of school sites alone. "Oh, but," it may be said, "the school sites of Garden City are extravagantly large, and would be out of the question in London, and it is altogether unfair to compare a small town like Garden City with London, the wealthy capital of a mighty Empire." I would reply, "It is quite true that the cost of land in London would [p. 48] make such sites extravagant, not to say prohibitive—they would cost about £40,000,000 sterling—but does not this of itself suggest a most serious defect of system, and that at a most vital part? Can children be better taught where land costs £9,500 an acre than where it costs £40? Whatever may be the real economic value of the London site, for other purposes—as to which we may have something to say at a later stage—for school purposes, wherein lies the advantage that the sites on which its schools are built are frequently surrounded by dingy factories or crowded courts and alleys? If Lombard Street is an ideal place for banks, is not a park like the Central Avenue of Garden City an ideal place for schools?—and is not the welfare of our children the primary consideration with any well-ordered community?" "But," it may be said, "the children must be educated near their homes, and these homes must be near the places where their parents work." Precisely; but does not the scheme provide for this in the most effective manner, and in that respect also are not the school sites of Garden City superior to those of London? The children will have to expend less than an average amount of energy in going to school, a matter, as all educationists admit, of immense importance, especially in the winter. But further, have we not heard from Professor Marshall (see heading to Chapter III.) that "150,000 people, in London, engaged in the clothes-making trades, are doing work which it is against all economic reason to have done where ground-rent is high"—in other words, that these 150,000 people *should not be in London at all;* and does not the consideration that the education of the children of such workers is carried on at once under inferior conditions [p. 49] and at enormous cost add weight and significance to the Professor's words? If these workers ought not to be in London, then their homes, for which, insanitary as they are, they pay heavy rents, ought not to be in London; a certain proportion of the shop-keepers who supply their wants should not be in London; and various other people to whom the wages earned by these persons in the clothes-making trade give employment should not be in London. Hence, there is a sense—and a very real one—in which it *is* fair to compare the cost of school sites in Garden City with the cost of school sites in London; because obviously if these people do, as suggested by Professor Marshall, migrate from London, they can at once effect (if they make, as I have suggested, proper provision beforehand) not only a great saving in respect of ground-rent for their work-shops, but also a vast saving in respect of sites for homes, schools, and other purposes; and this saving is obviously the difference between what is now paid and what would be paid under the new conditions, minus the loss incurred (if any), and plus the numerous gains secured as the result of such removal.

Let us for the sake of clearness make the comparison in another way. The people of London have paid a capital sum representing, when spread over the whole population of London (this being taken at 6,000,000), upwards of 11s. 6d. per head of population for school sites held by the London School Board, a sum which is, of course, exclusive of the sites for voluntary schools. The population of Garden City, 30,000 in number, have entirely saved that 11s. 6d. per head, making a total saving of £17,250, which at 3 per cent. involves an annual saving of £517 in perpetuity. And besides thus [p. 50] saving £517 a year as interest on cost of sites for schools, Garden City has secured sites for its schools incomparably better than those of London schools—sites which afford ample accommodation for all the children of the town, and not, as in the case of the London School Board, accommodation for only half of the children of the municipality. (The sites of the London School Board are 370 acres in extent, or about 1 acre to every 16,000 of the population, while the people of Garden City have obtained 24 acres or 1 acre for every 1,250.) In other words, Garden City secures sites which are larger, better placed, and in every way more suitable for educational purposes, at a mere fraction of the cost which in London is incurred for sites vastly inferior in every respect.

The economies with which we have thus dealt are, it will be seen, effected by the two simple expedients we have referred to. First, by buying the land before a new value is given to it by migration, the migrating people obtain a site at an extremely low figure, and secure the coming increment for themselves and those who come after them; and secondly, by coming to a new site, they do not have to pay large sums for old buildings, for compensation for disturbance, and for heavy legal charges. The practicability of securing for the poor workers of London the first of these great advantages appears to have been for the moment overlooked by Professor Marshall in his article in the *Contemporary Review*,[1] for the Professor remarks "Ultimately all would gain by the migration, *but most*" (the italics are [p. 51] my own) "*the landowners and the railroads connected with the colony.*" Let us then adopt the expedient here advocated of securing that the *landowners*, "*who . . . will gain most*" by a project specially designed to

---

[1] No one is, of course, better aware of this possibility than the Professor himself. (*See* "Principles of Economics," (2nd ed.) Book v., Chap. x. and xiii.)

benefit a class now low down in the social scale, *shall he those very people them-selves*, as members of a new municipality, and then a strong additional induce-ment will be held out to them to make a change, which nothing but the lack of combined effort has hitherto prevented. As to the benefit to be derived by the railways, while no doubt the building up of the town would specially benefit the main line of railway which passed through the estate, it is also true that the earnings of the people would not be diminished to the usual extent by railway freights and charges. (*See* Chap. ii., also Chap. v., page 60.)

We now come to deal with an element of economy which will be simply incalculable. This is to be found in the fact that the town is definitely planned, so that the whole question of municipal administration may be dealt with by one far-reaching scheme. It is not by any means necessary, and it is not, hu-manly speaking, possible, that the final scheme should be the work of one mind. It will no doubt be the work of many minds—the minds of engineers, of architects and surveyors, of landscape gardeners and electricians. But it is es-sential, as we have said, that there should be unity of design and purpose—that the town should be planned as a whole, and not left to grow up in a chaotic manner as has been the case with all English towns, and more or less so with the towns of all countries. A town, like a flower, or a tree, or an animal, should, at each stage of its growth, possess unity, symmetry, completeness, and the ef-fect of [p. 52] growth should never be to destroy that unity, but to give it greater purpose, nor to mar that symmetry, but to make it more symmetrical; while the completeness of the early structure should be merged in the yet greater completeness of the later development.

Garden City is not only planned, but it is planned with a view to the very latest of modern requirements;[1] and it is obviously always easier, and usually far more economical and completely satisfactory, to make out of fresh mate-rial a new instrument than to patch up and alter an old one. This element of economy will be perhaps best dealt with by a concrete illustration, and one of a very striking nature at once presents itself.

---

[1] "London has grown up in a chaotic manner, without any unity of design, and at the chance discretion of any persons who were fortunate enough to own land as it came into demand at successive periods for building operations. Sometimes a great landlord laid out a quarter in a manner to tempt the better class of residents by squares, gardens, or retired streets, often cut off from through traffic by gates and bars; but even in these cases London as a whole has not been thought of, and no main arteries have been provided for. In other and more frequent cases of small landowners, the only design of builders has been to crowd upon the land as many streets and houses as possible, regardless of anything around them, and without open spaces or wide ap-proaches. A careful examination of a map of London shows how absolutely wanting in any kind of plan has been its growth, and how little the convenience and wants of the whole population or the considerations of dignity and beauty have been consulted."—Right Hon. G. J. Shaw-Lefevre, *New Review*, 1891, p. 435.

In London the question of building a new street between Holborn and the Strand has been for many years under consideration, and at length a scheme is being carried out, imposing an enormous cost on the [p. 53] people of London. "Every such change in the street geography of London displaces thousands of the poor"—I quote from the *Daily Chronicle* of July 6, 1898—"and for many years all public or quasi-public schemes have been charged with the liability to re-house as many of them as possible. This is as it should be; but the difficulty begins when the public is asked to face the music and pay the bill. In the present case some three thousand souls of the working population have to be turned out. After some searching of heart, it is decided that most of them are so closely tied to the spot by their employment that it would be a hardship to send them more than a mile away. The result, in cash, is that London must spend in re-housing them about £100 a head—or £300,000 in all. As to those who cannot fairly be asked to go even a mile away—hangers-on to the market, or others tethered to the spot—the cost will be even higher. They will require to have parcels of the precious land cleared by the great scheme itself, and the result of that will be to house them at the handsome figure of £260 a-piece, or some £1,400 for every family of five or six. Financial statements convey little to the ordinary mind. Let us make it a little more intelligible. A sum of £1,400 means, in the house market, a rental of nearly £100 a year. It would buy an excellent, in fact a sumptuous, house and garden at Hampstead, such as the better middle-class delight in. It would purchase anywhere in the nearer suburbs such houses as men with £1,000 a year inhabit. If one went further afield, to the new neighbourhoods which the City clerk can easily reach by rail, a £1,400 house represents actual magnificence." But on what scale of comfort will the poor Covent Garden [p. 54] labourer with a wife and four children live? The £1,400 will by no means represent a fair standard of comfort, to say nothing of magnificence. "He will live in three rooms sufficiently small in a block at least three storeys high." Contrast this with what might be done on a new area, by carefully planning a bold scheme at the outset. Streets of greater width than this new street would be laid out and constructed at a mere fraction of the cost, while a sum of £1,400, instead of providing 1 family with "three rooms sufficiently small in blocks at least three storeys high," would provide 7 families in Garden City with a comfortable six-roomed cottage each, and with a nice little garden; and, manufacturers being concurrently induced to build on the sites set apart for them, each breadwinner would be placed within easy walking distance of his work.

There is another modern need which all towns and cities should be designed to meet—a need which has arisen with the evolution of modern sanitation, and which has of recent years been accentuated by the rapid growth of invention. Subways for sewerage and surface drainage, for water, gas, telegraph and telephone wires, electric lighting wires, wires for conveying motive power, pneumatic tubes for postal purposes, have come to be regarded as economic if not essential. But if they would be a source of economy in an old city, how much more so in new ones; for on a clean sheet it will be easy to use the very best appliances for their construction, and to avail ourselves to the fullest extent of the ever-growing advantages which they possess as the number of services which they accommodate increases. Before the subways can be constructed, trenches some- [p. 55] what wide and deep must be excavated. In making these the most approved excavating machinery could be employed. In old towns this might be very objectionable, if not, indeed, quite impossible. But here, in Garden City, the steam navvy would not make its appearance in the parts where people were living, but where they were coming to live after its work in preparing the way had been completed. What a grand thing it would be if the people of England could, by an actual illustration under their very eyes, be convinced that machinery can be so used as to confer not only an ultimate national benefit, but a direct and immediate advantage, and that not only upon those who actually own it or use it, but on others who are given work by its magic aid. What a happy day it would be for the people of this country, and of all countries, if they could learn, from practical experience, that machinery can be used on an extended scale to *give* employment as well as *to take it away*—to *implace* labour as well as to *displace* it—to free men as well as to *enslave* them. There will be plenty of work to be done in Garden City. That is obvious. It is also obvious that, until a large number of houses and factories are built, many of these things cannot be done, and that the faster the trenches are dug, the subways finished, the factories and the houses built, and the light and the power turned on, the sooner can this town, the home of an industrious and a happy people, be built, and the sooner can others start the work of building other towns, not like it, but gradually becoming as much superior to it as our present locomotives are to the first crude attempts of the pioneers of mechanical traction.

We have now shown four cogent reasons why a given [p. 56] revenue should, in Garden City, yield vastly greater results than under ordinary conditions.

(1) That no "landlord's rent" or interest in respect of freeholds would be payable other than the small amount which has been already provided for in estimating net revenue.

(2) That the site being practically clear of buildings and other works, but little expenditure would be incurred in the purchase of such buildings, or com-

pensation for business-disturbance, or legal and other expenses in connection therewith.

(3) The economy arising out of a definite plan, and one in accordance with modern needs and requirements, thus saving those items of expenditure which are incurred in old cities as it is sought to bring them into harmony with modern ideas.

(4) The possibility, as the whole site will be clear for operations, of introducing machinery of the very best and most modern type in road-making and other engineering operations.

There are other economies which will become apparent to the reader as he proceeds, but, having cleared the ground by discussing general principles, we shall be better prepared to discuss the question as to the sufficiency of our estimates in another chapter. [p. 57]

CHAPTER V.

FURTHER DETAILS OF EXPENDITURE ON GARDEN CITY.

To mike this chapter interesting to the general reader would be difficult, perhaps impossible; but if carefully studied, it will, I think, be found to abundantly establish one of the main propositions of this book—that the rate-rent of a well-planned town, built on an agricultural estate, will amply suffice for the creation and maintenance of such municipal undertakings as are usually provided for out of rates compulsorily levied.

The net available revenue of Garden City, after payment of interest on debentures and providing a sinking fund for the landed estate, has been already estimated at £50,000 per annum (see Chap. iii., page 42). Having, in the fourth chapter, given special reasons why a given expenditure in Garden City would be unusually productive, I will now enter into fuller details, so that any criticism which this book may elicit, having something tangible to deal with, may be the more valuable in preparing the ground for an experiment such as is here advocated. [p. 58]

			EXPENDITURE.	
			On Capital Account.	On Maintenance and Working Expenses.
(See Note A)		25 Miles road (city) at £4,000 a mile	£100,000	£2,500
(„	B)	6 Miles additional roads, country estate at £1,200	7,200	350
(„	C)	Circular railway and bridges, 5½ miles at £3,000	16,500	1,500
(„	D)	Schools for 6,400 children, or ¹/₅ of the total population, at £12 per school place for capital account, and £3 maintenance, etc.	76,800	(maintenance only) 19,200
(„	E)	Town Hall	10,000	2,000
(„	F)	Library	10,000	600
(„	G)	Museum	10,000	600
(„	H)	Parks, 250 acres at £50	12,500	1,250
(„	I)	Sewage disposal ...	20,000	1,000
			£263,000	£29,000
(„	K)	Interest on £263,000 at 4½ per cent.		11,835
(„	L)	Sinking Fund to provide for extinction of debt in 30 years		4,480
(„	M)	Balance available for rates levied by local bodies within the area of which the estate is situated		4,685
				£50,000

Besides the above expenditure, a considerable outlay would be incurred in respect of markets, water supply, lighting, tramways, and other revenue-yielding undertakings. But these items of expenditure are almost invariably attended with considerable profits, which go in aid of rates. No calculation, therefore, need be made in respect of these. [p. 59]

I will now deal separately with moat of the items in the above estimate.

A. Roads and Streets.

The first point to be observed under this head is that the cost of making new streets to meet the growth of population is generally not borne by the ground landlord nor defrayed out of the rates. It is usually paid by the building-owner before the local authorities will consent to take the road over as a free gift. It is obvious, therefore, that the greater part of the £100,000 *might* be struck out. Experts will also not forget that the cost of the road sites is elsewhere provided for. In considering the question of the actual sufficiency of the estimate, they will also remember that of the boulevards one-half and of the streets and avenues one-third may be regarded as in the nature of park, and the cost of laying out and maintenance of these portions of the roads is dealt with under the head "Parks." They will also note that road-making materials would probably be found near at hand, and that, the railway relieving the streets of most of the heavy traffic, the more expensive methods of paving need not be resorted to. The cost, £4,000 per mile, would, however, be doubtless inadequate if subways are constructed, as probably they ought to be. The following consideration, however, has led me not to estimate for these. Subways are, where useful, a source of economy. The cost of maintaining roads is lessened, as the continual breaking-up for laying and repairing of water, gas, and electric mains is avoided, while any waste from leaky pipes is quickly detected, and thus the subways *pay*. Their cost should, therefore, be [p. 60] debited rather to cost of water, gas, and electric supplies, and these services are almost invariably a source of revenue to the Company or Corporation which constructs them.

B. Country Roads.

These roads are only 40 feet wide, and £1,200 a mile is ample. The cost of sites has in this case to be defrayed out of estimate.

C. Circular Railway and Bridges.

The cost of site is elsewhere provided for (*see* p. 40). The cost of maintenance does not, of course, include working expenses, locomotives, etc. To cover these a charge based on cost might be made to traders using the line. It should also be noticed that, as in the case of roads, by showing that the expense of this undertaking could be defrayed out of the rate-rent, I am proving more than I undertook to prove. I am proving that the rate-rent is sufficient to provide for landlords' rent, for such purposes as are usually defrayed out of rent, *and also for greatly extending the area of municipal activity*.

It may here be well to point out that this circle railway not only will save the trader the expense of carting to and from his warehouse or factory, but will enable him to claim a rebate from the railway company. Section 4 of the Railway and Canal Tariff Act, 1894, enacts: "Whenever merchandise is received or delivered by a railway company at any siding or branch railway not belonging to the company, and a dispute arises between the railway company and the consignor or consignee of [p. 61] such merchandise, as to any allowance or rebate from the rates charged to such consignor or consignee, in respect that the railway company does not provide station accommodation or perform terminal services, the Railway and Canal Commissioners shall have jurisdiction to hear and determine what, if any, is a just and reasonable allowance or rebate."

D. Schools.

This estimate of £12 per school place represents what was only a few years ago (1892) the average cost per child of the London School Board for building, architect, and clerk of the works, and for furniture and fittings; and no one can doubt that buildings greatly superior to those in London could be obtained for this sum. The saving in sites has been already dealt with, but it may be remarked that in London the cost per child for sites has been £6 11s 10d.

As showing how ample this estimate is, it may be observed that the cost of schools which have been proposed to be built by a private company at Eastbourne, "with a view of keeping out the School Board," is estimated at £2,500 for 400 places, or but little more than half the sum per school place provided in the estimate for Garden City.

The cost of maintenance, £3 per head, is probably sufficient, in view of the fact that the "expenditure per scholar in actual average attendance" in England and Wales, as given in the Report of the Committee of Council on Education, 1896-97, c. 8545, is £2 11s. 11½d. It must be especially noticed, too, that the whole cost of educa- [p. 62] tion is, in these estimates, assumed to be borne by Garden City, though a considerable part would be, in the ordinary course, borne by the National Exchequer. The amount of income per scholar in actual average attendance in England and Wales, as given in the same report, is £1 1s. 2d. as against a rate in Garden City of £3. So that I am again, in the case of the schools, as in the case of roads and circle railway, proving more than I set out to prove.

E. Town Hall and Expenses of Management.

It is to be noticed that the estimates of the various undertakings are intended to cover professional direction and supervision of architects, engineers, teachers, etc. The £2,000 for maintenance and working expenses under this head is, therefore, intended to include only the salaries of town clerk and of officials other than those comprised under special heads, together with incidental expenses.

F. Library, and G. Museum.

The latter is usually and the former not infrequently elsewhere provided for out of funds other than rates. So, here again, I am more than proving my case.

H. Parks and Road Ornamentation.

This item of cost would not be incurred until the undertaking was in a thoroughly sound financial condition, and the park space for a considerable period might be a source of revenue as agricultural land. Further, [p. 63] much of the park space would probably be left in a state of nature. Forty acres of this park space is road ornamentation, but the planting of trees and shrubs would not entail great expense. Again, a considerable part of the area would be reserved for cricket-fields, lawn-tennis courts, and other playgrounds, and the clubs using public grounds might perhaps be called upon to contribute to the expense of keeping these in order, as is customary elsewhere.

I. Sewage.

All that need be said on this subject has been said in Chap. i., page 25, and Chap. ii., page 32.

K. Interest.

The money to construct the public works with which we have been dealing is supposed to be borrowed at 4½ per cent. The question here arises—a question partly dealt with in Chap. iv.—what is the security for those who lend money on the "B" debentures?

My answer is three-fold.

(1) Those who advance money to effect any improvements on land have a security the safety of which is in reality largely determined by the effectiveness with which the money so advanced is spent; and, applying this truism, I venture to say that, for effectiveness of expenditure, no money which the investing public has been for many years asked to subscribe for improvements of a like nature has an equal security, whether it be measured by miles of road, acres of park, or numbers of school children well provided for.

(2) Those who advance money to effect improvements [p. 64] on land have a security the safety of which is largely determined by the consideration, aye or no, are other and yet more valuable works to be simultaneously carried out by others at their own expense, which other works are to become a security in respect of the first-mentioned advance; and, applying this second truism, I say

that, as the money for effecting the public improvements here described would only be asked for as and when other improvements—factories, houses, shops, etc. (costing far more money than the public works necessary at any given period)—were about to be built or were in process of building, the quality of the security would be a very high one.

(3) It is difficult to name a better security than that offered when money is to be expended in converting an agricultural estate into an urban, and this of the very best known type.

That the scheme is in reality a 3 per cent. security, and would in its later stages become so, I entertain little doubt; but I do not forget that, though its points of novelty are the very elements which really make it secure, they may not make it *seem* so, and that those who are merely looking out for an investment may eye it with some distrust because of its novelty. We shall have in the first instance to look to those who will advance money with somewhat mixed motives—public spirit, love of enterprise, and possibly, as to some persons, with a lurking belief that they will be able to dispose of their debentures at a premium, as they probably will. Therefore, I put down 4½ per cent., but if anyone's conscience prick him he may tender at 2 or 2½, or may even advance money without interest. [p. 65]

L. Sinking Fund.

This sinking fund, which provides for the extinction of the debt in thirty years, compares most favourably with that usually provided by local bodies for works of so permanent a character. The Local Government Board frequently allows loans to be created with a sinking fund extending over much longer periods. It is to be remembered also that an additional sinking fund for the landed estate has been already provided (*see* Chapter iv., p. 42).

M. Balance available for Rates levied by Local Bodies within whose jurisdiction the estate is situated.

It will be seen that the whole scheme of Garden City will make extremely few demands upon the resources of outside local authorities. Roads, sewers, schools, parks, libraries, etc., will be provided out of the funds of the new "municipality," and in this way the whole scheme will come to the agriculturists at present on the estate very much like "a rate in aid"; for, as rates are only raised for the purpose of public expenditure, it follows that, there being little or no fresh call upon the rates while the number of ratepayers is greatly increased, the rate per head must fall. I do not, however, forget that there are some functions which such a voluntary organisation as Garden City could not take over, such as the police and the administration of the poor-law. As to the latter, it is believed that the whole scheme will in the long run make such rates unnecessary, as Garden City will provide, at all events from the time when the estate has been fully paid for, pensions for all its needy old citizens. Meantime and from the very outset it is doing its full [p. 66] share of charitable work. It has allotted sites of 30 acres for various institutions, and at a later stage will doubtless be prepared to assume the whole cost of maintaining them.

With regard to police rates, it is not believed that these can be largely increased by the coming into the town of 30,000 citizens, who, for the most part, will be of the law-abiding class; for, there being but one landlord, and this the community, it will not be difficult to prevent the creation of those surroundings which make the intervention of the police so frequently necessary. (*See* Chapter vii.)

I have, I think, now fully established my contention that the rate-rent which would be willingly offered by the tenants of Garden City, in respect of the advantages afforded them, would be amply sufficient, (1) to pay landlord's rent in the form of interest on debentures; (2) to provide a sinking fund for the entire abolition of landlord's rent; and (3) to provide for the municipal needs of the town without recourse to any Act of Parliament for the enforcement of rates—the community depending solely on the very large powers it possesses as a landlord.

N. Revenue-bearing Expenditure.

If the conclusion already arrived at—that the experiment advocated affords an outlet for an extremely effective expenditure of labour and capital—is sound in regard to objects the cost of which is usually defrayed out of rates, that conclusion must, I think, be equally sound in regard to tramways, lighting, water-supply, and the like, which, when carried on by municipalities, are [p. 67] usually made a source of revenue, thus relieving the rate-payer by making his rates lighter.[1] And as I have added nothing to the proposed revenue for any prospective profits on such undertakings, I do not propose to make any estimate of expenditure. [p. 68]

---

[1] "Birmingham rates are relieved to the extent of £50,000 a year out of profits on gas. The Electrical Committee of Manchester has promised to pay £10,000 this year to the city fund, in relief of rates out of a net profit of over £16,000."—*Daily Chronicle*, 9th June, 1897.

CHAPTER VI.
ADMINISTRATION.

I Have in the 4th and 5th chapters dealt with the fund at the disposal of the Board of Management, and have endeavoured to show, and I believe with success, that the rate-rents collected by the trustees in their capacity of landlords of the towns will suffice, (1) to provide interest on the debentures with which the estate is purchased, (2) to provide a sinking fund which will at a comparatively early date leave the community free from the burden of interest on such debentures, and (3) to enable the Board of Management to carry on such undertakings as are elsewhere, for the most part, carried out by means of rates compulsorily levied.

A most important question now arises regarding the extent to which municipal enterprise is to be carried, and how far it is to supersede private enterprise. We have already by implication stated that the experiment advocated does not involve, as has been the case in so many social experiments—the complete municipalisation of industry and the elimination of private enterprise. But what principle is to guide us in determining the line which shall separate municipal from private control and management? Mr. Joseph Chamberlain has said: "The true field for municipal activity is limited to those things [p. 69] which the community can do better than the individual." Precisely, but that is a truism, and does not carry us one whit further, for the very question at issue is as to *what those things are* which the community can do better than the individual; and when we seek for an answer to this question we find two directly conflicting views—the view of the socialist, who says: Every phase of wealth-production and distribution can be best performed by the community; and the view of the individualist, who contends these things are best left to the individual. But probably the true answer is to be found at neither extreme, is only to be gained by experiment, and will differ in different communities and at different periods. With a growing intelligence and honesty in municipal enterprise, with greater freedom from the control of the Central Government, it may be found—especially on municipally-owned land—that the field of municipal activity may grow so as to embrace a very large area, and yet the municipality claim no rigid monopoly and the fullest rights of combination exist.

Bearing this in mind, the municipality of Garden City will, at the outset, exercise great caution, and not attempt too much. The difficulty of raising the necessary funds with which to carry on municipal undertakings would be greatly increased if the Board of Management attempted to do everything; and, in the prospectus to be ultimately issued, a clear statement will be made of what the Corporation undertakes to do with the moneys entrusted to it, and this will at first embrace little more than those things which experience has proved municipalities can perform better than individuals. Tenants, too, will, it is obvious, be far more ready to offer adequate "rate-rents" [p. 70] if they are given distinctly to understand to what purpose those "rate-rents" are to be devoted, and after those things are done, and done well, little difficulty will be placed in the way of further appropriate extensions of the field of municipal enterprise.

Our answer, then, to the question, what field is to be covered by municipal enterprise, is this. Its extent will be measured simply by the willingness of the tenants to pay rate-rents, and will grow in proportion as municipal work is done efficiently and honestly, or decline as it is done dishonestly or inefficiently. If, for example, the tenants find that a very small additional contribution, recently made in the shape of "rate-rent," has enabled the authorities to provide an excellent supply of water for all purposes, and they are convinced that so good a result at so small a cost would not have been achieved through the agency of any private undertaking working for a profit, they will naturally be willing and even anxious that further hopeful-looking experiments in municipal work should be undertaken. The site of Garden City may, in this respect, be compared with Mr. and Mrs. Boffin's famous apartment, which, the reader of Dickens will remember, was furnished at one end to suit the taste of Mrs. Boffin, who was "a dab at fashion," while at the other end it was furnished to conform to the notions of solid comfort which so gratified Mr. Boffin, but with the mutual understanding between the parties that if Mr. B. should get by degrees to be "a high-flyer" at fashion, then Mrs. B.'s carpet would gradually "come for'arder," whilst if Mrs. B. should become "less of a dab at fashion," Mrs. B.'s carpet would "go back'arder." So, in Garden City, if the inhabitants become greater [p. 71] "dabs" at co-operation, the municipality will "come for'arder"; if they become less "dabs" at co-operation, the municipality will "go back'arder"; while the relative number of positions occupied by municipal workers and non-municipal workers at any period will very fairly reflect the skill and integrity of the public administration and the degree of value which is therefore associated with municipal effort.

But the municipality of Garden City, besides setting its face against any attempt to embark upon too large a field of enterprise, will so frame its constitution that the responsibility for each branch of the municipal service will be thrown directly upon the officers of that branch and not be practically lost sight of because loosely thrown upon the larger central body—a plan which makes it difficult for the public to perceive where any leakage or friction may be taking place. The constitution is modelled upon that of a large and well-appointed business, which is divided into various departments, each department being expected to justify its own continued existence—its officers being selected, not so much for their knowledge of the business generally as for their special fitness for the work of their department.

THE BOARD OF MANAGEMENT

consists of—

> (1) The Central Council.
>
> (2) The Departments.

THE CENTRAL COUNCIL (*see* Diagram 5).

In this council (or its nominees) are vested the rights and powers of the community as sole landlord of Garden [p. 72] City. Into its treasury are paid (after provision has been made for landlord's rent and sinking fund) all rate-rents received from its tenants, as well as the profits derived from its various municipal undertakings, and these, we have seen, are amply sufficient to discharge all public burdens without any resort to the expedient of compulsory rates. The powers possessed by the Central Council are, it may be noticed in passing, more ample than those possessed by other municipal bodies, for whilst most of these enjoy only such powers as are expressly conferred on them by Acts of Parliament, the Central Council of Garden City exercises on behalf of the people those wider rights, powers and privileges which are enjoyed by landlords under the common law. The private owner of land can do with his land and with the revenue he derives from it what he pleases so long as he is not a nuisance to his neighbour; while, on the other hand, public bodies which acquire land or obtain power to levy rates by Acts of Parliament, can only use that land or spend those rates for such purposes as are expressly prescribed by those Acts. But Garden City is in a greatly superior position, for, by stepping as a *quasi* public body into the rights of a private landlord, it becomes at once clothed with far larger powers for carrying out the will of the people than are possessed by other local bodies, and thus solves to a large extent the problem of local self-government.

But the Central Council, though possessing these large powers, delegates many of them, for convenience of administration, to its various departments, retaining, however, responsibility for—

(1) The general plan on which the estate is laid out. [p. 73]

(2) The amount of money voted to each of the various spending departments, as schools, roads, parks, etc.

(3) Such measure of oversight and control of the departments as is necessary to preserve a general unity and harmony, but no more.

THE DEPARTMENTS.

These are divided into various groups—for example:

> (A) Public Control.
> (B) Engineering.
> (C) Social Purposes.

GROUP A, PUBLIC CONTROL.

This group may consist of the following sub-groups:

> Finance.   Assessment.
> Law.   Inspection.

Finance.

Into this department are paid, after making provision for landlord's rent and sinking fund, all rate-rents; and out of it the necessary sums for the various departments are voted by the Central Council.

Assessment.

This department receives all applications from would-be tenants, and fixes the rate-rent to be paid—such rate-rents not, however, being fixed arbitrarily by the department, but upon the essential principle adopted by other Assessment Committees—the really determining factor [p. 74] being the rate-rent which an average tenant is found willing to pay.[1]

Law.

This department settles the terms and conditions under which leases shall be granted, and the nature of the covenants to be entered into by and with the Central Council.

Inspection.

This department carries out such reasonable duties in relation to inspection as the municipality, in its capacity of landlord, may with the tenants of the municipality mutually agree upon.

GROUP B, ENGINEERING.

This group may consist of the following departments—some of which would be later creations.

Roads.	Parks and open spaces.
Subways.	Drainage.
Sewers.	Canals.
Tramways.	Irrigation.
Municipal Railway.	Water-supply.
Public Buildings (other than schools).	Motive-power & Lighting.
	Messages.

GROUP C, SOCIAL AND EDUCATIONAL.

This group is also divided into various departments, dealing with: —

Education.	Libraries.
Baths and Wash-houses.	
Music.	Recreation. [p. 75]

Election of Members of Board of Management.

Members (who may be men or women) are elected by the rate-renters to serve on one or more departments, and the Chairmen and Vice-Chairmen of the departments constitute the Central Council.

Under such a constitution it is believed that the community would have the readiest means of rightly estimating the work of its servants, and, at elec-

---

[1] This individual is known to Assessment Committees under the name of the "hypothetical tenant."

tion times, would have clear and distinct issues brought before it. The candidates would not be expected to specify their views upon a hundred and one questions of municipal policy upon which they had no definite opinions, and which would probably not give rise within their term of office to the necessity for recording their votes, but would simply state their views as to some special question or group of questions, a sound opinion upon which would be of urgent importance to the electors, because immediately connected with the welfare of the town. [p. 76]

CHAPTER VII.

SEMI-MUNICIPAL ENTERPRISE—LOCAL OPTION—TEMPERANCE REFORM.

IN the last chapter we saw that no line could be sharply drawn between municipal and individual enterprise, so that one could definitely say of one or the other, "Hitherto shalt thou come, but no further"; and this ever-changing character of the problem can be usefully illustrated in our examination of the industrial life of Garden City by reference to a form of enterprise there carried on which is neither distinctly municipal nor distinctly individualistic, but partaking, as it does, of the character of both, may be termed "semi-municipal."

Among the most reliable sources of revenue possessed by many of our existing municipalities are their so-called "public markets." But it is important to notice that these markets are by no means public in the same full sense as are our public parks, libraries, water under-takings, or those numerous other branches of municipal work which are carried on upon public property, by public officials, at the public expense, and solely with a view to the public advantage. On the contrary, our so-called "public markets" are, for the most part, carried on by private individuals, who pay tolls for the parts of the buildings which they occupy, but who are not, except on [p. 77] a few points, controlled by the municipality, and whose profits are personally enjoyed by the various dealers. Markets may, therefore, be fitly termed *semi-municipal* enterprises.

It would, however, have been scarcely necessary to touch on this question, but that it naturally leads up to the consideration of a form of semi-municipal enterprise which is one of the characteristic features of Garden City. This is to be found in the Crystal Palace, which, it will be remembered, is a wide arcade, skirting the Central Park, in which the most attractive wares on sale in Garden City are exhibited, and, this being a winter garden as well as the great shopping centre, is one of the most favourite resorts of the townspeople. The business at the shops is carried on, not by the municipality, but by various individuals and societies, the number of traders being, however, limited by the principle of local option.

The considerations which have led to this system arise out of the distinction between the cases on the one hand of the manufacturers, and on the other of the distributive societies and shopkeepers who are invited to the town. Thus, for example: —In the case of the manufacturer, say, of boots, though he may be glad of the custom of the people of the town, he is by no means dependent on it; his products go all over the world; and he would scarcely wish that the number of boot manufacturers within the area should be specially limited. He would, in fact, lose more than he would gain by restrictions of this kind. A manufacturer frequently prefers to have others carrying on the same trade in his vicinity; for this gives him a larger choice [p. 78] of skilled workmen or workwomen, who themselves desire it also, because it gives them a larger range of employers.

But in the case of shops and stores the case is entirely different. An individual or a society proposing to open in Garden City, say a drapery store, would be most anxious to know what, if any, arrangements were to be made for limiting the number of his competitors, for he would depend almost entirely on the trade of the town or neighbourhood. Indeed it frequently happens that a private landlord, when laying out a building estate, makes arrangements with his shopkeeping tenants designed to prevent them from being swamped by others in the same trade starting on his estate.

The problem, therefore, seems to be how to make such suitable arrangements as will at once—

(1) Induce tenants of the shopkeeping class to come and start in business, offering to the community adequate rate-rents.

(2) Prevent the absurd and wasteful multiplication of shops referred to in the note at the foot of page 81.

(3) Secure the advantages usually gained (or supposed to be) by competition—such as low prices, wide range of choice, fair dealing, civility, etc.

(4) Avoid the evils attending monopoly.

All these results may be secured by a simple expedient, which will have the effect of converting competition from an active into a latent force to be brought into play or held in reserve. It is, as we have said, an application of the principle of local option. To explain: [p. 79] —Garden City is the sole landlord, and it can grant to a proposed tenant—we will suppose a co-operative society or an individual trader in drapery or fancy goods—a long lease of a certain amount of space in the Grand Arcade (Crystal Palace), at a certain annual rate-rent; and it can say, in effect, to its tenant, "That site is the only space in that ward which we for the present intend to let to any tenant engaged in your trade. The Arcade is, however, designed to be not only the great shopping centre of the town and district, and the permanent exhibition in which the manufacturers of the town display their wares, but a summer and winter garden. The space this Arcade covers will, therefore, be considerably greater than is actually required for the purposes of shops or stores, if these are kept within reasonable limits. Now, so long as you give satisfaction to the people of the town, none of the space devoted to these recreative purposes will be let to anyone engaged in your calling. It is necessary, however, to guard against monopoly. If, therefore, the people become dissatisfied with your methods of trading, and desire that the force of competition shall be actively brought into play against you, then, on the requisition of a certain number, the necessary space in the Arcade will be allotted by the municipality to some one desirous of starting an opposition store."

Under this arrangement it will be seen the trader will depend upon the good-will of his customers. If he charges prices which are too high; if he misrepresents the quality of his goods; if he does not treat his employees with proper consideration in regard to hours of labour, wages, or other matters, he will run a great risk of losing the good-will of his customers, and the people of the town will have a [p. 80] method of expressing their sentiments regarding him which will be extremely powerful; they will simply invite a new competitor to enter the field. But, on the other hand, as long as he perform his functions wisely and well, his good-will resting on the solid basis of the good-will of his customers, he will be protected. His advantages are, therefore, enormous. In other towns a competitor might enter the field against him at any moment without warning, perhaps at the very time when he had purchased some expensive goods, which, unless sold during the season, could only be realised at an enormous sacrifice. In Garden City, on the other hand, he has full notice of his danger—time to prepare for it and even to avert it. Besides, the members of the community, except for the purpose of bringing a trader to reason, will not only have no interest in bringing a competitor into the field, but their interests will be best served by keeping competition in the background as long as possible. If the fire of competition is brought to bear upon a trader, they must suffer with him. They will lose space they would far rather see devoted to some other purpose—they will be bound to pay higher prices than those at which the first trader could supply them if he would, and they will have to render municipal services to two traders instead of to one, while the two competitors could not afford to pay so large a sum in rate-rent as could the original trader. For in many cases the effect of competition is to make a rise in price absolutely necessary. Thus, A. has a trade of 100 gallons of milk a day, and can, we will suppose, pay his expenses, earn a bare living, and supply his customers with milk, say, at 4d. a quart. But if a competitor enters the field, [p. 81] then A. can only sell *milk and water* at 4d. a quart if he is to continue to pay his way. Thus the competition of shopkeepers absolutely tends not only to ruin the competitors, but to maintain and even to raise prices, and so to lower real wages.[1]

Under this system of local option it will be seen that the tradesmen of the town—be they co-operative societies or individuals—would become, if not strictly or technically so, yet in a very real sense, municipal servants. But they would not be bound up in the red-tape of officialism, and would have the fullest rights and powers of initiation. It would not be by any literal conformity to cast-iron and inflexible rules, but by their skill and judgment in forecasting the wishes and in anticipating the tastes of their constituents, as well as by their integrity and courtesy as business men and women, that they would win and maintain their good-will. They would run certain risks, as all tradesmen must, and in return they would be paid, not of course in the form of salary, but in profits. But the risks they would run would be far less than they must be where competition is unchecked and uncontrolled, while their annual profits in propor- [p. 82] tion to capital invested might also be greater. They might even sell considerably below the ordinary rate prevailing elsewhere, but yet, having an assured trade and being able very accurately to gauge demand, they might turn their money over with remarkable frequency. Their working expenses, too, would be absurdly small. They would not have to advertise for customers, though they would doubtless make announcements to them of any novelties; but all that waste of effort and of money which is so frequently expended by tradesmen in order to secure customers or to prevent their going elsewhere, would be quite unnecessary.

And not only would each trader be in a sense a municipal servant, but those in his employ would be also. It is true such a trader would have the fullest right to engage and dismiss his servants; but if he acted arbitrarily or harshly, if

---

[1] "It has been calculated by Mr. Neale" ("Economics of Co-operation") "that there are 41,735 separate establishments for 22 of the principal retail trades in London. If for each of these trades there were 648 shops—that is 9 to the square mile, no one would have to go more than a quarter of a mile to the nearest shop. There would be 14,256 shops in all. Assuming that this supply would be sufficient, there are in London 251 shops for every hundred that are really wanted. The general prosperity of the country will be much increased when the capital and labour that are now wastefully employed in the retail trade are set free for other work."—"Economics of Industry," A. and M. P. Marshall, Chap. ix., sec. 10.

he paid insufficient wages, or treated his employees inconsiderately, he would certainly run the risk of losing the good-will of the majority of his customers, even although in other respects he might prove himself an admirable public servant. On the other hand, if the example were set of profit-sharing, this might grow into a custom, and the distinction between master and servant would be gradually lost in the simple process of all becoming co-operators.[1]

This system of local option as applied to shopkeeping is not only business-like, but it affords an opportunity for [p. 83] the expression of that public conscience against the sweater which is now being stirred, but which scarcely knows how to effectually respond to the new impulse. Thus there was established in London some years ago the Consumers' League, the object of which was not, as its name might lead one to suspect, to protect the consuming public against the unscrupulous producer, but it was to protect the sweated, over-driven producer against a consuming public over-clamorous for cheapness. Its aim was to assist such of the public as hate and detest the sweating system to avail themselves of the League's carefully compiled information, so that they might be able to studiously avoid the products which had passed through sweaters' hands. But such a movement as the Consumers' League advocated could make but little headway without the support of the shopkeeper. That consumer must be an uncommonly earnest opponent of sweating who insists upon knowing the source whence every article he purchases has come, and a shopkeeper under ordinary circumstances would scarcely be disposed either to give such information or to guarantee that the goods he sold were produced under "fair" conditions; while to establish shops in large cities, which are already overcrowded with distributive agencies, and to do this with the special object of putting down sweating, is to court failure. Here in Garden City, however, there will be a splendid opportunity for the public conscience to express itself in [p. 84] this regard, and no shopkeeper will, I hope, venture to sell "sweated goods."

There is another question with which the term "local option" is most closely associated which may be dealt with here. I refer to the temperance question. Now it will be noticed that the municipality, in its position of sole landlord, has the *power* of dealing in the most drastic manner possible with the liquor traffic.

---

[1] This principle of local option, which is chiefly applicable to distributive callings, is perhaps applicable to production in some of its branches. Thus bakeries and laundries, which would largely depend upon the trade of the locality, seem to present instances where it might with some caution be applied. Few businesses seem to require more thorough supervision and control than these, and few have a more direct relation to health. Indeed, a very strong case might be made out for municipal bakeries and municipal laundries, and it is evident that the control of an industry by the community is a half-way house to its assumption of it, should this prove desirable and practicable.

There are, as is well known, many landlords who will not permit a public-house to be opened on their estate, and the landlord of Garden City—the people themselves—*could* adopt this course. But would this be wise? I think not. First, such a restriction would keep away the very large and increasing class of moderate drinkers, and would also keep away many of those who are scarcely moderate in their use of alcohol, but as to whom reformers would be most anxious that they should be brought under the healthful influences which would surround them in Garden City. The public-house, or its equivalent, would, in such a community, have many competitors for the favour of the people; while, in large cities, with few opportunities of cheap and rational enjoyment, it has its own way. The experiment, as one in the direction of temperance reform, would, therefore, be more valuable if the traffic were permitted under reasonable regulations than if it were stopped; because, while, in the former case, the effects in the direction of temperance would be clearly traceable to the more natural and healthy form of life, if the latter course were adopted it could only prove, what no one now denies, that it may be possible, by restrictive measures, to entirely keep away the traffic from one small area while intensifying the evils elsewhere. [p. 85]

But the community would certainly take care to prevent the undue multiplication of licensed houses, and it would be free to adopt any one of the various methods which the more moderate of temperance reformers suggest. The municipal authorities might conduct the liquor traffic themselves, and employ the profits in relief of rates. There is, however, much force in the objection that it is not desirable that the revenue of a community should be so derived, and, therefore, it might be better that the profits should be entirely applied to purposes which would compete with the traffic, or in minimising its evil effects by establishing asylums for those affected with alcoholism.[1] On this subject, as on all points involved, I earnestly invite correspondence from those who have, practical suggestions to offer; and, although the town is but a small one, it would perhaps not be impracticable to test various promising suggestions in the different wards. [p. 86]

[1] Since "To-Morrow" was published, various Companies have been formed by the Public House Trust Association, 116 Victoria Street, Westminster, S.W., with the object of carrying on the trade on principles advocated by the Bishop of Chester. A limited dividend of 5 per cent. is fixed; all profits beyond are expended in useful public enterprises, and the Managers have no interest whatever in pushing the trade in intoxicating liquors. It may be interesting also to observe that Mr. George Cadbury, in the Deed of Foundation of the Bourneville Trust, provides for the complete restriction of the traffic at the outset. But as a practical man, he sees that as the Trust grows (and its power of growth is among its most admirable features) it may be necessary to remove such complete restrictions. And he provides that in that event "all the net profits arising from the sale and co-operative distribution of intoxicating liquors shall be devoted to securing recreation and counter attractions to the liquor trade as ordinarily conducted."

CHAPTER VIII.
PRO-MUNICIPAL WORK.

THERE will be found in every progressive community societies and organisations which represent a far higher level of public spirit and enterprise than that possessed or displayed by such communities in their collective capacity. It is probable that the government of a community can never reach a higher tone or work on a higher plane than the average sense of that community demands and enforces; and it will greatly conduce to the well-being of any society if the efforts of its State or municipal organisations are inspired and quickened by those of its members whose ideals of society duty rise higher than the average.[1]

And so it may be in Garden City. There will be discovered many opportunities for public service which [p. 87] neither the community as a whole, nor even a majority of its members, will at first recognise the importance of, or see their way to embrace, and which public services it would be useless, therefore, to expect the municipality to undertake; but those who have the welfare of society at heart will, in the free air of the city, be always able to experiment on their own responsibility, and thus quicken the public conscience and enlarge the public understanding.

The whole of the experiment which this book describes is indeed of this character. It represents pioneer work, which will be carried out by those who have not a merely pious opinion, but an effective belief in the economic, sanitary, and social advantages of common ownership of land, and who, therefore, are not satisfied merely to advocate that those advantages should be secured

[1] "Only a proportion of each in one society can have nerve enough to grasp the banner of a new truth, and endurance enough to bear it along rugged and untrodden ways. . . . To insist on a whole community being made at once to submit to the reign of new practices and new ideas which have just begun to commend themselves to the most advanced speculative intelligence of the time—this, even if it were a possible process, would do much to make life impracticable and to hurry on social dissolution. . . . A new social state can never establish its ideas unless the persons who hold them confess them openly and give them an honest and effective adherence."—Mr. John Morley, "On Compromise," Chap. v.

on the largest scale at the national expense, but are impelled to give their views shape and form as soon as they can see their way to join with a sufficient number of kindred spirits. And what the whole experiment is to the nation, so may what we term "pro-municipal" undertakings be to the community of Garden City or to society generally. Just as the larger experiment is designed to lead the nation into a juster and better system of land tenure and a better and more common-sense view of how towns should be built, so are the various pro-municipal undertakings of Garden City devised by those who are prepared to lead the way in enterprises designed to further the well-being of the town, but who have not as yet succeeded in getting their plans or schemes adopted by the Central Council.

Philanthropic and charitable institutions, religious [p. 88] societies, and educational agencies of various kinds occupy a very large part in this group of pro-municipal or pro-national agencies, and these have been already referred to, and their nature and purposes are well known. But institutions which aim at the more strictly material side of well-being, such as banks and building societies, may be found here too. Just as the founders of the Penny Bank paved the way for the Post Office Savings Bank, so may some of those who study carefully the experiment of building up Garden City see how useful a bank might be, which, like the Penny Bank, aims not so much at gain for its founders as at the well-being of the community at large. Such a bank might arrange to pay the whole of its net profits or all its profits over a certain fixed rate, into the municipal exchequer, and give to the authorities of the town the option of taking it over should they be convinced of its utility and its general soundness.

There is another large field for pro-municipal activity in the work of building homes for the people. The municipality would be attempting too much if it essayed this task, at least at the outset. To do so would be perhaps to depart too widely from the path which experience has justified, however much might be said in favour of such a course on the part of a municipal body in command of ample funds. The municipality has, however, done much to make the building of bright and beautiful homes for the people possible. It has effectually provided against any overcrowding within its area, thus solving a problem found insoluble in existing cities, and it offers sites of ample size at an average rate of £6 per annum for ground-rent and rates. Having done so much, the municipality will [p. 89] pay heed to the warning of an experienced municipal reformer, whose desire for the extension, of municipal enterprise cannot be doubted (Mr. John Burns, M.P., L.C.C.), who has said: "A lot of work has been thrown upon the Works Committee of the London County Council by councillors who are so anxious for its success that they would choke it by a burden of work."

There are, however, other sources to which the workers may look for means to build their own homes. They may form building societies or induce cooperative societies, friendly societies, and trade unions to lend them the necessary money, and to help them to organise the requisite machinery. Granted the existence of the true social spirit, and not its mere letter and name, and that spirit will manifest itself in an infinite variety of ways. There are in this country—who can doubt it?—many individuals and societies who would be ready to raise funds and organise associations for assisting bodies of workmen secure of good wages to build their own homes on favourable terms.

A better security the lenders could scarcely have, especially having regard to the ridiculously small landlord's rent paid by the borrowers. Certain it is that if the building of the homes for these workmen is left to speculative builders of a strongly-pronounced individualistic type, and these reap golden harvests, it will be the fault, amongst others, of those large organisations of working-men which now place their capital in banks, whence it is withdrawn by those who with it "exploit" the very men who have placed it there. It is idle for working-men to complain of this self-imposed exploitation, and to talk of nationalising the entire land and capital of [p. 90] this country under an executive of their own class, until they have first been through an apprenticeship at the humbler task of organising men and women with their own capital in constructive work of a less ambitious character—until they have assisted far more largely than they have yet done in building up capital, not to be wasted in strikes, or employed by capitalists in fighting strikers, but in securing homes and employment for themselves and others on just and honourable terms. The true remedy for capitalist oppression where it exists, is not the strike of *no work*, but the strike of *true work*, and against this last blow the oppressor has no weapon. If labour leaders spent half the energy in co-operative organisation that they now waste in co-operative disorganisation, the end of our present unjust system would be at hand. In Garden City such leaders will have a fair field for the exercise of pro-municipal functions—functions which are exercised for the municipality, though not by it—and the formation of building societies of this type would be of the greatest possible utility.

But would not the amount of capital required for the building of the dwelling-houses of a town of 30,000 be enormous? Some persons with whom I have discussed the question look at the matter thus. So many houses in Garden City at so many hundred of pounds a-piece, capital required so much.[1]

---

[1] The position was so stated by Mr. Buckingham in "National Evils and Practical Remedies,"

This is, of course, quite a mistaken way of regarding the problem. Let us test the matter thus. How many houses have been built in London within the last ten years? Shall we say, at the very roughest of guesses 150,000, costing on an average [p. 91] £300 a-piece—to say nothing of shops, factories, and warehouses. Well, that is £45,000,000. Was £45,000,000 raised for this purpose? Yes, certainly, or the houses would not have been built. But the money was not raised all at once, and if one could recognise the actual sovereigns that were raised for the building of these 150,000 houses, one would often find the very same coins turning up again and again. So in Garden City. Before it is completed, there will be 5,500 houses at, say, £300 a-piece, making £1,650,000. But this capital will not be raised all at once, and here, far more than in London, the very same sovereigns would be employed in building many houses. For observe, money is not lost or consumed when it is spent. It merely changes hands. A workman of Garden City borrows £200 from a pro-municipal building society, and builds a house with it. That house costs him £200, and the 200 sovereigns disappear so far as he is concerned, but they become the property of the brickmakers, builders, carpenters, plumbers, plasterers, etc., who have built his house, whence those sovereigns would find their way into the pockets of the tradesmen and others with whom such workmen deal, and thence would pass into the pro-municipal bank of the town, when presently, those 200 identical sovereigns might be drawn out and employed in building another house. Thus there would be presented the apparent anomaly of two, and then three, and then four or more houses, each costing £200, being built with 200 sovereigns.[1] But there is no real anomaly about it. The coins, of course, [p. 92] did not build the houses in any of the supposed cases. The coins were but the measure of value, and like a pair of scales and weights, may be used over and over again without any perceptible lessening of their worth. What built the houses was really labour, skill, enterprise, working up the free gifts of nature; and though each of the workers might have his reward weighed out to him in coins, the cost of all buildings and works in Garden City must be mainly determined by the skill and energy with which its labours are directed. Still, so long as gold and silver are recognised as the medium of exchange, it will be necessary to use them, and of great importance to use them skilfully—for the skill with which they are used, or their unnecessary use dispensed with, as in a banker's clearing house, will have a most important bearing upon the cost of the town, and upon the annual tax levied in the shape of interest on borrowed capital. Skill must be therefore di-

---

see Chap. x.

[1] A similar line of argument to this is very fully elaborated in a most able work entitled "The Physiology of Industry," by Mummery and Hobson (MacMillan & Co.).

rected to the object of so using coins that they may quickly effect their object of measuring one value, and be set to work to measure another—that they may be turned over as many times as possible in the year, in order that the amount of labour measured by each coin may be as large as possible, and thus the amount represented by interest on the coins borrowed, though paid at the normal or usual rate, shall bear as small a proportion as possible to the amount paid to labour. If this is done effectively, then a saving to the community in respect of interest as great as the more easily demonstrated saving in landlord's rent may probably be effected.

And now the reader is asked to observe how admirably, and, as it were, automatically, a well-organised migratory movement to land held in common lends itself [p. 93] to the economic use of money, and to the making of one coin serve many purposes. Money, it is often said, is "a drug in the market." Like labour itself, it seems enchanted, and thus one sees millions in gold and silver lying idle in banks facing the very streets where men are wandering workless and penniless. But here, on the site of Garden City, the cry for employment on the part of those willing to work will no more be heard in vain. Only yesterday it may have been so, but to-day the enchanted land is awake, and is loudly call-ing for its children. There is no difficulty in finding work—profitable work—work that is really urgently, imperatively needed—the building of a home-city, and, as men hasten to build up this and the other towns which must inevitably follow its construction, the migration to the towns—the old, crowded, chaotic slum-towns of the past—will be effectually checked, and the current of popu-lation set in precisely the opposite direction—to the new towns, bright and fair, wholesome and beautiful. [p. 94]

CHAPTER IX.
SOME DIFFICULTIES CONSIDERED.

HAVING now, in a concrete rather than an abstract form, stated the objects and purposes of our scheme, it may be well to deal, though somewhat briefly, with an objection which may arise in the thought of the reader: "Your scheme may be very attractive, but it is but one of a great number, many of which have been tried and have met with but little success. How do you distinguish it from those? How, in the face of such a record of failure, do you expect to secure that large measure of public support which is necessary ere such a scheme can be put into operation?"

The question is a very natural one, and demands an answer. My reply is: It is quite true that the pathway of experiment towards a better state of society is strewn with failures. But so is the pathway of experiment to any result that is worth achieving. Success is, for the most part, built on failure. As Mrs. Humphrey Ward remarks in "Robert Elsmere": "All great changes are preceded by numbers of sporadic, and, as the bystander thinks, intermittent efforts." A successful invention or discovery is usually a slow growth, to which new elements are added, and from which old elements are removed, first in the thought of the inventor, and subsequently in an outward form, until at last precisely the right elements [p. 95] and no others are brought together. Indeed, it may be truly said that if you find a series of experiments continued through many years by various workers, there will eventually be produced the result for which so many have been industriously searching. Long-continued effort, in spite of failure and defeat, is the fore-runner of complete success. He who wishes to achieve success may turn past defeat into future victory by observing one condition. He must profit by past experiences, and aim at retaining all the strong points without the weaknesses of former efforts.

To deal at all exhaustively here with the history of social experiments would be beyond the scope of this book; but a few leading features may be noticed with a view of meeting the objection with which this chapter opens.

Probably the chief cause of failure in former social experiments has been a misconception of the principal element in the problem—human nature itself. The degree of strain which average human nature will bear in an altruistic direction has not been duly considered by those who have essayed the task of suggesting new forms of social organisation. A kindred mistake has arisen from regarding one principle of action to the exclusion of others. Take Communism, for instance. Communism is a most excellent principle, and all of us are Communists in some degree, even those who would shudder at being told so. For we all believe in communistic roads, communistic parks, and communistic libraries. But though Communism is an excellent principle. Individualism is no less excellent. A great orchestra which enraptures us with its delightful music is [p. 96] composed of men and women who are accustomed not only to play together, but to practise separately, and to delight themselves and their friends by their own, it may be comparatively, feeble efforts. Nay, more: isolated and individual thought and action are as essential, if the best results of combination are to be secured, as combination and co-operation are essential, if the best results of isolated effort are to be gained. It is by isolated thought that new combinations are worked out; it is through the lessons learned in associated effort that the best individual work is accomplished; and that society will prove the most healthy and vigorous where the freest and fullest opportunities are afforded alike for individual and for combined effort.

Now, do not the whole series of communistic experiments owe their failure largely to this—that they have not recognised this duality of principle, but have carried one principle, excellent enough in itself, altogether too far? They have assumed that because common property is good, all property should be common; that because associated effort can produce marvels, individual effort is to be regarded as dangerous, or at least futile, some extremists even seeking to abolish altogether the idea of the family or home. No reader will confuse the experiment here advocated with any experiment in absolute Communism.

Nor is the scheme to be regarded as a socialistic experiment. Socialists, who may be regarded as Communists of a more moderate type, advocate common property in land and in all the instruments of production, distribution, and exchange—railways, machinery, factories, docks, banks, and the like; but they would preserve [p. 97] the principle of private ownership in all such things as have passed in the form of wages to the servants of the community, with the proviso, however, that these wages shall not be employed in organised creative effort, involving the employment of more than one person; for all forms of employment with a view to remuneration should, as the Socialists contend, be under the direction of some recognised department of the Government, which is to claim a rigid monopoly. But it is very doubtful whether this principle of the Socialist, in which there is a certain measure of recognition of the individual side of man's nature as well as of his social side, represents a basis on which an experiment can fairly proceed with the hope of permanent success. Two chief difficulties appear to present themselves. First, the self-seeking side of man—his too frequent desire to produce, with a view to possessing for his own personal use and enjoyment; and, secondly, his love of independence and of initiative, his personal ambition, and his consequent unwillingness to put himself under the guidance of others for the whole of his working day, with little opportunity of striking out some independent line of action, or of taking a leading part in the creation of new forms of enterprise.

Now, even if we pass over the first difficulty—that of human self-seeking—even if we assume that we have a body of men and women who have realised the truth that concerted social effort will achieve far better results in enjoyable commodities for each member of the community than can possibly be achieved by ordinary competitive methods—each struggling for himself—we have still the other difficulty, arising out of the higher and not the [p. 98] lower nature of the men and women who are to be organised—their love of independence and of initiative. Men love combined effort, but they love individual effort, too, and they will not be content with such few opportunities for personal effort as they would be allowed to make in a rigid socialistic community. Men do not object to being organised under competent leadership, but some also want to be leaders, and to have a share in the work of organising; they like to lead as well as to be led. Besides, one can easily imagine men filled with a desire to serve the community in some way which the community as a whole did not at the moment appreciate the advantage of, and who would be precluded by the very constitution of the socialistic state from carrying their proposals into effect.

Now, it is at this very point that a most interesting experiment at Topolobampo has broken down. The experiment, which was initiated by Mr. A. K. Owen, an American civil engineer, was started on a considerable tract of land obtained under concession from the Mexican Government. One principle adopted by Mr. Owen was that "all employment must be through the Department for the Diversity of Home Industries. One member cannot directly employ another member, and only members can be employed through the settlement."[1] In other words, if A. and B. were dissatisfied with the man-

---

[1] "Integral Co-operation at Work," A. K. Owen (U.S. Book Co., 150 Worth St., N.Y.).

agement, whether owing to doubts as to its competency or honesty, they could not arrange to work with each other, even though their sole desire might be the common good; but they must leave the settlement. And [p. 99] this is what they accordingly did in very considerable numbers.

It is at this point that a great distinction between the Topolobampo experiment and the scheme advocated in this work is evident. In Topolobampo the organisation claimed a monopoly of all productive work, and each member must work under the direction of those who controlled that monopoly, or must leave the organisation. In Garden City no such monopoly is claimed, and any dissatisfaction with the public administration of the affairs of the town would no more necessarily lead to a widespread split in Garden City than in any other municipality. At the outset, at least, by far the larger part of the work done will be by individuals or combinations of individuals quite other than municipal servants, just as in any other municipality, at present existing, the sphere of municipal work is still very small as compared with the work performed by other groups.

Other sources of failure in some social experiments are the considerable expense incurred by migrants before they reach the scene of their future labours, the great distance from any large market, and the difficulty of previously obtaining any real knowledge of the conditions of life and labour there prevailing. The one advantage gained—cheap land—seems to be altogether insufficient to compensate for these and other disadvantages.

We now come to what is perhaps the chief difference between the scheme advocated in this work and most other schemes of a like nature which have been hitherto advocated or put into actual practice. That difference is this: While others have sought to weld into one large organisation individuals who have not yet been combined [p. 100] into smaller groups, or who must leave those smaller groups on their joining the larger organisation, my proposal appeals not only to individuals but to co-operators, manufacturers, philanthropic societies, and others experienced in organisation, and with organisations under their control, to come and place themselves under conditions involving no new restraints but rather securing wider freedom. And, further, a striking feature of the present scheme is that the very considerable number of persons already engaged on the estate will not be displaced (except those on the town site, and these gradually), but these will themselves form a valuable nucleus, paying in rents, from the very inception of the enterprise, a sum which will go very far towards the interest on the money with which the estate is purchased—rents which they will be more willing to pay to a landlord who will treat them with perfect equity, and who will bring to their doors consumers for their produce. The work of organisation is, therefore, in a very large measure accomplished. The army is now in existence; it has but to be mobilised; it is with no undisciplined mob that we have to deal. Or the comparison between this experiment and those which have preceded it is like that between two machines—one of which has to be created out of various ores which have first to be gathered together and then cast into various shapes, while for the other all the parts are ready to hand and have but to be fitted together. [p. 101]

CHAPTER X.
A UNIQUE COMBINATION OF PROPOSALS.

In the last chapter, I pointed out the great differences of principle between the project placed before the reader of this work and some of those schemes of social reform which, having been put to the test of experience, have ended in disaster, and I urged that there were features of the proposed experiment which so completely distinguished it from those unsuccessful schemes that they could not be fairly regarded as any indication of the results which would probably follow from launching this experiment.

It is my present purpose to show that though the scheme taken as a whole is a new one, and is, perhaps, entitled to some consideration on that account, its chief claim upon the attention of the public lies in the fact that it combines the important features of several schemes which have been advocated at various times, and so combines them as to secure the best results of each, without the dangers and difficulties which sometimes, even in the minds of their authors, were clearly and distinctly seen.

Shortly stated, my scheme is a combination of three, distinct projects which have, I think, never been united before. These are—(1) The proposals for an organised [p. 102] migratory movement of population of Wakefield and of Professor Marshall; (2) the system of land tenure first proposed by Thos. Spence and afterwards (though with an important modification) by Mr. Herbert Spencer; and (3) the model city of Jas. S. Buckingham.[1]

Let us take these proposals in the order named. Wakefield, in his "Art of Colonisation" (London: J. W. Parker, 1849), urged that colonies when

---

[1] I may, perhaps, state as showing how in the search for truth men's minds run in the same channels, and as, possibly, some additional argument for the soundness of the proposals thus combined, that, till I had got far on with my project, I had not seen either the proposals of Professor Marshall or of Wakefield (beyond a very short reference to the latter in J. S. Mill's "Elements of Political Economy"), nor had I seen the work of Buckingham, which, published nearly fifty years ago, seems to have attracted but little attention.

formed—he was not thinking of home colonies—should be based on scientific principles. He said (page 109): "We send out colonies of the limbs, without the belly and the head, of needy persons, many of them mere paupers, or even criminals; colonies made up of a *single class of persons* in the community, and that the most helpless and the meet unfit to perpetuate our national character, and to become the fathers of a race whose habits of thinking and feeling shall correspond to those which, in the meantime, we are cherishing at home. The ancients, on the contrary, sent out *a representation of the parent State—colonists from all ranks.* We stock the farm with creeping and climbing plants, without any trees of firmer growth for them to entwine round. A hop-ground without poles, the plants matted confusedly together, and scrambling on the ground in tangled heaps, with here and [p. 103] there some clinging to rank thistles and hemlock, would be an apt emblem of a modern colony. The ancients began by nominating to the honourable office of captain or leader of the colony one of the chief men, if not the chief man of the State, like the queen bee leading the workers. Monarchies provided a prince of the royal blood; an aristocracy its choicest nobleman; a democracy its most influential citizen. These naturally carried along with them some of their own station in life—their companions and friends; some of their immediate dependents also—of those between themselves and the lowest class; and were encouraged in various ways to do so. The lowest class again followed with alacrity, because they found themselves moving *with* and not *away from* the state of society in which they had been living. It was the same social and political union under which they had been born and bred; and to prevent any contrary impression being made, the utmost solemnity was observed in transferring the rites of pagan superstition. They carried with them their gods, their festivals, their games—all, in short, that held together and kept entire the fabric of society as it existed in the parent state. Nothing was left behind that could be moved of all that the heart or eye of an exile misses. The new colony was made to appear as if time or chance had reduced the whole community to smaller dimensions, leaving it still essentially the same home and country to its surviving members. It consisted of a general contribution of members from all classes, and so became, on its first settlement, a mature state, with all the component parts of that which sent it forth. It was a transfer of population, therefore, which gave rise to no sense of degradation, as if the colonist [p. 104] were thrust out from a higher to a lower description of community."

J. S. Mill, in his "Elements of Political Economy," Book I., Chap. viii., §3, says of this work: "Wakefield's theory of colonisation has excited much attention, and is doubtless destined to excite much more. . . . His system consists of arrangements for securing that each colony shall have from the first a town population bearing due proportion to the agricultural, and that the cultivators of the soil shall not be so widely scattered as to be deprived by distance of the benefit of that town population as a market for their produce."

Professor Marshall's proposals for an organised migratory movement of population from London have been already noticed, but the following passage from the article already referred to may be quoted:—

"There might be great variety of method, but the general plan would probably be for a committee, whether formed specially for the purpose or not, to interest themselves in the formation of a colony in some place well beyond the range of London smoke. After seeing their way to building or buying suitable cottages there, they would enter into communication with some of the employers of low-waged labour. They would select, at first, industries that used very little fixed capital; and, as we have seen, it fortunately happens that most of the industries which it is important to move are of this kind. They would find an employer—and there must be many such—who really cares for the misery of his employees. Acting with him and by his advice, they would make themselves the friends of people employed or fit to be employed in his trade; they would show them the advantages of [p. 105] moving, and help them to move, both with counsel and money. They would organise the sending of work backwards and forwards, the employer perhaps opening an agency in the colony. But after being once started it ought to be self-supporting, for the cost of carriage, even if the employees went in sometimes to get instructions, would be less than the saving made in rent—at all events, if allowance be made for the value of the garden produce. And more than as much gain would probably be saved by removing the temptation to drink which is caused by the sadness of London. They would meet with much passive resistance at first. The unknown has terrors to all, but especially to those who have lost their natural spring. Those who have lived always in the obscurity of a London court might shrink away from the free light; poor as are their acquaintanceships at home, they might fear to go where they knew no one. But, with gentle insistence, the committee would urge their way, trying to get those who knew one another to move together, by warm, patient sympathy, taking off the chill of the first change. It is only the first step that costs; every succeeding step would be easier. The work of several firms, not always in the same business, might, in some cases, be sent together. Gradually a prosperous industrial district would grow up, and then, mere self-interest would induce employers to bring down their main workshops, and even to start factories in the colony. Ultimately all would gain, but most the landowners and the railroads connected with the colony."

What could more strongly point than the last sentence of that quotation from Professor Marshall's proposal to the necessity of first *buying* the land, so that the most admir- [106] able project of Thomas Spence can be put into practice, and thus prevent the terrible rise in rent which Professor Marshall forsees? Spence's proposal, put forward more than a hundred years ago, at once suggests how to secure the desired end. Here it is: —

"Then you may behold the rent which the people have paid into the parish treasuries employed by each parish in paying the Government its share of the sum which the Parliament or National Congress at any time grants; in maintaining and relieving its own poor and people out of work; in paying the necessary officers their salaries; in building, repairing, and adorning its houses, bridges, and other structures; in making and maintaining convenient and delightful streets, highways, and passages, both for foot and carriages; in making and maintaining canals and other conveniences for trade and navigation; in planting and taking in waste grounds; in premiums for the encouragement of agriculture or anything else thought worthy of encouragement; and, in a word, in doing whatever the people think proper, and not, as formerly, to support and spread luxury, pride, and all manner of vice. . . . There are no tolls or taxes of any kind paid among them by native or foreigner but the aforesaid rent, which every person pays to the parish, according to the quantity, quality, and conveniences of the land . . . he occupies in it. The government, poor, roads, etc., . . . are all maintained with the rent, on which account all wares, manufactures, allowable trade employments or actions are entirely duty-free."—From a lecture read at the Philosophical Society in Newcastle, on November 8th, 1775, for printing which the Society did the author the honour to expel him. [p. 107]

It will be observed that the only difference between this proposal and the proposals as to land reform put forward in this book, is not a difference of system, but a difference (and a very important one) as to the *method* of its inauguration. Spence appears to have thought that the people would, by a fiat, dispossess the existing owners and establish the system at once and universally throughout the country; while, in this work, it is proposed to purchase the necessary land with which to establish the system on a small scale, and to trust to the inherent advantages of the system leading to its gradual adoption.

Writing some seventy years after Spence had put forward his proposal, Mr. Herbert Spencer (having first laid down the grand principle that all men are equally entitled to the use of the earth, as a corollary of the law of equal liberty generally), in discussing this subject, observes, with his usual force and clearness: —

"But to what does this doctrine that men are equally entitled to the use of the earth, lead? Must we return to the times of unenclosed wilds, and subsist on roots, berries, and game? Or are we to be left to the management of Messrs. Fourrier, Owen, Louis Blanc & Co.? Neither. Such a doctrine is consistent with the highest civilisation, may be carried out without involving a community of goods, and need cause no very serious revolution in existing arrangements. The change required would be simply a change of landlords. Separate ownership would merge in the joint-stock ownership of the public. Instead of being in the possession of individuals, the country would be held by the great corporate body—society. Instead of leasing his acres from an isolated proprietor, the farmer would lease them from the [p. 108] nation. Instead of paying his rent to the agent of Sir John and His Grace, he would pay it to an agent or deputy agent of the community. Stewards would be public officials instead of private ones, and tenancy the only land tenure. A state of things so ordered would be in perfect harmony with the moral law. Under it all men would be equally landlords; all men would be alike free to become tenants. A., B., C. and the rest might compete for a vacant farm as now, and one of them might take that farm without in any way violating the principles of pure equity. All would be equally free to bid; all would be equally free to refrain. And when the farm had been let to A., B., or C, all parties would have done that which they willed, the one in choosing to pay a given sum to his fellow-men for the use of certain lands—the others in refusing to pay the sum. Clearly, therefore, on such a system the earth might be enclosed, occupied, and cultivated in entire subordination to the law of equal freedom."—"Social Statics," Chap. ix., sec 8.

But having thus written, Mr. Herbert Spencer at a later period, having discovered two grave difficulties in the way of his own proposal, unreservedly withdrew it. The first of these difficulties was the evils which he considered as inseparable from State ownership (see "Justice," published in 1891, appendix B., p. 290); the second, the impossibility, as Mr. Spencer regarded it, of acquiring the land on terms which would be at once equitable to existing owners and remunerative to the community.

But if the reader examines the scheme of Spence, which preceded the now-withdrawn proposals of Mr. [p. 109] Herbert Spencer, he will see that Spence's scheme was entirely freed (as is the one put forward in this little book), from the objections which might probably attend control by the State.[1] The rents

---

1 Though Mr. Herbert Spencer, as if to rebuke his own theory that State control is inherently bad, says, "Political speculation which sets out with the assumption that the State has in all cases

were, under Spence's proposals, as in my own, not to be levied by a *Central Government* far removed from contact with the people, but by the very parish (in my scheme the municipality) in which the people reside. As to the other difficulty which presented itself to Mr. Herbert Spencer's mind—that of acquiring the land on equitable terms, and of yet making it remunerative to the purchasers—a difficulty which Mr. Herbert Spencer, seeing no way out of, rashly concluded to be insuperable—that difficulty is entirely removed by my proposal of buying agricultural or sparsely-settled land, letting it in the manner advocated by Spence, and then bringing about the scientific migratory movement advocated by Wakefield and (though in a somewhat less daring fashion) by Professor Marshall.

Surely a project, which thus brings what Mr. Herbert Spencer still terms "the dictum of absolute ethics"—that all men are equally entitled to the use of the earth—into the field of practical life, and makes it a thing immediately realisable by those who believe in it, must be one of the greatest public importance. When a great philosopher in effect says, we cannot conform our life to the highest moral principles because men have laid an immoral [p. 110] foundation for us in the past, but "if, while possessing those ethical sentiments which social discipline has now produced, men stood in possession of a territory not yet individually portioned out, they would no more hesitate to assert equality of their claims to the land than they would hesitate to assert equality of their claims to light and air"[1]— one cannot help wishing—so inharmonious does life seem—that the opportunity presented itself of migrating to a new planet where the "ethical sentiments which social discipline has now produced" might be indulged in. But a new planet, or even "a territory not yet individually portioned out," is by no means necessary if we are but in real earnest; for it has been shown that an organised, migratory movement from over-developed, high-priced land to comparatively raw and unoccupied land, will enable all who desire it to live this life of equal freedom and opportunity; and a sense of the possibility of a life on earth at once orderly and free dawns upon the heart and mind.

The third proposal which I have combined with those of Spence and Mr. Herbert Spencer, of Wakefield and Professor Marshall, embraces one essential feature of a scheme of James S. Buckingham,[2] though I have purposely omit-

---

the same nature must end in profoundly erroneous conclusions."

[1] "Justice," Chap. xi., p. 85.

[2] Buckingham's scheme is set forth in a work entitled "National Evils and Practical Remedies," published by Peter Jackson, St. Martins le Grand, about 1849.

ted some of the essential features of that scheme. Mr. Buckingham says (p. 25): "My thoughts were thus directed to the great defects of all existing towns, and the desirability of forming at least one model [p. 111] town which should avoid the most prominent of these defects, and substitute advantages not yet possessed by any." In his work he exhibits a ground plan and a sketch of a town of about 1,000 acres, containing a population of 25,000, and surrounded by a large agricultural estate. Buckingham, like Wakefield, saw the great advantages to be derived by combining an agricultural community with an industrial, and urged: "Wherever practicable, the labours of agriculture and manufacture to be so mingled and the variety of fabrics and materials to be wrought upon also so assorted as to make short periods of labour on each alternately with others produce that satisfaction and freedom from tedium and weariness which an unbroken round of monotonous occupation so frequently occasions, and because also variety of employment develops the mental as well as physical faculties much more perfectly than any single occuption."

But though on these points the scheme is strikingly like my own, it is also a very different one. Buckingham having traced, as he thought, the evils of society to their source in competition, intemperance, and war, proposed to annihilate competition by forming a system of complete or integral co-operation; to remove intemperance by the total exclusion of intoxicants; to put an end to war by the absolute prohibition of gunpowder. He proposed to form a large company, with a capital of £4,000,000; to buy a large estate, and to erect churches, schools, factories, warehouses, dining-halls, dwelling-houses, at rents varying from £30 a year to £300 a year; and to carry on all productive operations, whether agricultural or industrial, as one large undertaking covering the whole field and permitting no rivals. [p. 112]

Now it will be seen that though in outward form Buckingham's scheme and my own present the same feature of a model town set in a large agricultural estate, so that industrial and farming pursuits might be carried on in a healthy, natural way, yet the inner life of the two communities would be entirely different—the inhabitants of Garden City enjoying the fullest rights of free association, and exhibiting the most varied forms of individual and co-operative work and endeavour, the members of Buckingham's city being held together by the bonds of a rigid cast-iron organisation, from which there could be no escape but by leaving the association, or breaking it up into various sections.

To sum up this chapter. My proposal is that there should be an earnest attempt made to organise a migratory movement of population from our overcrowded centres to sparsely-settled rural districts; that the mind of the public should not be confused, or the efforts of organisers wasted in a premature attempt to accomplish this work on a national scale, but that great thought and attention shall be first concentrated on a single movement yet one sufficiently large to be at once attractive and resourceful; that the migrants shall be guaranteed (by the making of suitable arrangements before the movement commences) that the whole increase in land-values due to their migration shall be secured to them; that this be done by creating an organisation, which, while permitting its members to do those things which are good in their own eyes (provided they infringe not the rights of others) shall receive all "rate-rents" and expend them in those public works which the migratory movement renders necessary or expedient—thus eliminating [p. 113] rates, or, at least, greatly reducing the necessity for any compulsory levy; and that the golden opportunity afforded by the fact that the land to be settled upon has but few buildings or works upon it, shall be availed of in the fullest manner, by so laying out a Garden City that, as it grows, the free gifts of Nature—fresh air, sunlight, breathing room and playing room—shall be still retained in all needed abundance, and by so employing the resources of modern science that Art may supplement Nature, and life may become an abiding joy and delight. And it is important to notice that this proposal, so imperfectly put forward, is no scheme hatched in a restless night in the fevered brain of an enthusiast, but is one having its origin in the thoughtful study of many minds, and the patient effort of many earnest souls, each bringing some element of value, till, the time and the opportunity having come, the smallest skill avails to weld those elements into an effective combination. [p. 114]

CHAPTER XI

THE PATH FOLLOWED UP.

"How can a man learn to know himself? By reflection never—only by action. In the measure that thou seekest to do thy duty shalt thou know what is in thee. But what is thy duty? The demand of the hour."—*Goethe*.

THE reader is now asked to kindly assume, for the sake of argument, that our Garden City experiment has been fairly launched, and is a decided success, and to consider briefly some of the more important effects which such an object-lesson, by the light which it will throw upon the pathway of reform, must inevitably produce upon society, and then we will endeavour to trace some of the broader features of the after-development.

Among the greatest needs of man and of society to-day, as at all times, are these: A worthy aim and opportunity to realise it; work and ends worth working for. All that a man is, and all that he may become, is summed up in his aspirations, and this is no less true of society than of the individual. The end I venture to now set before the people of this country and of other countries is no less "noble and adequate" than this, that they should forthwith gird themselves to the task of building up clusters of beautiful home-towns, each zoned by gardens, for those who now dwell in crowded, slum-infested cities. We have already seen how *one* such town [p. 115] may be built; let us now see how the true path of reform, once discovered, will, if resolutely followed, lead society on to a far higher destiny than it has ever yet ventured to hope for, though such a future has often been foretold by daring spirits.

There have in the past been inventions and discoveries on the making of which society has suddenly leaped upward to a new and higher plane of existence. The utilisation of steam—a force long recognised, but which proved somewhat difficult to harness to the task it was fitted to accomplish—effected mighty changes; but the discovery of a method for giving effect to a far greater force than the force of steam—to the long pent-up desire for a better and nobler social life here on earth—will work changes even more remarkable.

What clearly marked economic truth is brought into view by the successful issue of such an experiment as we have been advocating? This: —That there is a broad path open, through a creation of new wealth forms, to a new industrial system in which the productive forces of society and of nature may be used with far greater effectiveness than at present, and in which the distribution of the wealth forms so created will take place on a far juster and more equitable basis. Society may have more to divide among its members, and at the same time the greater dividend may be divided in a juster manner.

Speaking broadly, industrial reformers may be divided into two camps. The first camp includes those who urge the primary importance of paying close and constant attention to the necessity of *increased production:* the second includes those whose special aim is directed to *more just and equitable division.* The [p. 116] former are constantly saying, in effect, "Increase the national dividend, and all will be well"; the latter, "The national dividend is fairly sufficient were it but divided equitably." The former are for the most part of the individualistic, the latter of the socialistic type.

As an instance of the former point of view, I may cite the words of Mr. A. J. Balfour, who, at a Conference of the National Union of Conservative Associations held at Sunderland on 14th November, 1894, said: "Those who represented society as if it consisted of two sections disputing over their share of the general produce were utterly mistaken as to the real bearing of the great social problem. We had to consider that the produce of the country was not a fixed quantity, of which, if the employers got more, the employed would get less, or if the employed got more, the employers would get less. The real question for the working-classes of this country was not primarily or fundamentally a question of division: it was a question of production." As an instance of the second point of view, take the following: "The absurdity of the notion of raising the poor without, to a corresponding degree, depressing the rich will be obvious."—"Principles of Socialism made plain," by Frank Fairman (William Reeves, 83 Charing Cross Road, W.C.), page 33.

I have already shown, and I hope to make this contention yet more clear, that there is a path along which sooner or later, both the Individualist and the Socialist must inevitably travel; for I have made it abundantly clear that on a small scale society may readily become more individualistic than now—if by Individualism is meant a society in which there is fuller and freer opportunity for its members to do and to produce what they [p. 117] will, and to form free associations, of the most varied kinds; while it may also become more socialistic—if by Socialism is meant a condition of life in which the well-being of the community is safe-guarded, and in which the collective spirit is manifested by a wide extension of the area of municipal effort. To achieve these desirable ends, I have taken a leaf out of the books of each type of reformer and bound them together by a thread of practicability. Not content with *urging* the necessity of increased production, I have shown *how it can he achieved;* while the other and equally important end of more equitable distribution is, as I have shown, easily possible, and in a manner which need cause no ill-will, strife, or bitterness; is constitutional; requires no revolutionary legislation; and involves no direct attack upon vested interests. Thus may the desires of the two sections of reformers to whom I have referred be attained. I have, in short, followed out Lord Rosebery's suggestion, and "borrowed from Socialism its large conception of common effort, and its vigorous conception of municipal life, and from Individualism the preservation of self-respect and self-reliance," and, by a concrete illustration, I have, I think, disproved the cardinal contention of Mr. Benjamin Kidd in his famous book, "Social Evolution," that "the interests of the social organism and of the individuals comprising it at any particular time are actually antagonistic; they can never be reconciled; they are inherently and essentially irreconcilable" (page 85).

Most socialistic writers appear to me to exhibit too keen a desire to appropriate old forms of wealth, either by purchasing out or by taxing out the owners, and they seem to have little conception that the truer method is to [p. 118] create new forms and to create them under juster conditions. But this latter conception should inevitably follow an adequate realisation of the ephemeral nature of most forms of wealth; and there is no truth more fully recognised by economic writers than that nearly all forms of material wealth, except, indeed, the planet on which we live and the elements of nature, are extremely fugitive and prone to decay. Thus for instance, J. S. Mill, in "Elements of Political Economy," Book 1, Chapter v., says: "The greater part in value of the wealth now existing in England has been produced by human hands within the last twelve months. A very small proportion indeed of that large aggregate was in existence ten years ago; —of the present productive capital of the country, scarcely any part except farm-houses and manufactories and a few ships and machines; and even these would not in most cases have survived so long if fresh labour had not been employed within that period in putting them into repair. The land subsists, and the land is almost the only thing that subsists." The leaders of the great socialistic movement, of course, know all this perfectly well; yet this quite elementary truth seems to fade from their minds when they are discussing methods of reform, and they appear to be as anxious to seize upon present forms of wealth as if they regarded them as of a really lasting and permanent nature.

But this inconsistency of socialistic writers is all the more striking when one remembers that these writers are the very ones who insist most strongly upon the view that a very large part of the wealth-forms now in existence are not really *wealth* at all—that they are "ilth," and that any form of society which represents even a step [p. 119] towards their ideal must involve the sweeping away of such forms and the creation of new forms in their place. With a degree of inconsistency that is positively startling, they exhibit an insatiable desire to become possessed of these forms of wealth which are not only rapidly decaying, but are in their opinion absolutely useless or injurious.

Thus Mr Hyndman, at a lecture delivered at the Democratic Club, 29th March, 1893, said: —"It was desirable that they should map out and formulate socialistic ideas which they should desire to see brought about when the so-called Individualism of the present day has broken down, as it inevitably would do. One of the first things that they as Socialists would have to do would be to depopulate the vast centres of their over-crowded cities. Their large towns had no longer any large agricultural population from which to recruit their ranks, and through bad and insufficient food, vitiated atmosphere, and other insanitary conditions, the physique of the masses of the cities was rapidly deteriorating, both materially and physically." Precisely; but does not Mr. Hyndman see that in striving to become possessed of present wealth forms, he is laying siege to the wrong fortress? If the population of London, or a large part of the population of London, is to be transplanted elsewhere, when some future event has happened, would it not be well to see if we cannot induce large numbers of these people to transplant themselves *now*, when the problem of London administration and of London reform would, as we shall shortly discover, present itself in a somewhat startling fashion?

A similar inconsistency is to be noticed in a little [p. 120] book which has had an enormous and well-deserved sale, "Merrie England" (Clarion Offices, Fleet Street). The author, "Nunquam," remarks at the outset: "The problem we have to consider is: —Given a country and a people, find how the people may make the best of the country and themselves." He then proceeds to vigorously condemn our cities, with their houses ugly and mean, their narrow streets, their want of gardens, and emphasises the advantages of out-door occupations. He condemns the factory system, and says: "I would set men to grow wheat and fruit, and rear cattle and poultry for our own use. Then I would develop the fisheries, and construct great fish-breeding lakes and harbours. Then I would

restrict our mines, furnaces, chemical works, and factories to the number actually needed for the supply of our own people. Then I would stop the smoke
nuisance by developing water-power and electricity. *In order to achieve these
ends, I would make all the lands, mills, mines, factories, works, shops, ships, and
railways the property of the people.*" That is (the italics are my own), the people
are to struggle hard to become possessed of factories, mills, works, and shops,
at least half of which must be closed if Nunquam's desires are attained; of ships
which will become useless if our foreign trade is to be abandoned, (*see* "Merrie
England," Chap. iv.); and of railways, which, with an entire redistribution of
population such as Nunquam desires, must for the most part become derelict.
And how long is this useless struggle to last? Would it not—I ask Nunquam to
consider this point carefully—be better to study a smaller problem first, and, to
paraphrase his words, "Given, say, 6,000 acres of land, let us endeavour to make
the best use of [p. 121] it"? For then, having dealt with this, we shall have educated
ourselves to deal with a larger area.

Let me state again in other terms this fugitiveness of wealth forms, and
then suggest the conclusion to which that consideration should lead us. So
marked are the changes which society exhibits—especially a society in a progressive state—that the outward and visible forms which our civilisation presents to-day, its public and private buildings, its means of communication, the
appliances with which it works, its machinery, its docks, its artificial harbours,
its instruments of war and its instruments of peace, have most of them under-
gone a complete change, and many of them several complete changes, within
the last sixty years. I suppose not one person in twenty in this country is living
in a house which is sixty years old; not one sailor in a thousand is sailing a ship,
not one artisan or labourer in a hundred is engaged in a workshop or handling
tools or driving a cart which was in existence sixty years ago. It is now sixty
years since the first railway was constructed from Birmingham to London,
and our Railway Companies possess one thousand millions of invested capital,
while our systems of water supply, of gas, of electric lighting, and of sewerage
are, for the most part, of recent date. Those material relics of the past which
were created more than sixty years ago, though some of them are of infinite
value as mementos, examples, and heirlooms, are, for the most part, certainly
not of a kind which we need wrangle over or fight about. The best of them are
our universities, schools, churches, and cathedrals, and these should certainly
teach us a different lesson.

But can any reasonable person, who reflects for a [p. 122] moment on the
recent unexampled rate of progress and invention, doubt that the next sixty

years will reveal changes fully as remarkable? Can any person suppose that these mushroom forms, which have sprung up as it were in a night, have any real permanence? Even apart from the solution of the labour problem, and the finding of work for the thousands of idle hands which are eager for it—a solution, the correctness of which I claim to have demonstrated—what possibilities are opened up by the bare contemplation of the discovery of new motive powers, new means of locomotion, perhaps, through the air, new methods of water supply, or a new distribution of population, which must of itself render many material forms altogether useless and effete! Why, then, should we squabble and wrangle about what man *has* produced? Why not rather seek to learn what man *can* produce; when, aiming to do that, we may perhaps discover a grand opportunity for producing not only better forms of wealth, but how to produce them under far juster conditions? To quote the author of "Merrie England": "We should first of all ascertain what things are desirable for our health and happiness of body and mind, and then organise our people with the object of producing those things in the best and easiest way."

Wealth forms, then, in their very nature are *fugitive*, and they are besides liable to constant displacement by the better forms which in an advancing state of society are constantly arising. There is, however, one form of material wealth which is most permanent and abiding; from the value and utility of which our most wonderful inventions can never detract one jot, but will serve only to make more clear, and to render more [p. 123] universal. The planet on which we live has lasted for millions of years, and the race is just emerging from its savagery. Those of us who believe that there is a grand purpose behind nature cannot believe that the career of this planet is likely to be speedily cut short now that better hopes are rising in the hearts of men, and that, having learned a few of its less obscure secrets, they are finding their way, through much toil and pain, to a more noble use of its infinite treasures. The earth for all practical purposes may be regarded as abiding for ever.

Now, as every form of wealth must rest on the earth as its foundation, and must be built up out of the constituents found at or near its surface, it follows (because foundations are ever of primary importance) that the reformer should first consider how best the earth may be used in the service of man. But here again our friends, the Socialists, miss the essential point. Their professed ideal is to make society the owner of land *and of all instruments of production*; but they have been so anxious to carry both points of their programme that they have been a little too slow to consider the special importance of the land question, and have thus missed the true path of reform.

There is, however, a type of reformers who push the land question very much to the front, though, as it appears to me, in a manner little likely to commend their views to society. Mr. Henry George, in his well-known work, "Progress and Poverty," urges with much eloquence, if not with complete accuracy of reasoning, that our land laws are responsible for all the economic evils of society, and that as our landlords are little better [p. 124] than pirates and robbers, the sooner the State forcibly appropriates their rents the better, for when this is accomplished the problem of poverty will, he suggests, be entirely solved. But is not this attempt to throw the whole blame of and punishment for the present deplorable condition of society on to a single class of men a very great mistake? In what way are landlords as a class less honest than the average citizen? Give the average citizen the opportunity of becoming a landlord and of appropriating the land values created by his tenants, and he will embrace it to-morrow. If then, the average man is a potential landlord, to attack landlords as individuals is very like a nation drawing up an indictment against itself, and then making a scape-goat of a particular class.[1] But to endeavour to change our land system is a very different matter from attacking those individuals who represent it. But how is this change to be effected? I reply—By the force of example, that is, by setting up a better system, and by a little skill in the grouping of forces and manipulation of ideas. It is quite true that the average man is a potential landlord, and as ready to appropriate the unearned increment as to cry out against its appropriation. But the average man has very little chance of ever becoming a landlord and of appropriating rent-values created by others; and he is, therefore, the better able to consider, quite dispassionately, whether such a proceeding is really honest, and whether it may not be possible to gradually establish a new and more equitable system under which, without enjoying the privilege of appropriating rent-values created by others, [p. 125] he may himself be secured against expropriation of the rent-values which he is now constantly creating or maintaining. We have demonstrated how this may be done on a small scale; we have next to consider how the experiment may be carried out on a much wider scale, and this we can best do in another chapter. [p. 126]

---

[1] I hope it is not ungrateful in one who has derived much inspiration from "Progress and Poverty" to write thus.

CHAPTER XII.
SOCIAL CITIES.

"Human nature will not flourish, any more than a potato, if it be planted and re-planted for too long a series of generations in the same worn-out soil. My children have had other birth-places, and, so far as their fortunes may be within my control, shall strike their roots into unaccustomed earth."—"The Scarlet Letter," Nathaniel Hawthorne.

THE problem with which we have now to deal, shortly stated, is this: How to make our Garden City experiment the stepping-stone to a higher and better form of industrial life generally throughout the country. Granted, the success of the initial experiment, and there must inevitably arise a widespread demand for an extension of methods so healthy and so advantageous; and it will be well, therefore, to consider some of the chief problems which will have to be faced in the progress of such extension.

It will, I think, be well, in approaching this question, to consider the analogy presented by the early progress of railway enterprise. This will help us to see more clearly some of the broader features of the new development which is now so closely upon us if only we show ourselves energetic and imaginative. Railways were first made without any statutory powers. They were con- [p. 127] structed on a very small scale, and, being of very short lengths, the consent of only one or at the most a few landowners was necessary; and what private agreement and arrangement could thus easily compass was scarcely a fit subject for an appeal to the Legislature of the country. But when the "Rocket" was built, and the supremacy of the locomotive was fully established, it then became necessary, if railway enterprise was to go forward, to obtain legislative powers. For it would have been impossible, or at least very difficult, to make equitable arrangements with all the landowners whose estates might lie between points many miles distant; because one obstinate landlord might take advantage of his position to demand an altogether exorbitant price for his land, and thus practically stifle such an enterprise. It was necessary, therefore, to obtain power to secure the land compulsorily at its market value, or at a price not too extravagantly removed from such value; and, this being done, railway enterprise went forward at so rapid a rate that in one year no less than £132,600,000 was authorised by Parliament to be raised for the purpose of railway construction.[1]

Now, if Parliamentary powers were necessary for the extension of railway enterprise, such powers will certainly be also needed when the inherent practicability of building new, well-planned towns, and of the population moving into them from the old slum cities as naturally, and, in proportion to the power to be exercised, almost as easily as a family moves out of a rotten old tenement into a new and comfortable dwelling, is once fairly recog- [p. 128] nised by the people. To build such towns, large areas of land must be obtained. Here and there a suitable site may be secured by arrangement with one or more land-owners, but if the movement is to be carried on in anything like a scientific fashion, stretches of land far larger than that occupied by our first experiment must be obtained. For, just as the first short railway, which was the germ of railway enterprise, would convey to few minds the conception of a net-work of railways extending over the whole country, so, perhaps, the idea of a well-planned town such as I have described will not have prepared the reader for the later development which must inevitably follow—the planning and building of town clusters—each town in the cluster being of different design from the others, and yet the whole forming part of one large and well-thought-out plan.

Let me here introduce a very rough diagram, representing, as I conceive, the true principle on which all towns should grow. Garden City has, we will suppose, grown until it has reached a population of 32,000. How shall it grow? How shall it provide for the needs of others who will be attracted by its numerous advantages? Shall it build on the zone of agricultural land which is around it, and thus for ever destroy its right to be called a "Garden City"? Surely not. This disastrous result would indeed take place if the land around the town were, as is the land around our present cities, owned by private individuals anxious to make a profit out of it. For then, as the town filled up, the agricultural land would become "ripe" for building purposes, and the beauty and healthfulness of the town would be quickly destroyed. But the land around Garden City is, fortunately, not in the [p. 129] hands of private individuals: it is in the hands of the people: and is to be administered, not in the supposed interests of the few, but in the real interests of the whole community. Now, there are few objects which the people so jealously guard as their parks and open spaces; and we may, I think, feel confident that the people of Garden City will not for a moment

---

[1] Clifford's "History of Private Bill Legislation" (Butterworth, 1885), Introduction, p. 88.

permit the beauty of their city to be destroyed by the process of growth. But it may be urged—If this be true, will not the inhabitants of Garden City in this way be selfishly preventing the growth of their city, and thus preclude many from enjoying its advantages? Certainly not. There is a bright, but overlooked, alternative. The town *will* grow; but it will grow in accordance with a principle which will result in this—that such growth shall not lessen or destroy, but ever add to its social opportunities, to its beauty, to its convenience. Consider for a moment the case of a city in Australia which in some measure illustrates the principle for which I am contending. The city of Adelaide, as the accompanying sketch map shows, is surrounded by its "Park Lands." The city is built up. How does it grow? It grows by leaping over the "Park Lands" and establishing North Adelaide. And this is the principle which it is intended to follow, but improve upon, in Garden City.

Our diagram may now be understood. Garden City is built up. Its population has reached 32,000. How will it grow? It will grow by establishing—under Parliamentary powers probably—another city some little distance beyond its own zone of "country," so that the new town may have a zone of country of its own. I have said 'by establishing another city," and, for administra- [p. 130] tive purposes there would be *two* cities; but the inhabitants of the one could reach the other in a very few minutes; for rapid transit would be specially provided for, and thus the people of the two towns would in reality represent one community.

And this principle of growth—this principle of always preserving a belt of country round our cities would be ever kept in mind till, in course of time, we should have a cluster of cities, not of course arranged in the precise geometrical form of my diagram, but so grouped around a Central City that each inhabitant of the whole group, though in one sense living in a town of small size, would be in reality living in, and would enjoy all the advantages of, a great and most beautiful city; and yet all the fresh delights of the country—field, hedgerow, and woodland—not prim parks and gardens merely—would be within a very few minutes walk or ride. And *because the people in their collective capacity own the land* on which this beautiful group of cities is built, the public buildings, the churches, the schools and universities, the libraries, picture galleries, theatres, would be on a scale of magnificence which no city in the world whose land is in pawn to private individuals can afford.

I have said that rapid railway transit would be realised by those who dwell in this beautiful city or group of cities. Reference to the diagram will show at a glance the main features of its railway system. There is, first, an inter-municipal railway connecting all the towns of the outer ring—20 miles in circumference—so that to get from any town to its most distant neighbour requires one to cover a distance of only 10 miles, which could be accomplished in, say, 12 minutes. These trains would [p. 131] not stop between the towns—means of communication for this purpose being afforded by electric tramways which traverse the high-roads, of which, it will be seen, there are a number—each town being connected with every other town in the group by a direct route.

There is also a system of railways by which each town is placed in direct communication with Central City. The distance from any town to the heart of Central City is only 3¼ miles, and this could be readily covered in 5 minutes.

Those who have had experience of the difficulty of getting from one suburb of London to another will see in a moment what an enormous advantage those who dwell in such a group of cities as here shown would enjoy, because they would have a railway *system* and not a railway *chaos* to serve their ends. The difficulty felt in London is of course due to want of forethought and pre-arrangement. On this point, I may quote with advantage a passage from the Presidential address of Sir Benjamin Baker to the Institute of Civil Engineers, Nov. 12th, 1895: "We Londoners often complain of the want of system in the arrangement of the railways and their terminal stations in and around the Metropolis, which necessitates our performing long journeys in cabs to get from one railway system to another. That this difficulty exists, arises, I feel sure, chiefly from the want of forethought of no less able a statesman than Sir Robert Peel, for, in 1836, a motion was proposed in the House of Commons that all the Railway Bills seeking powers for terminals in London should be referred to a Special Committee, so that a complete scheme might be evolved out of the numerous [p. 132] projects before Parliament, and that property might not be unnecessarily sacrificed for rival schemes. Sir Robert Peel opposed the motion on the part of the Government, on the grounds that 'no railway project could come into operation till the majority of Parliament had declared that its principles and arrangements appeared to them satisfactory, and its investments profitable. It was a recognised principle in these cases that the probable profits of an undertaking should be shown to be sufficient to maintain it in a state of permanent utility before a Bill could be obtained, and landlords were perfectly justified in expecting and demanding such a warranty from Parliament.' In this instance, incalculable injury was unintentionally inflicted upon Londoners by not having a grand central station in the Metropolis, and events have shown how false was the assumption that the passing of an Act implied any warranty as to the financial prospects of a railway."

N⁰ 4.

── ADELAIDE ──

SHOWING PARK LANDS ALL ROUND
CITY, AND ITS MODE OF GROWTH.

But are the people of England to suffer for ever for the want of foresight of those who little dreamed of the future development of railways? Surely not. It was in the nature of things little likely that the first network of railways ever constructed should conform to true principles; but now, seeing the enormous progress which has been made in the means of rapid communication, it is high time that we availed ourselves more fully of those means, and built our cities upon some such plan as that I have crudely shown. We should then be, for all purposes of quick communication, nearer to each other than we are in our crowded cities, while, at the same time, we should be surrounding ourselves with the most healthy and the most advantageous conditions. [p. 133]

Some of my friends have suggested that such a scheme of town clusters is well enough adapted to a new country, but that in an old-settled country, with its towns built, and its railway "system" for the most part constructed, it is quite a different matter. But surely to raise such a point is to contend, in other words, that the existing wealth forms of the country are permanent, and are forever to serve as hindrances to the introduction of better forms; that crowded, ill-ventilated, unplanned, unwieldy, unhealthy cities—ulcers on the very face of our beautiful island—are to stand as barriers to the introduction of towns in which modern scientific methods and the aims of social reformers may have the fullest scope in which to express themselves. No, it cannot be; at least, it cannot be for long. What Is may hinder What Might Be for a while, but cannot stay the tide of progress. These crowded cities have done their work; they were the best which a society largely based on selfishness and rapacity could construct, but they are in the nature of things entirely unadapted for a society in which the social side of our nature is demanding a larger share of recognition—a society where even the very love of self leads us to insist upon a greater regard for the well-being of our fellows. The large cities of to-day are scarcely better adapted for the expression of the fraternal spirit than would a work on astronomy which taught that the earth was the centre of the universe be capable of adaptation for use in our schools. Each generation should build to suit its own needs; and it is no more in the nature of things that men should continue to live in old areas because their ancestors lived in them, than it is that they should cherish the old beliefs which a wider faith and a more [p. 134] enlarged understanding have outgrown. The reader is, therefore, earnestly asked not to take it for granted that the large cities in which he may perhaps take a pardonable pride are necessarily, in their present form, any more permanent than the stage-coach system which was the subject of so much admiration just at the very moment when it was about to be supplanted by the railways.[1] The simple issue to be faced, and faced resolutely, is—Can better results be obtained by starting on a bold plan on comparatively virgin soil than by attempting to adapt our old cities to our newer and higher needs? Thus fairly faced, the question can only be answered in one way; and when that simple fact is well grasped, the social revolution will speedily commence.

That there is ample land in this country on which such a cluster as I have here depicted could be constructed with *comparatively* small disturbance of

---

[1] See, for instance, the opening chapter of "The Heart of Midlothian" (Sir Walter Scott).

Nº 5.

— DIAGRAM —

ILLUSTRATING CORRECT PRINCIPLE
OF A CITY'S GROWTH – OPEN COUNTRY
EVER NEAR AT HAND, AND RAPID
COMMUNICATION BETWEEN OFF-SHOOTS.

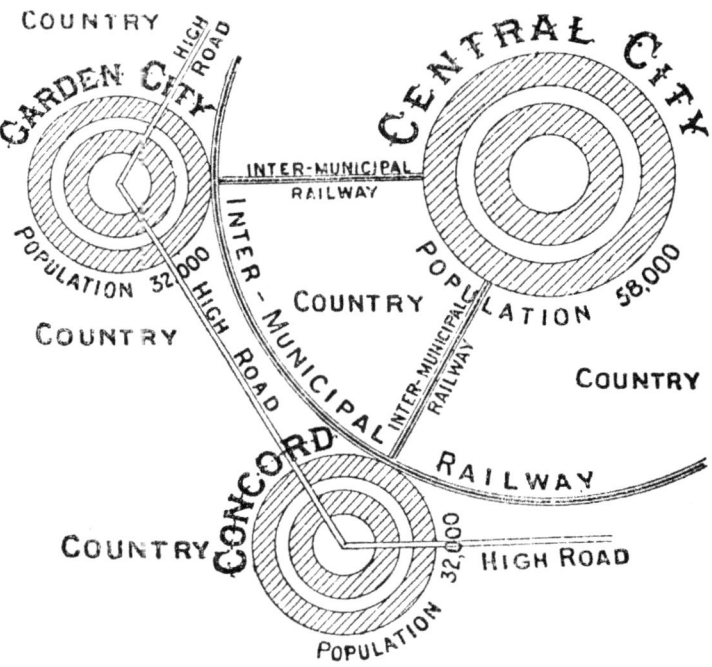

vested interests, and, therefore, with but little need for compensation, will be obvious to anyone; and, when our first experiment has been brought to a successful issue, there will be no great difficulty in acquiring the necessary Parliamentary powers to purchase the land and carry out the necessary works step by step. County Councils are now seeking larger powers, and an overburdened Parliament is becoming more and more anxious to devolve some of its duties upon them. Let such powers be given more and more freely. Let larger and yet larger measures of local self-government be granted, and then all that my diagram depicts—only on a far better plan, because the [p. 135] result of well-concerted and combined thought,—will be easily attainable.

But it may be said, "Are you not, by thus frankly avowing the very great danger to the vested interests of this country which your scheme indirectly threatens, arming vested interests against yourself, and so making any change by legislation impossible?" I think not. And for three reasons. First, because those vested interests which are said to be ranged like a solid phalanx against progress, will, by the force of circumstances and the current of events, be for once divided into opposing camps. Secondly, because property owners, who are very reluctant to yield to threats, such as are sometimes made against them by Socialists of a certain type, will be far more ready to make concessions to the logic of events as revealing itself in an undoubted advance of society to a higher form; and, thirdly, because the largest and most important, and, in the end, the most influential of all vested interests—I mean the vested interests of those who work for their living, whether by hand or brain—will be naturally in favour of the change when they understand its nature.

Let me deal with these points separately. First, I say vested-property interests will be broken in twain, and will range themselves in opposite camps. This sort of cleavage has occurred before. Thus, in the early days of railway legislation, the vested interests in canals and stage coaches were alarmed, and did all in their power to thwart and hamper what threatened them. But other great vested interests brushed this opposition easily on one side. These interests were chiefly two—capital seeking investment, and land desiring to sell itself. (A [p. 136] third vested interest—namely, labour seeking employment—had then scarcely begun to assert its claims.) And notice now how such a successful experiment as Garden City may easily become will drive into the very bed-rock of vested interests a great wedge, which will split them asunder with irresistible force, and permit the current of legislation to set strongly in a new direction. For what will such an experiment have proved up to the very hilt? Among other things too numerous to mention, it will have proved that far more healthy and economic conditions can be secured on raw uncultivated land (if only that land be held on just conditions) than can be secured on land which is at present of vastly higher market value; and in proving this it will open wide the doors of migration from the old crowded cities with their inflated and artificial rents, back to the land which can be now secured so cheaply. Two tendencies will then display themselves. The first will be a strong tendency for city ground values to fall, the other a less marked tendency for agricultural land to rise.[1] The

---

[1] The chief reason for this is that agricultural land as compared with city land is of vastly larger

holders of agricultural land, at least those who are willing to sell—and many of them are even now most anxious to do so—will welcome the extension of an experiment which promises to place English agriculture once again in a position of prosperity: the holders of city lands will, so far as their merely selfish interests prevail, greatly fear it. In this way, landowners throughout the country will be divided into two opposing factions, and the path of land reform—the foundation on which all other reforms must be built—will be made comparatively easy. [p. 137]

Capital in the same way will be divided into opposite camps. Invested capital—that is, capital sunk in enterprises which society will recognise as belonging to the old order—will take the alarm and fall in value enormously, while, on the other hand, capital seeking investment will welcome an outlet which has long been its sorest need. Invested capital will in its opposition be further weakened by another consideration. Holders of existing forms of capital will strive—even though it be at a great sacrifice—to sell part of their old time-honoured stocks, and invest them in new enterprises, on municipally-owned land, for they will not wish to "have all their eggs in one basket"; and thus will the opposing influences of vested property neutralise each other.

But vested-property interests will be, as I believe, affected yet more remarkably in another way. The man of wealth, when he is personally attacked and denounced as an enemy of society, is slow to believe in the perfect good faith of those who denounce him, and, when efforts are made to tax him out by the forcible hand of the State, he is apt to use every endeavour, lawful or unlawful, to oppose such efforts—and often with no small measure of success. But the average wealthy man is no more an unmixed compound of selfishness than the average poor man; and if he sees his houses or lands depreciated in value, not by force, but because those who lived in or upon them have learned how to erect far better homes of their own, and on land held on conditions more advantageous to them, and to surround their children with many advantages which cannot be enjoyed on his estate, he will philosophically bow to the inevitable, and, in his better moments, even welcome a change [p. 138] which will involve him in far greater pecuniary loss than any change in the incidence of taxation is likely to inflict. In every man there is some measure of the reforming instinct; in every man there is some regard for his fellows; and when these natural feelings run athwart his pecuniary interests, then the result is that the spirit of opposition is inevitably softened, in some degree in all men, while in others it is entirely replaced by a fervent desire for the country's good, even at the sacrifice of many cherished possessions. Thus it is that what will not be yielded to a force from without may readily be granted as the result of an impulse from within.

And now let me deal for a moment with the greatest, the most valuable, and the most permanent of all vested interests—the vested interests of skill, labour, energy, talent, industry. How will these be affected? My answer is, The force which will divide in twain the vested interests of land and capital will unite and consolidate the interests of those who live by work, and will lead them to unite their forces with the holders of agricultural land and of capital seeking investment, to urge upon the State the necessity for the prompt opening up of facilities for the reconstruction of society; and, when the State is slow to act, then to employ voluntary collective efforts similar to those adopted in the Garden City experiment, with such modifications as experience may show to be necessary. Such a task as the construction of a cluster of cities like that represented in our diagram may well inspire all workers with that enthusiasm which unites men, for it will call for the very highest talents of engineers of all kinds, of architects, artists, medical men, [p. 139] experts in sanitation, landscape gardeners, agricultural experts, surveyors, builders, manufacturers, merchants and financiers, organisers of trades unions, friendly and co-operative societies, as well as the very simplest forms of unskilled labour, together with all those forms of lesser skill and talent which lie between. For the vastness of the task which seems to frighten some of my friends, represents, in fact, the very measure of its value to the community, if that task be only undertaken in a worthy spirit and with worthy aims. Work in abundance is, as has been several times urged, one of the greatest needs of to-day, and no such field of employment has been opened up since civilisation began as would be represented by the task which is before us of reconstructing anew the entire external fabric of society, employing, as we build, all the skill and knowledge which the experience of centuries has taught us. It was "a large order" which was presented in the early part of this century to construct iron highways throughout the length and breadth of this island, uniting in a vast network all its towns and cities. But railway enterprise, vast as has been its influence, touched the life of the people at but few points compared with the newer call to build home-towns for slum cities; to plant gardens for crowded courts; to construct beautiful water-ways in flooded valleys; to establish a scientific system of distribution to take the place of a chaos, a just system of land tenure for one representing the selfishness which we hope is passing away; to found pensions with liberty for our aged poor, now imprisoned in workhouses; to banish despair and awaken hope in the breasts of those who have fallen; to silence the harsh voice of anger, and to awaken the soft notes of brotherliness and [p. 140] goodwill; to place in strong hands implements of peace and construction, so that implements of war and destruction may drop uselessly down. Here is a task which may well unite a vast army of workers to utilise that power, the present waste of which is the source of half our poverty, disease, and suffering. [p. 141]

CHAPTER XIII.
THE FUTURE OF LONDON.

It will now be interesting to consider some of the more striking effects which will be produced on our now overcrowded cities by the opening-up in new districts of such a vast field of employment as the reader's mind will, it is hoped, be now able to realise with some degree of clearness. New towns and groups of towns are springing up in parts of our islands hitherto well-nigh deserted; new means of communication, the most scientific the world has yet seen, are being constructed; new means of distribution are bringing the producer and the consumer into closer relations, and thus (by reducing railway rates and charges, and the number of profits) are at once raising prices to the producer and diminishing them to the consumer; parks and gardens, orchards and woods, are being planted in the midst of the busy life of the people, so that they may be enjoyed in the fullest measure; homes are being erected for those who have long lived in slums; work is found for the workless, land for the landless, and opportunities for the expenditure of long pent-up energy are presenting themselves at every turn. A new sense of freedom and joy is pervading the hearts of the people as their individual faculties are awakened, and they discover, in a social life which permits alike of the completest concerted action and of [p. 142] the fullest individual liberty, the long-sought-for means of reconciliation between order and freedom—between the well-being of the individual and of society.

The effects produced on our over-crowded cities, whose forms are at once, by the light of a new contrast, seen to be old-fashioned and effete, will be so far-reaching in their character that, in order to study them effectively, it will be well to confine our attention to London, which, as the largest and most unwieldy of our cities, is likely to exhibit those effects in the most marked degree.

There is, as I said at the outset, a well-nigh universal current of opinion that a remedy for the depopulation of our country districts and for the overcrowding of our large cities is urgently needed. But though every one recommends that a remedy should be diligently sought for, few appear to believe that such a remedy will ever be found, and the calculations of our statesmen and reformers proceed upon the assumption that not only will the tide of population never actually turn from the large cities countryward, but that it will continue to flow in its present direction at a scarcely diminished rate for a long time to come.[1] Now it can hardly be supposed that any [p. 143] search made in the full belief that the remedy sought for will not be discovered is likely to be carried on with great zeal or thoroughness; and, therefore, it is perhaps not surprising to find that though the late chairman of the London County Council (Lord Rosebery) declared that the growth of this huge city was fitly comparable to the growth of a tumour (see p. 11)—few venturing to deny the correctness of the analogy—yet the various members of that body, instead of bending their energies to reforming London by means of a reduction of its population, are boldly advocating a policy which involves the purchase of vast undertakings on behalf of the municipality, at prices which must prove far higher than they will be worth if only the long-sought-for remedy is found.

Let us now assume (simply as an hypothesis, if the reader is still sceptical) that the remedy advocated in this work is effective; that new garden-cities are springing up all over the country on sites owned by the municipalities—the rate-rents of such corporate property forming a fund ample for the carrying on of municipal undertakings representing the highest skill of the modern engineer and the best aspirations of the enlightened reformer; and that in these cities, healthier, wholesomer, cleaner and more just and sound economic conditions prevail. What, then, must in the nature of things be the more noticeable effects upon London and the population of London; upon its land values; upon its municipal debt, and its municipal assets; upon London as a labour market; upon the homes of its people; upon its open spaces, and upon the great undertakings which our socialistic and municipal reformers are at the present moment so anxious to secure? [p. 144]

First, notice that ground values will fall enormously! Of course, so long as the 121 square miles out of the 58,000 square miles of England exercise a mag-

---

[1] It is scarcely necessary to give instances of what is meant; but one that occurs to my mind is that this assumption of the continued growth of London forms one of the fundamental premises of the Report of the Royal Commission on Metropolitan Water Supply, 1893. On the contrary, it is satisfactory to note that Mr. H. G. Wells has recently entirely changed his views as to the future growth of London (see "Anticipations," chap. ii.). Read also "The Distribution of Industry," by P. W. Wilson, in "the Heart of the Empire" (Fisher Unwin), and Paper by Mr. W. L. Madgen, M.I.E.E., on "Industrial Redistribution," Society of Arts Journal, February, 1902. See also note on page 31.

netic attraction so great as to draw to it one-fifth of the whole population, who compete fiercely with each other for the right to occupy the land within that small area, so long will that land have a monopoly price. But de-magnetise that people, convince large numbers of them that they can better their condition in every way by migrating elsewhere, and what becomes of that monopoly value? Its spell is broken, and the great bubble bursts.

But the life and earnings of Londoners are not only in pawn to the owners of its soil, who kindly permit them to live upon it at enormous rents—£16,000,000 per annum, representing the present ground value of London, which is yearly increasing; but they are also in pawn to the extent of about £40,000,000, representing London's municipal debts.

But notice this. A municipal debtor is quite different from an ordinary debtor in one most important respect. *He can escape payment by migration.* He has but to move away from a given municipal area, and he at once, *ipso facto,* shakes off not only all his obligations to his landlord, but also all his obligations to his municipal creditors. It is true, when he migrates he must assume the burden of a new municipal rent, and of a new municipal debt; but these in our new cities will represent an extremely small and diminishing fraction of the burden now borne, and the temptation to migrate will, for this and many other reasons, be extremely strong.

But now let us notice how each person in migrating [p. 145] from London, while making the burden of *ground-rents* less heavy for those who remain, will (unless there be some change in the law), make the burden of *rates* on the rate-payers of London yet heavier. For, though each person in migrating will enable those who remain to make better and yet better terms with their landlords; on the other hand, the municipal debt remaining the same, the interest on it will have to be borne by fewer and yet fewer people, and thus the relief to the working population which comes from *reduced rent* will be largely discounted by *increased rates,* and in this way the temptation to migrate will continue, and yet further population will remove, making the debt ever a larger and larger burden, till at length, though accompanied by a still further reduction of rent, it may become intolerable. Of course this huge debt need never have been incurred. Had London been built on municipally-owned land, its rents would not only have easily provided for all current expenditure, without any need for a levy of rates or for incurring loans for long periods, but it would have been enabled to own its own water-supply and many other useful and profit-bearing undertakings, instead of being in its present position with vast debts and small assets. But a vicious and immoral system is bound ultimately to snap, and when the breaking-point is reached, the owners of London's bonds will, like the owners of London's land, have to make terms with a people who can apply the simple remedy of migrating and building a better and brighter civilisation elsewhere, if they are not allowed to rebuild on a just and reasonable basis on the site of their ancient city.

We may next notice, very briefly, the bearing of this [p. 146] migration of population upon two great problems—the problem of the housing of the people of London, and the problem of finding employment for those who remain. The rents now paid by the working population of London, for accommodation most miserable and insufficient, represents each year a larger and larger proportion of income, while the cost of moving to and from work, continually increasing, often represents in time and money a very considerable tax. But imagine the population of London falling, and falling rapidly; the migrating people establishing themselves where rents are extremely low, and where their work is within easy-walking distance of their homes! Obviously, house-property in London will fall in rental value, and fall enormously. Slum property will sink to zero, and the whole working population will move into houses of a class quite above those which they can now afford to occupy. Families which are now compelled to huddle together in one room will be able to rent five or six, and thus will the housing problem temporarily solve itself by the simple process of a diminution in the numbers of the tenants.

But what will become of this slum property? Its power to extort a large proportion of the hard earnings of the London poor gone for ever, will it yet remain an eye-sore and a blot, though no longer a danger to health and an outrage on decency? No. These wretched slums will be pulled down, and their sites occupied by parks, recreation grounds, and allotment gardens. And this change, as well as many others, will be effected, not at the expense of the ratepayers, but almost entirely at the expense of the landlord class: in this sense, at least, that [p. 147] such ground rents as are still paid by the people of London in respect of those classes of property which retain some rental value will have to bear the burden of improving the city. Nor will, I think, the compulsion of any Act of Parliament be necessary to effect this result: it will probably be achieved by the voluntary action of the landowners, compelled, by a Nemesis from whom there is no escape, to make some restitution for the great injustice which they have so long committed.

For observe what must inevitably happen. A vast field of employment being opened outside London, unless a corresponding field of employment is opened within it, London must die,—when the landowners will be in a sorry plight. Elsewhere new cities are being built: London then must be transformed. Elsewhere the town is invading the country: here the country must invade the town. Elsewhere cities are being built on the terms of paying low prices for land, and of then vesting such land in the new municipalities: in London corresponding arrangements must be made or no one will consent to build. Elsewhere, owing to the fact that there are but few interests to buy out, improvements of all kinds can go forward rapidly and scientifically: in London similar improvements can only be carried out if vested interests recognise the inevitable and accept terms which may seem ridiculous, but are no more so than those which a manufacturer often finds himself compelled to submit to, who sells for a ridiculously low price the machine which has cost a very large sum, for the simple reason that there is a far better one in the market, and that it no longer *pays*, in the face of keen competition, to work the inferior machine. The displacement of capital will, no [p. 148] doubt, be enormous, but the implacement of labour will be yet greater. A few may be made comparatively poor, but the many will be made comparatively rich—a very healthy change, the slight evils attending which society will be well able to mitigate.

There are already visible symptoms of the coming change—rumblings which precede the earthquake. London at this very moment may be said to be on strike against its landowners. Long-desired London improvements are awaiting such a change in the law as will throw some of the cost of making them upon the landowners of London. Railways are projected, but in some cases are not built—for instance, The Epping Forest Railway—because the London County Council, most properly anxious to keep down the fares by workmen's trains, press for and secure, at the hands of a Parliamentary Committee, the imposition of terms upon the promoters which seem to them extremely onerous and unremunerative, but which would pay the company extremely well were it not for the prohibitive price asked for land and other property along the line of its projected route. These checks upon enterprise must affect the growth of London even now, and make it less rapid than it otherwise would be; but when the people now living in London discover how easily vested interests, without being attacked, may be circumvented, then the landowners of London and those who represent other vested interests had better quickly make terms, or London, besides being what Mr. Grant Allen termed "a squalid village," will also become a deserted one.

But better counsels, let us hope, will prevail, and a [p. 149] new city rise on the ashes of the old. The task will indeed be difficult. Easy, comparatively, is it to lay out on virgin soil the plan of a magnificent city, such as represented on our

Diagram 5. Of far greater difficulty is the problem—even if all vested interests freely effaced themselves—of rebuilding a new city on an old site, and that site occupied by a huge population. But this, at least, is certain, that the present area of the London County Council ought not (if health and beauty, and that which is too frequently put in the front rank—rapid production of wealth forms—are to be considered) to contain more than, say, one-fifth of its present population; and that new systems of railways, sewerage, drainage, lighting, parks, etc., must be constructed if London is to be saved, while the whole system of production and of distribution must undergo changes as complete and as remarkable as was the change from a system of barter to our present complicated commercial system.

Proposals for the reconstruction of London have already been projected. In 1883 the late Mr. William Westgarth offered the Society of Arts the sum of £1,200 to be awarded in prizes for essays on the best means of providing dwellings for the London poor, and on the reconstruction of Central London—an offer which brought forward several schemes of some boldness.[1] More recently a book by Mr. Arthur Cawston, entitled "A Comprehensive Scheme for Street Improvements in London," was published by Stanford, which contains in its introduction the following striking passage: —"The literature relating to London, extensive as it is, contains [p. 150] no work which aims at the solution of one problem of vast interest to Londoners. They are beginning to realise, partly by their more and more extensive travels, and partly through their American and foreign critics, that the gigantic growth of their capital, without the controlling guidance of a municipality, has resulted in not only the biggest, but in probably the most irregular, inconvenient, and unmethodical collection of houses in the world. A comprehensive plan for the transformation of Paris has been gradually developed since 1848; slums have disappeared from Berlin since 1870; eighty-eight acres in the centre of Glasgow have been remodeled; Birmingham has transformed ninety-three acres of squalid slums into magnificent streets flanked by architectural buildings; Vienna, having completed her stately outer ring, is about to remodel her inner city: and the aim of the writer is to show, by example and illustration, in what way the means successfully employed for improving these cities can be best adapted to the needs of London."

The time for the complete reconstruction of London—which will eventually take place on a far more comprehensive scale than that now exhibited in Paris, Berlin, Glasgow, Birmingham, or Vienna—has, however, not yet come. A simpler problem must first be solved. One small Garden City must be built

[1] See "Reconstruction of Central London" (George Bell and Sons).

as a working model, and then a group of cities such as that dealt with in the last chapter. These tasks done, and done well, the reconstruction of London must inevitably follow, and the power of vested interests to block the way will have been I almost, if not entirely, removed.

Let us, therefore, first bend all our energies to the smaller of these tasks, thinking only of the larger tasks [p. 151] which lie beyond as incentives to a determined line of immediate action, and as a means of realising the great value of little things if done in the right manner and in the right spirit.

THE END.

INDEX

POSTSCRIPT.

"To-Morrow," of which this book is substantially a reproduction, having been published towards the end of 1898, the reader who has followed me thus far will be interested to learn what has been done, and what is proposed to be done to realise the project which was there set forth. I will endeavour to answer these questions.

At the outset, I perceived that the first thing was to make the project widely known—that the city which was pictured so vividly in my own mind must be pictured more or less vividly by many, and that a strong and widespread desire for its up-rearing must be created before a single step could be wisely taken to put the project in a concrete form. For the task before me was, I was fully conscious, a most difficult one, and demanded the hearty co-operation of men and of women[1] experienced in very numerous departments of human activity; and many of these had to be reached and enlisted. City building, as a deliberately thought-out enterprise, is indeed a lost art, in this country at least, and this art has not only to be revived, but has to be carried to finer issues than those who have before practised it ever dreamt of. Autocrats like Alexander the Great and Philip II. could build cities according to [p. 162] well-thought out and carefully-matured plans, because they could impose their will by force; but a city which is to be the outward expression of a strong desire to secure the best interests of all its inhabitants can, among a self-governing people, only arise as the outcome of much patient and well-sustained effort. Moreover, the building of the first of such cities necessarily involves co-operation on new lines—in untried ways; and, as it is essential that the freedom of the individual as well as the interests of the community should be preserved, very much work must needs be done to prepare the way for the successful launching of such an experiment.

---

[1] Woman's influence is too often ignored. When Garden City is built, as it shortly will be, woman's share in the work will be found to have been a large one. Women are among our most active missionaries.

My task—hardly a self-imposed one, for, when I commenced my investigations many years ago, I little dreamed where they would lead me—was rendered especially difficult by the nature of my professional work, which it was impossible for me to give up; and I could, therefore, only give odds and ends of time and energies largely exhausted to the work. But, fortunately, I was not left without help. First the press came to my aid. "To-Morrow" was very widely noticed. Many books have been more fully reviewed, but few have been noticed, and favourably noticed, in such a variety of types of journals as "To-Morrow" has been. Besides the daily and weekly papers of London and the provinces, the project has been favourably commented upon in journals representing widely different points of view. I may mention, merely as illustrations of this—"Commerce," "Country Gentleman," "Spectator," "Leisure Hour," "Court Circular," "Clarion," "Builder's Journal," "Commonwealth," "Young Man," "Councillor and Guardian," "Ladies' Pictorial," [p. 163] "Public Health Engineer," "Municipal Journal," "Argus," "Vegetarian," "Journal of Gas Lighting," "Labour Copartnership," "Hospital," "Brotherhood," "Municipal Reformer."

Nor was the reason of this widespread interest difficult to discover. The project, indeed, touches life at every point, and when once carried out will be an object-lesson which must have far-reaching and beneficial results.

But, although approval of my aims was general, doubts were often, especially at first, expressed as to their realisabilty. Thus, the "Times" said: "The details of administration, taxation, etc., work out to perfection. The only difficulty is to create the city, but that is a small matter to Utopians." If this be so, then, by the "Times'" own showing, I am no Utopian, for to me the building of the city is what I have long set my mind upon, and it is with me no "small matter." A few months after this, however, the "Journal of Gas Lighting" put my case very forcibly thus: "Why should the creation of a town be an insuperable difficulty. It is nothing of the kind. Materials for a tentative realisation of Mr Howard's ideal city exist in abundance in London at the present moment. Time and again it is anounced that some London firm have transferred their factory to Rugby, or Dunstable, or High Wycombe for business reasons. It ought not to be impossible to systematise this movement and give the old country some new towns in which intelligent design shall direct the social workings of economic forces."

In my spare time I lectured on the Garden City, the first lecture after publication being given in Decem- [p. 164] ber, 1898, at the Rectory Road Congregational Church, Stoke Newington, N. In the chair was Mr. T. E. Young, past President, Institute of Actuaries, and I was supported also by Dr. Forman,

A.L.C.C.; Rev. C. Fleming Williams, A.L.C.C.; Mr. James Branch, L.C.C.; and Mr. Lampard, L.C.C. The lecture was well reported in a local journal, and I speedily found that, by means of lectures, interest in the project could be widened, because the subject made "good copy." I, therefore, as far as possible, have always given lectures when requested, and have spoken in London, Glasgow, Manchester, and many provincial towns. Friends, too, began to help, the Rev. J. Bruce Wallace, M.A., of Brotherhood Church being among the first to lecture upon the project; nor shall I ever forget the pleasure I felt at hearing his simple and forcible exposition of it.

Soon after the publication of "To-Morrow," I began to receive many letters, and these often from business men. One of the first of these was from Mr. W. R. Bootland, of Daisy Bank Mills, Newchurch, near Warrington, who wrote heartily commending the project as "sound business," and yet as likely to confer great public benefits.

After a few months of such fitful work as I could undertake, I consulted a friend, Mr F. W. Flear, and we decided it would be well to form an Association with a view to securing supporters in a more systematic manner, and of formulating the scheme more completely, so that, at as early a date as possible, a suitable organisation might be created for carrying it out. Accordingly, on the 10th June, 1899, a few friends met at the offices of Mr. Alexander W. Payne, Chartered Accountant, 70 [p. 165] Finsbury Pavement, E.C., Mr Fred. Bishop, of Tunbridge Wells, in the chair, and the Garden City Association was formed—Mr. Payne being its first Hon. Treasurer, and Mr. F. W. Steere, a barrister, who had written a very useful summary of "To-Morrow" in Uses, its first Hon. Secretary. On the 21st of the same month, a public meeting was held at the Memorial Hall, Farringdon Street, E.C., which was presided over by Sir John Leng, M.P., who, at a very short notice, gave an interesting outline of the project, and urged those present to support me in my very difficult task. At this meeting a Council was formed, and at the first sittings of that body Mr. T. H. W. Idris, J.P., L.C.C., was elected chairman, a post which he resigned at a later stage on account of ill-health, though remaining as firmly convinced as ever of the soundness of the Garden City idea.

Lecturers now began to come forward in different parts of the country, and additional interest was afforded by lantern slides and diagrams. The Association steadily grew, and three months after its formation I was able to write to the "Citizen": —"The Association numbers amongst its members, Manufacturers, Co-operators, Architects, Artists, Medical Men, Financial Experts, Lawyers, Merchants, Ministers of Religion, Members of the L.C.C., Moderate and Progressive; Socialists and Individuals, Radicals and Conservatives."

Our subscriptions, however, were very small. We had put the minimum at the democratic shilling, so that none should be shut out, but, unfortunately, some who could afford much more were content to subscribe that sum, and, from the formation of the Association until August 13, 1901—a little more than two years—the total [p. 166] subscriptions to the general funds of the Association only reached £241 13s. 9d.

A change suddenly came over the Association. I learned early in 1901 that Mr. Ralph Neville, K.C., had written in "Labour Copartnership" expressing his full approval of the essential principles of the Garden City project, and when I called upon him he at once consented to join our Council, and, shortly afterwards, was unanimously elected its chairman. At about the same time, though our financial position hardly justified such a step, we took an office of our own, and engaged a paid secretary, who agreed to devote his whole time to the work.

And here the Garden City Association was very fortunate. It secured the services of Mr. Thomas Adams, a young Scotchman, who has proved active, energetic, and resourceful—to whose suggestion was due the Conference held last September at Mr. Cadbury's beautiful village of Bournville, which has done more than anything else to make the Garden City Association and its project known to the great public, and to give to our members ocular proof of the feasibility—indeed, the wonderful success—of a scheme in so many respects like our own.[1]

Since our Annual Meeting in December our membership has increased—thanks mainly to a special effort of members—from 530 to 1,300; and, as many of our friends, anxious to put the project to the test of experiment at an early date, are offering to subscribe very considerable sums, a Joint Stock Company, to be called the [p. 167] Garden City Pioneer Company, Limited, with a small capital of about £20,000, is being formed for the purpose of securing the option of a site, and of preparing and presenting to the public a complete scheme adapted to the development of the site thus selected—a scheme which will be in accordance with the general principles set forth in this book, but differing, of course, in many details. Subscribers to this preliminary Company will, of course, run considerable risk; and, as the profits, even in the event of the most complete success, will only be nominal, the appeal will be addressed only to those who take an interest in the project as public-spirited citizens. The Secretary of the Garden City Association will give the latest information on this

---

[1] Through the kindness of Messrs. Lever Brothers, a conference is being arranged for July this year at Port Sunlight, a most admirably planned industrial village in Cheshire.

subject, and will also gladly enrol members.

No one can possibly be under a greater obligation than he who has an idea which he earnestly wishes to see carried out and who finds others helping him to make visible that which exists only as a thought. Under this greatest of debts am I. By writing; by speaking; by organising public meetings and drawing-room meetings; by suggestion, encouragement, and advice; by secretarial and other work; by making the project known among their friends; by subscribing funds for propaganda work; and, now, by offering to subscribe considerable sums for practical steps, many have helped and are helping me to do that which, without their aid, must have been quite impossible. They have thus multiplied my strength a thousandfold; and from the very bottom of my heart I thank them for the assurance of speedy success which their efforts have thus given me. Ere long, I trust we shall meet in Garden City.

GARDEN CITY ASSOCIATION.

VICE-PRESIDENTS.

The Countess of Warwick.
The Earl of Carrington, G.C.M.G., L.C.C.
The Earl of Meath, L.C.C.
The Bishop of London.
The Bishop of Hereford.
The Bishop of Rochester.
Percy Alden, M.A.
Dr. Tempest Anderson (York).
Yarborough Anderson.
L. A. Atherley-Jones, K.C., M.P.
William Baker.
R. A. Barrett (Ashton-under-Lyne).
J. Williams Benn, J.P., L.C.C.
Sir M. M. Bhownaggree, K.C.I.E., M.P.
W. R. Bootland (Manchester).
Rev. Stopford Brooke, M.A.
The Right Hon. James Bryce, M.P.
W. P. Byles, J.P. (Bradford).
George Cadbury, J.P. (Bournville).
W. S. Caine, M.P.
Robert Cameron, M P.
Professor Chapman (Manchester).
Rev. Thomas Child.
Dr. John Clifford, M.A.
Miss Marie Corelli.
Walter Crane.
Alderman W. H. Dickinson, L.C.C.
Canon Moore Ede (Sunderland).
Samuel Edwards, J.P. (Birmingham).
The Master of Elibank, M.P.
Alfred Emmott, M.P.
F. J. Farquharson, J.P
Mrs. Anna Farquharson.
Michael Flürscheim.
Lady Forsyth.
Sir Walter Foster, M P.
Madame Sarah Grand.
Corrie Grant, M.P.
W. Winslow Hall, M.D., M.R.C.S.
G. A. Hardy, L.C.C.
Cecil Harmsworth.
R. Leicester Harmsworth, M.P.
Henry B. Harris.
Anthony Hope Hawkins.
The Hon. Claude G. Hay, M.P.
Sir Robert Head, Bart.
C. E. Hobhouse, M.P.
Henry Holiday.

Canon Scott Holland.
George Jacob Holyoake.
Rev. Alfred Hood.
T. H. W. Idris, J.P.
Ben. Jones (Chairman C.W.S. London).
Mrs. Ashton Jonson.
Dean Kitchin (Durham).
George Lampard, L.C.C.
A. L. Leon, L.C.C.
Sir John Leng, M.P.
W. H. Lever (Port Sunlight).
J. W. Logan, M.P.
Dr. T. J. Macnamara, M.P.
Walter T. Macnamara.
Mrs. Magrath.
R. Biddulph Martin, M.P.
Professor Alfred Marshall (Cambridge).
Rev. F. B. Meyer
Edward R. P. Moon, M.P.
Mrs. Morgan-Browne.
Harington Morgan.
The Hon Dadabhai Naoroji.
Mrs. Overy.
Gilbert Parker, M.P.
F. Platt-Higgins, M.P.
Sir Robert Pullar (Perth).
Joseph Rowntree (York).
C. E. Schwann, M.P.
Arthur Sherwell.
Albert Spicer, J.P.
Henry C. Stephens, J.P.
Miss Julie Sutter.
A. C. Swinton.
Ivor H. Tuckett (Cambridge).
J. Elliott Viney.
Professor A. R. Wallace, D.C.L., F.R.S.
J. Bruce Wallace, M.A.
H. G. Wells.
Richard Whiteing.
J. H. Whitley, M.P.
Aneurin Williams.
Alderman Rev. Fleming Williams, L.C.C.
Robert Williams, F.R.I.B.A., L.C.C.
Henry J. Wilson, M.P.
Wm. Woodward, A.R.I.B.A.
Robert Yerburgh, M.P.
T. E. Young, B.A., F.R.A.S.
J. H. Yoxall, M.P.

COUNCIL.

Chairman—Ralph Neville, K.C.   *Hon. Treasurer*—A. W. Payne, F.C.A., F.S.S.

A. S. E. Ackerman. A.M. Inst. C.E.
C. M. Bailhache, L.L.B.
G. M. Bishop.
Arthur Blott.
Miss Edith Bradley (Lady Warwick
    Hostel).
James Branch, J.P., L.C.C.
William Carter.
J. Cleghorn.
G. Croscer.
F. W. Flear.
J. C. Gray (Secretary, Co-op. Union
    Manchester).
Ebenezer Howard.
Mrs. Ebenezer Howard.

James P. Hurst.
H. C. Lander, A.R.I.B.A.
Fred. W. Lawrence, M.A.
H. D. Pearsall, M.Inst.C.E.
T. P. Ritzema, J.P. (Blackburn).
Edward Rose.
Hon. Rollo Russell.
W. H. Gurney Salter.
Sydney Schiff (Chester).
W. S. Sherrington, M.A., L.L.M.
Edward T. Sturdy.
Alderman W. Thompson.
Herbert Warren, B.A.
Aneurin Williams.

(The full Council will consist of 30 Members.)

Honorary Provincial Secretaries.

Manchester District— R. Morrell, Moston Lane, New Moston, Manchester.

Liverpool and Cheshire District—J. Norton, 1 Morningside Road, Bootle, near Liverpool.

N.E.—F. W. Bricknell, Guyscliffe, Hessle, East Yorks.

Midlands—Rev. J. B. Higham, 25 Copthorne Road, Wolverhampton.

Scotland—Robert MacLaurin, 39 Caldercuilt Road, Maryhill, Glasgow.

James Allport, 15 Montpelier, Edinburgh.

General Secretary—
THOMAS ADAMS, 77 Chancery Lane, London, W.C.

Objects.

To promote the discussion of the project suggested by Mr. Ebenezer Howard in "To-morrow"[1], and ultimately to formulate a practical scheme on the lines of that project, with such modifications as may appear desirable.

Membership.

Payment of an Annual Subscription of not less than 1s. confers Membership. A Subscription of 2s. 6d., or more, entitles the Subscriber to all literature published by the Association. More funds are required for the immediate purpose of bringing our proposals prominently before the public, and an average

---

[1] Now published by Swan Sonnenschein & Co. (London), under the title "Garden Cities of To-morrow."

subscription of 5s. per member is necessary to meet current expenditure. The income for the first half year 1901-02 was ten times that of the same period of the previous year. The Membership is over 1,300, being an increase of 700 since January 1st, 1902. It is hoped that all who are desirous of improving, by constitutional means, the present physical, social, and industrial conditions of life in town and country, will help to immediately increase this number.

Sectional Committees.

Committees have been or are being appointed to consider questions of detail, such as Land Tenure, Manufactures and Trade, Co-operative Societies, Labour, Housing and Public Health, Liquor Traffic, Education, Smoke Abatement, Art, etc. Members desirous of taking part in the work of any section are requested to communicate with the General Secretary.

Publications.

The Association publishes a number of tracts which are forwarded to members on joining. A list of publications and some explanatory literature will be sent free on application. A few reports of the Bournville Conference may still be had, price 6d., post free. These reports consist of 80 pages, and contain reports of speeches by—Earl Grey, Mr. Ralph Neville, K.C.; Mr. George Cadbury, Mr. Aneurin Williams, the Mayor of Camberwell, Sir M. M. Bhownaggree, M.P.; Mr. R. B. Martin, M.P.; Mr. Ebenezer Howard, Dr. Mansfield Robinson, and others.

All communications should be addressed to the Secretary, Garden City Association, 77 Chancery Lane, London, W.C. Cheques and postal orders should be crossed London City and Midland Bank, Fore Street.

Printed at the Rosemount Press;
London Office: 149 Fleet Street, E.C.

EDITOR'S POSTSCRIPT

Ebenezer Howard's "Garden Cities of To-Morrow" is a remarkably compact and informationally dense volume that deserves a bit of clarification and elaboration, especially for the modern reader. As the author states, his work is nearly a direct reissue of "To-Morrow: A Peaceful Path to Real Reform," published four years earlier in 1898. And yet, the later edition had several differences that are worth highlighting. Interestingly, several diagrams present in the 1898 issue were eliminated from or substantially altered in the later edition.

First, Howard's original diagram "No. 4," or "The Vanishing Point of Landlord's Rent" is an interesting figurative representation of his concept of land ownership and municipal taxation via rate-rents. This figure illustrates how rents decrease over the proposed thirty year window, with each circle corresponding to a point in time and showing the breakdown of total rents (being rent, land purchase, and fees for municipal services) into constituent parts. By way of comparison, Howard calculates that an average Londoner of the time pays £4 10s. per year in total rent, with more than sixty percent (£88,000 out of a total of £144,000 for a Garden City size municipality) going towards landlord's rent—with no decrease over time and no tangible benefit to the renter.

As Howard's diagram illustrates, his Garden City concept requires substantially less total rent, the per-capita average being only £2 annually. More importantly, he shows how the portion allocated for landlord's rent actually decreases over time so that a larger and larger percentage of each citizen's overall rent goes toward municipal purposes, including the eventual repayment of the land purchase outright. Howard's eliminated figure "No. 4" is an interesting graphical presentation of the concept, albeit one that he explains in narrative format throughout the course of Chapters II and III, collectively titled "The Revenue of Garden City."

Curiously, Howard's original "Diagram 5," entitled "Diagram of Administration" is actually referenced in the later edition, next to the heading of "The

Central Council" on page 71, even though it was not included in that version. Through this illustration, Howard shows the division of his Garden City administration into the Municipal, Semi-Municipal, Pro-Municipal, and Cooperative & Individualistic Groups, as he describes in the text. This diagram actually helps explain the proposed organization, and these organizational units serve as the titles for subsequent chapters of the work. Howard proposes a central council to manage the three municipal groups: public control, social

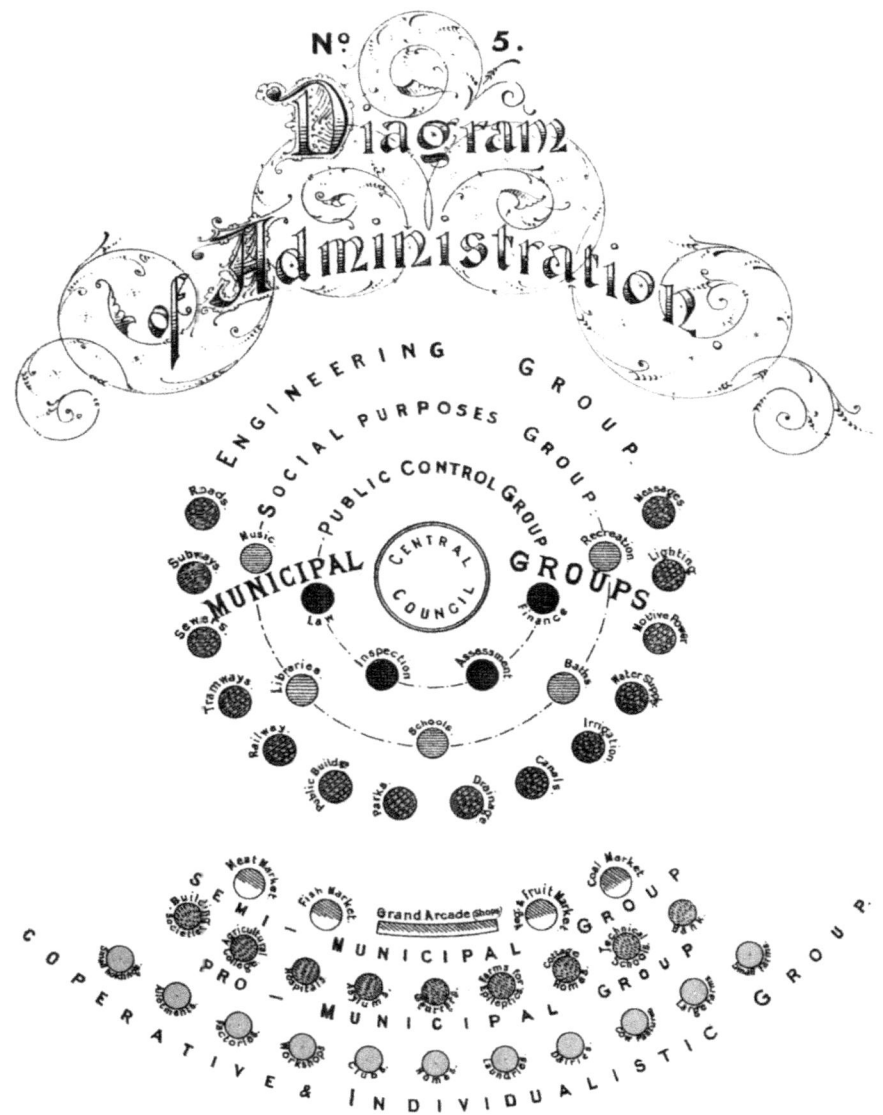

purposes, and engineering. As the diagram shows, the semi-municipal, pro-municipal, and cooperative and individualistic groups span further from the control of the central council—essentially a public- to private-control continuum.

The elaborate and iconic figure "No. 7," or "Group of Slumless, Smoke-less Cities" was replaced by a much simpler Figure Five in the 1902 edition. The original Figure Seven illustrates how the Garden City concept could be

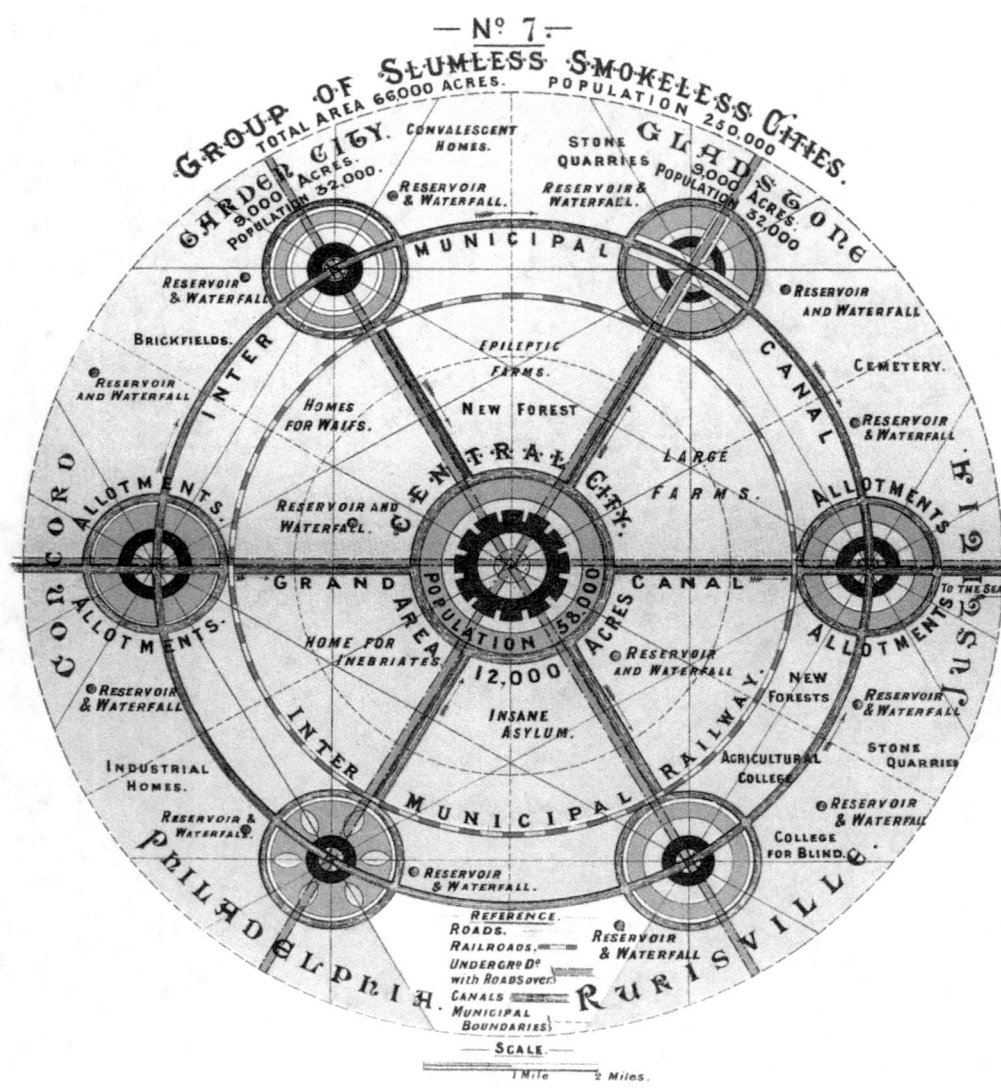

extended to produce a larger interconnected arrangement of cities with a total population of 250,000. This diagram is especially interesting due to the creativity of specialized land uses listed, such as "epileptic farms," "home for inebriates," "new forests," "reservoir and waterfall," "homes for waifs," and so on. The original figure "No. 7" was placed in the "Social Cities" chapter, after page 130 (using 1902 edition page numbering). Figure "No. 5" of the later edition is a simplified version of the upper left quadrant of this "No. 7," showing Concord" and "Garden City" on spokes originating from "Central City."

One additional diagram, figure "No. 6," or "A New System of Water Supply" was included in the 1898 edition. This illustration was intended to accompany the appendix to that edition, titled "Water Supply." Neither the appendix nor the diagram were included in the 1902 edition, and thus are not shown here.

FINANCIAL PROJECTIONS.

The modern reader of Howard's "Garden Cities of To-Morrow" is also faced with a daunting task of interpreting financial figures from the late nineteenth and early twentieth centuries. In an effort to make these figures more relatable, an effort has been made to project key figures forward to the present. While it is nearly impossible to do so accurately, an average consumer cost inflation figure of 90-times has been assumed.[1] For U.S. dollar estimates, an equivalent is provided based on an average of the last decade's exchange rate between the pound and the dollar, or £1 = $1.71.

From Chapters II and III, the tables on pages 36, 41, and 42 would be combined and updated to reflect the following:

Total "rate-rent" from agricultural estates, being		£877,500
Original rent paid by tenants of 5,000 acres, say	£585,000	
Add 50 per cent. for contributions to rates and sinking fund	292,500	
Rate-rent from 5,500 home building lots at £540 per lot		2,970,000
Rate-rent from business premises 10,625 persons employed at an average of £180 per head		1,912,500
Total gross revenue of the entire estate		£5,760,000
This sum would be available as follows: —		
For landlord's rent or interest on purchase money £21,600,000 at 4 per cent.		£864,000
For sinking fund (30 years)		396,000
For such purposes as are elsewhere defrayed out of rates		4,500,000
		£5,760,000

The expenditure table from page 58 of Howard's work has been similarly converted below. The first provides present-day pounds, and the second an es-

---

[1] Estimated from 1898 to 2004 figures provided in "Consumer Price Inflation since 1750," issued by the Office for National Statistics in *Economic Trends 604*, March 2004.

		EXPENDITURE.	
		On Capital Account.	On Maintenance and Working Expenses.
(See Note A)	25 Miles road (city) at £360,000 a mile ...	£9,000,000	£225,000
(„ B)	6 Miles additional roads, country estate at £108,000	648,000	31,500
(„ C)	Circular railway and bridges, 5½ miles at £270,000	1,485,000	135,000
(„ D)	Schools for 6,400 children, or ¹/₅ of the total population, at £1,080 per school place for capital account, and £270 maintenance, etc.	6,912,000	135,000 (maintenance only) 1,728,000
(„ E)	Town Hall	900,000	180,000
(„ F)	Library	900,000	54,000
(„ G)	Museum	900,000	54,000
(„ H)	Parks, 250 acres at £4,500	1,125,000	112,500
(„ I)	Sewage disposal ...	1,800,000	90,000
		£23,670,000	£2,610,000
(„ K)	Interest on £23,670,000 at 4½ per cent.		1,065,150
(„ L)	Sinking Fund to provide for extinction of debt in 30 years		403,200
(„ M)	Balance available for rates levied by local bodies within the area of which the estate is situated		421,650
			£4,500,000

Conversion of Chapter V Expenditures to Current-day Pounds Sterling.

timate in U.S. dollars.

While these figures certainly appear to be more plausible, two factors might still lead to a remaining under-estimation. First, land values have almost certainly exceeded the rate of consumer inflation over the past hundred years, especially for what we would consider "suburban" land adjacent to larger metropolitan areas. Similarly, the rate of wage increases over the last century has outweighed price inflation as minimum wages and dramatically improved working conditions have prevailed. Wage increases would be reflected most heavily in the construction costs and ongoing maintenance of a new town. Conversely, however, higher wages create additional purchasing power on the behalf of potential participants, and so on.

	EXPENDITURE.	
	On Capital Account.	On Mainten- ance and Working Ex- penses.
(See Note A) 25 Miles road (city) at $615,600 a mile ...	$15,390,000	$384,750
(„ B) 6 Miles additional roads, country estate at $184,680	1,108,080	53,865
(„ C) Circular railway and bridges, 5½ miles at $461,700	2,539,350	230,850
(„ D) Schools for 6,400 chil- dren, or ¹/₅ of the total population, at $1,847 per school place for capital account, and $462 main- tenance, etc.	11,819,520	(maintenance only) 2,954,880
(„ E) Town Hall	1,539,000	307,800
(„ F) Library	1,539,000	92,340
(„ G) Museum	1,539,000	92,340
(„ H) Parks, 250 acres at $7,695	1,923,750	192,375
(„ I) Sewage disposal ...	3,078,000	153,900
	$40,475,700	$4,463,100
(„ K) Interest on $40,475,700 at 4½ per cent.		1,821,407
(„ L) Sinking Fund to provide for extinc- tion of debt in 30 years		689,472
(„ M) Balance available for rates levied by local bodies within the area of which the estate is situated		721,022
		$7,695,000

Conversion of Chapter V Expenditures to Current-day U.S. Dollars.

Perhaps, as a matter of course, these estimates are off by another factor of 1½- to 3-times...a consideration which is left for the reader. A more thorough analysis and calculation of the present-day costs of Howard's scheme is outside the scope of this volume. Nevertheless, it is interesting to see Howard's figures translated into current-day estimates that appear more concrete to the average reader.

THE
GARDEN CITY MOVEMENT
UP-TO-DATE

BY

EWART G. CULPIN

(Secretary to the Garden Cities and Town Planning Association)

THE GARDEN CITIES AND TOWN PLANNING ASSOCIATION
3, GRAY'S INN PLACE, LONDON, W.C.
1913

A PROPHET'S PLEA FOR GARDEN CITIES.

"As I sit at my work at home, which is at Hammersmith, close to the river, I often hear some of that ruffianism go past the window of which a good deal has been said in the papers of late, and has been said before at recurring periods. As I hear the yells and shrieks and all the degradation cast on the glorious tongue of Shakespeare and Milton, as I see the brutal, reckless faces and figures go past me, it rouses the recklessness and brutality in me also, and fierce wrath takes possession of me, till I remember that it was my good luck only of being born respectable and rich, that has put me on this side of the window among delightful books and lovely works of art, and not on the other side, in the empty street, the drink-steeped liquor-shops, the foul and degraded lodgings. I know by my own feelings and desires what these men want, what would have saved them from this lowest depth of savagery; employment which would foster their self-respect and win the praise and sympathy of their fellows, and dwellings which they could come to with pleasure, surroundings which would soothe and elevate them; reasonable labour, reasonable rest."

WILLIAM MORRIS, at Burslem, 1881.

iii

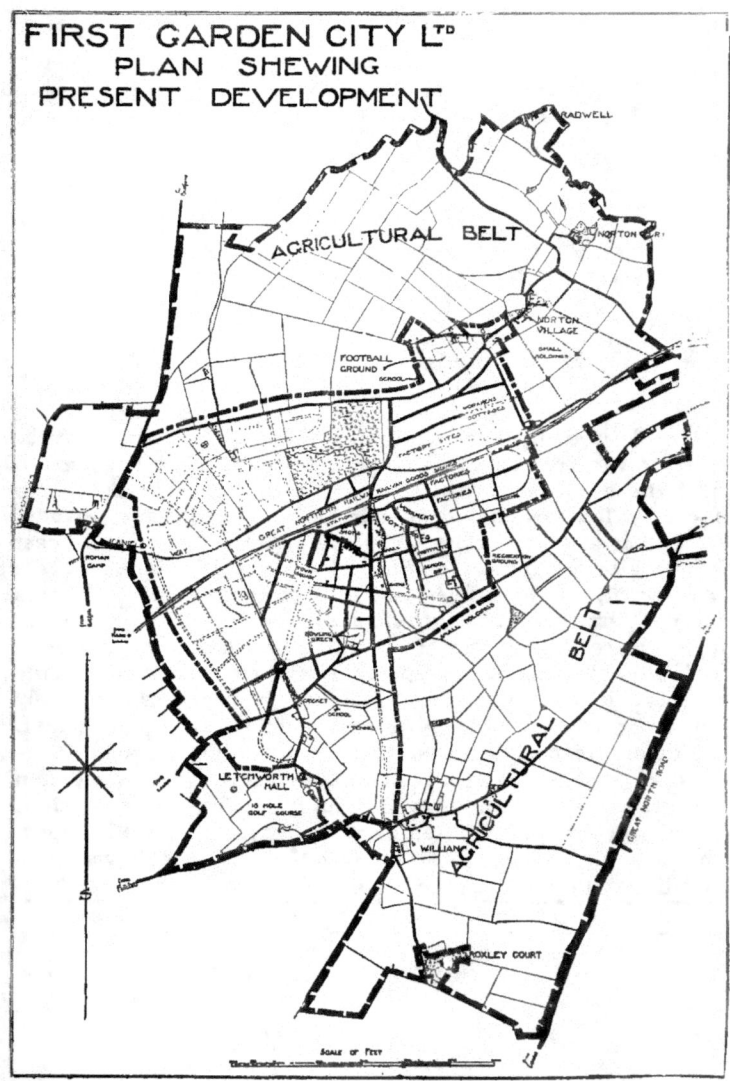

PLAN OF LETCHWORTH GARDEN CITY.

This plan illustrates some of Mr. Ebenezer Howard's main proposals. The whole area is 4,566 acres, of which the town area, shown by the broken line, occupies about 1,500 acres, the remainder forming the Agricultural Belt, which entirely surrounds the urban land. The present population is 8,500, against some 400 souls who lived in the villages of Radwell, Norton, Letchworth, and Willian, the position of which is indicated above. The ultimate population provided for on the town area is 30,000, together with 5,000 on the agricultural belt.

iv

CONTENTS.

Map showing developments on Garden City lines in Great Britain where a limitation
of dividend is observed.

vi

THE GARDEN CITY MOVEMENT UP-TO-DATE

1899—1914

WHEN fifteen years ago the Garden City Association was first formed, it was necessary in the literature that was published from time to time to point out in graphic form and detail the necessity for action along the lines which were advocated by Mr. Ebenezer Howard. Thirteen years of propaganda have, however, brought home to the minds of the thinking part of the population the fact of the awful wastage that is going on through the ill-housing of the people, and through the haphazard growth of our centres of population. Month by month the pages of GARDEN CITIES AND TOWN PLANNING, the organ of the Garden City and Town Planning Movement, has contained information shedding new light on the varied phases of this difficult question, and it may fairly be claimed that the knowledge of garden city principles has spread into every civilised nation under the sun. There is, therefore, not the same necessity that there was to quote statistics to prove we are rearing in our slums an enfeebled rickety race, and that by our neglect a slum population is growing up which is foredoomed to degeneration. The following particulars will, however, show graphically the effect upon health, and especially upon the health of the child, of life in the slums and life in a properly planned community.

Since the first efforts of the Garden City Association, which followed upon the excellent work done at Bournville and Port Sunlight, numerous examples of garden suburb and garden village work have branched out in various parts of Great Britain, and an endeavour is here made to supply the salient facts relating to each. It may be that some schemes are omitted, and it is hoped that, if this is the case, particulars will be forwarded for a succeeding issue. Every effort has been made to obtain the utmost degree of accuracy, and the figures given have been supplied by the companies or societies concerned.

Although growing out of the garden city movement, not all of these ventures are upon the lines pursued by Mr. Ebenezer Howard in his original book " Garden Cities of To-morrow "; in fact, Letchworth is the only garden city in existence. Several garden suburbs and garden villages have grown up, while, in addition to this, there are quite a number of schemes which take the title "Garden City" promiscuously, without having any claim whatever to use the name, their objects being as foreign as possible to the conceptions of the founder of the movement.

THE ESSENTIALS OF A GARDEN CITY.

It may be well to set out at the beginning the essentials of a garden city as distinguished from a garden suburb, and from ordinary development. These may be stated as follows :—

1. That before a sod is cut, or a brick is laid, the town must in its broad outlines be properly planned with an eye to the convenience of the community as a whole, the preservation of natural beauties, the securing of the utmost degree of healthfulness, and proper regard to communication with the surrounding district.

I

2. That in the town area the number of houses to each acre should be strictly limited, so that every dwelling should have ample light and air, with a suitable garden, and that public recreation ground and open space should be provided generously.

3. That the town area should for ever be surrounded by a belt of agricultural and park land, so that while in the centre the urban problem is being dealt with, the rural portion, which should be the larger part of the estate, may be available for farms and small holdings, in order that the small holder and market gardener may have a new market direct to hand for the sale of produce.

4. That the return on capital should be limited to, say, 5 per cent., any profit above that amount being applied to the estate itself for the benefit of the community.

5. That the town should be not merely residential, but also commercial and industrial, that provision should exist for taking the worker and his work away from the crowded centres into the fresh air of the country district, where not only should the land be cheaply obtainable for the employer, but the worker should have a comfortable cottage at a convenient distance from his labour.

It is, therefore, essential that the land should be of considerable area, and its development should be in the hands of one controlling body, which, in Mr. Howard's scheme, should have for its ultimate object, not the making of huge profits, but the improvement of the conditions of life for all who live on the area. The estate should be somewhere from six to ten square miles in area, and in order to give effect to the desire for the combination of town and country, about two-thirds should be reserved for the rural area.

CITIES, SUBURBS, AND VILLAGES.

In view of the many distorted ideas of what a Garden City is and the confusion which has resulted between Garden Cities, Garden Suburbs, and Garden Villages, it may be well to quote a succinct definition of the three phrases :—

A " Garden City " is a self-contained town, industrial, agricultural, residential— planned as a whole—and occupying land sufficient to provide garden-surrounded homes for at least 30,000 persons, as well as a wide belt of open fields. It combines the advantages of town and country, and prepares the way for a national movement, stemming the tide of the population now leaving the countryside and sweeping into our overcrowded cities.

A " Garden Suburb " provides that the normal growth of existing cities shall be on healthy lines ; and, when such cities are not already too large, such suburbs are most useful, and even in the case of overgrown London they may be, though on the other hand they tend to drive the country yet further afield, and do not deal with the root evil—rural depopulation.

" Garden Villages," such as Bournville and Port Sunlight, are Garden Cities in miniature, but depend upon some neighbouring city for water, light and drainage ; they have not the valuable provision of a protective belt, and are usually the centre of one great industry only.

The Garden City therefore stands as the preventive, not as the palliative.

There is general agreement that the housing of the people and the evil environment of that housing are very potent factors of our social maladies. The aggregation of population is in itself an evil. Wherever more than a certain number of people are housed on a given area of land, no matter whether they be in the best of " model dwellings," there the vital statistics show the progress of the evil.

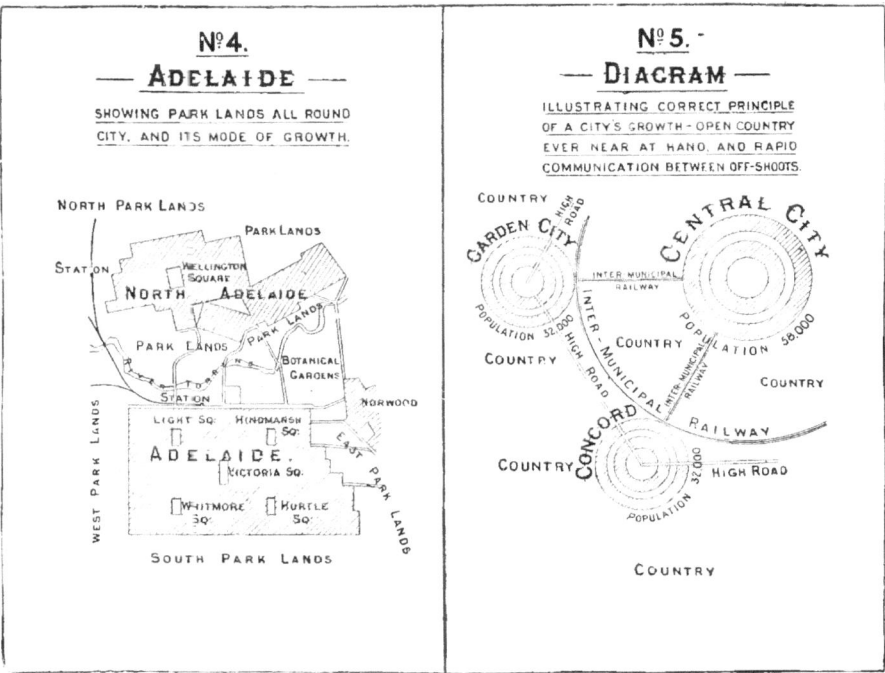

One of Mr. Howard's original diagrams illustrating the principle of the agricultural belt, and his suggestions for extension when the first Garden City has reached its limit of population.

Croft Lane, Letchworth, on the Agricultural Belt.

The central area of Letchworth, showing the new railway station and the shopping area.

Hillshott, Letchworth.

One of the problems most seriously affecting civilised humanity to-day is the twin problem of the overcrowding of the towns and the depopulation of the countryside. Wherever we inquire, whether it be in the industrial countries of the old world or the more newly developed settlements of the new, the same state of things is to be found—everywhere the towns are becoming too large and, particularly noticeable in the old countries, the rural population is decreasing at such a rate as seriously to jeopardise the proper carrying on of husbandry.

TOWN AND COUNTRY—ADVANTAGES AND DISADVANTAGES.

The industrial revolution of the last century, while it led to much material advantage and greatly increased the financial prosperity of the country, was responsible for many evils, which, although not perceived at the time, are none the less pernicious in their results.

Fifty or sixty years ago the bulk of the population of this country lived in rural conditions, but it is estimated that at the present time six-sevenths is born and bred in large towns and cities. The growth of mechanical industries and the higher money wages which resulted, caused the rural dwellers to flock into the towns and to neglect the countryside, where at eighteen years of age a man was earning as much as he ever would earn as an agricultural labourer. Too often country life presented a picture of helplessness and hopelessness ; there was no opportunity for improved conditions of employment, for recreation, for education, or for social life. Housing conditions presented features as horrible as the worst slum can show ; sanitation, lighting, water, and the other services which the town-dweller has come to regard as a necessity are altogether lacking, and it is not to be wondered at that the lights of the town and its gold-paved streets have proved a fatal fascination to the hundreds of thousands who have come to swell the already overcrowded labour market.

And the town, with all the advantages of commerce and high monetary wages, with education, amusement, and all the services of civilisation, has its dark underworld, whose real inwardness is hardly known to those whose lot is cast in more pleasant places. The march of science, the increasing activity of sanitary authorities, and the efficiency of their officials, backed by an enormous expenditure of money, has resulted in much improvement in the condition of our large cities, but still there is the slum and the overcrowding, still disease, dirt, and degradation. And even where in their extreme these conditions do not prevail, we find dreariness, monotony, inconvenience, and absolute divorce from the beauties of nature : we are trying to breed an imperial race out of the material which makes for ruin and decay.

A satisfactory solution of the problem thus presented must therefore go a long way towards the prevention of destitution. Anything which brings a new hope to humanity, any force which may be expended on creating a new condition of life, and any new economic truth which is capable of adaptation to the varying needs of the dwellers in town and in country, in old worlds and in new worlds, must be hailed as leading to that prophetic day and that ideal city which the dreamers of every age have dreamt of from the time of Isaiah down to William Morris.

THE FOUNDER.

As is the case with so many great movements, the Garden City idea was the outcome of the man of the people—unknown beyond his immediate circle, and without the resources of wealth and privilege to forward his project. It is not too much to say that Mr. Ebenezer Howard, the founder of the Garden City movement, will be remembered in history when the names of many prominent politicians and soldiers have been forgotten, for of him alone can it be said in modern times that he founded a city, and not only founded one city but that by his practical enthusiasm and his clear-sighted idealism he gave to the world an idea which has resulted in a few years in a complete change of the ordinary methods of town extension and estate development. It was only in 1898 that, after studying for many years the social problems of the country, and observing the results which had come with the improved environment of the people, he published a book called "To-morrow: A Peaceful Path to Real Reform," subsequently issued as "Garden Cities of To-morrow."

The problem which Mr. Ebenezer Howard set himself out to solve was to show that by starting entirely new towns in rural districts, free from the vicious inheritance of generations of town life and slum degeneracy, an opportunity would be given for a fuller, freer, life, and that the mental, moral, and intellectual development would follow as surely as the physical. It was not an easy problem, although it is so much taken for granted nowadays. It was really the creation of new economic conditions. First, it involved town planning, then quite a new idea in this country, but through Mr. Howard's initial work and the labours of those who gathered round him, now an accepted necessity and embodied in an Act of Parliament.

Before a sod was cut or a brick was laid, in its main outlines at least, the new city must take its form upon paper. By so doing, traffic difficulties would be avoided in the future. By the proper restriction of areas, schemes of lighting, drainage, and water supply could be planned out from the beginning, with no uncertainty as to the whereabouts of the future population. The limitation of the number of houses was an essential point ; in many districts to-day the municipal by-laws allow fifty-six and even sixty houses to be crowded on to an acre of land, giving a population, even in cottage property, of some three hundred people to the acre, while in tenement dwellings the number comes up still higher.

Profiting by investigations that have been made by scientists, a limit of twelve houses to the net acre was determined upon, and this, with the provision of ample open spaces, parks, and recreation grounds, and allowing for generous grass-lined roadways, will mean on the average of five people to a house, no greater population than thirty people to the acre.

But it was not enough to plan where the town should grow ; it was necessary to say where it should stop. It is being borne in upon the minds of thinkers that our big towns are too big, and that where you go along adding village to town and town to city, so that you have huge conglomerations like London—or, as in south-east Lancashire, practically one great town twenty-five or thirty miles long and eight or ten miles wide—and where your population is numbered by the hundred thousand, you have practically shut out the benefits of fresh air and pure sunlight from the great mass of the dwellers. The idea, therefore, in creating garden cities is to aim at towns with populations of between thirty thousand, lower than which it would not be possible to go to enable the necessary provisions to be made, and sixty or seventy thousand, beyond which access to the countryside begins to be in danger.

THE INDUSTRIAL ASPECT.

To secure the proper restriction of the town, Mr. Howard conceived the idea of the agricultural belt of land encircling the town area and providing upon its farms and small holdings an opportunity for the solution there of rural problems, while in the town area urban questions were being settled.

But it was useless to talk about fresh air and sunlight to the man who has to earn his daily bread by the sweat of his brow, unless you give him an opportunity of continuing his employment. This meant the provision of work near to his home.

4

Few people have realised the enormous economic waste involved in carrying work people to and from their work. Not only is much time wasted, but the conditions of workmen's trains are such that serious physical results must follow, and we are probably thereby laying up a store of nervous disorders.

But apart from that, with improved forms of transit, it is not necessary for mechanical industries all to be carried on at one centre, and all in big towns. Years before the Garden City movement came to birth individual manufacturers were finding that it paid them to take their works out into the country districts, where the cheapness of land and the lower expenditure on rates, etc., amply repaid them for their outlay. It is true there were failures, and there have been failures since then ; but this is where the Garden City movement met the problem and solved it by organising the migration of manufacturers. Only the largest firms could provide housing, sewerage, water, gas, and other facilities for their workpeople, and the failures were deterring further experiments when Mr. Howard showed how, under the Garden City scheme, the combination of manufacturers in conjunction with residential development, could do what was not possible to individuals. The cheapness of land enabled factories to be built all on one floor, and with proper lighting ; it enabled cottages to be built cheaply and reasonably near the factories ; and it also provided that each house should have an ample amount of garden ground around it. Working in a London factory often means living in a slum, with the children's playground in the gutter, or on the stairs of a " model dwelling "; it means an exorbitant rent in the centre, and if the worker lives in the suburbs what he saves on rent he spends on railway fare.

The financial side of the question was given very careful thought and study, because it was realised from the beginning that even if sufficient money could be found to equip such a venture at the start, unless it could be proved a commercial success, no one else would be likely to make the experiment, and it would be impossible to impress upon the country, and upon the State, the value of development upon these lines. In order to adjust the claims of capital and of production it was proposed that the dividend on capital should be limited to 5 per cent., and that all profits above this sum should be devoted to the benefit of the community. The land would be bought as a whole at agricultural prices, and a freehold retained by the company. As the population increased, so would the value go up, and this value would be for the benefit of the people themselves. The developing company was to act as a sort of trustee, and when the estate was sufficiently advanced to run on its own legs it was hoped that it would be possible to hand over the whole concern to some body which should act as permanent trustees for the community at the original price which had been paid for the estate, which should henceforth be carried on in the interests of the dwellers on the spot.

The promulgation of these principles thirteen years ago was received with that kindly cynicism with which most changes are greeted. " Utopian," " beautiful but impracticable," " wildly visionary," and many another epithet is found on looking through the newspaper press of that day. Except in a few quarters, the scheme was hailed as idyllic ; few deemed it possible of success. But the few have proved the truer prophets.

THE WORK OF THE GARDEN CITY ASSOCIATION.

After a few years' propagandist work by the Garden City Association (now the Garden Cities and Town Planning Association), which was called into being to foster the new idea, a pioneer company was formed to make investigations, and in 1903 First Garden City Ltd. was formed to develop the estate of nearly four thousand acres at Letchworth. Here many of Mr. Howard's original ideas have been put into practice, modified, of course, by the

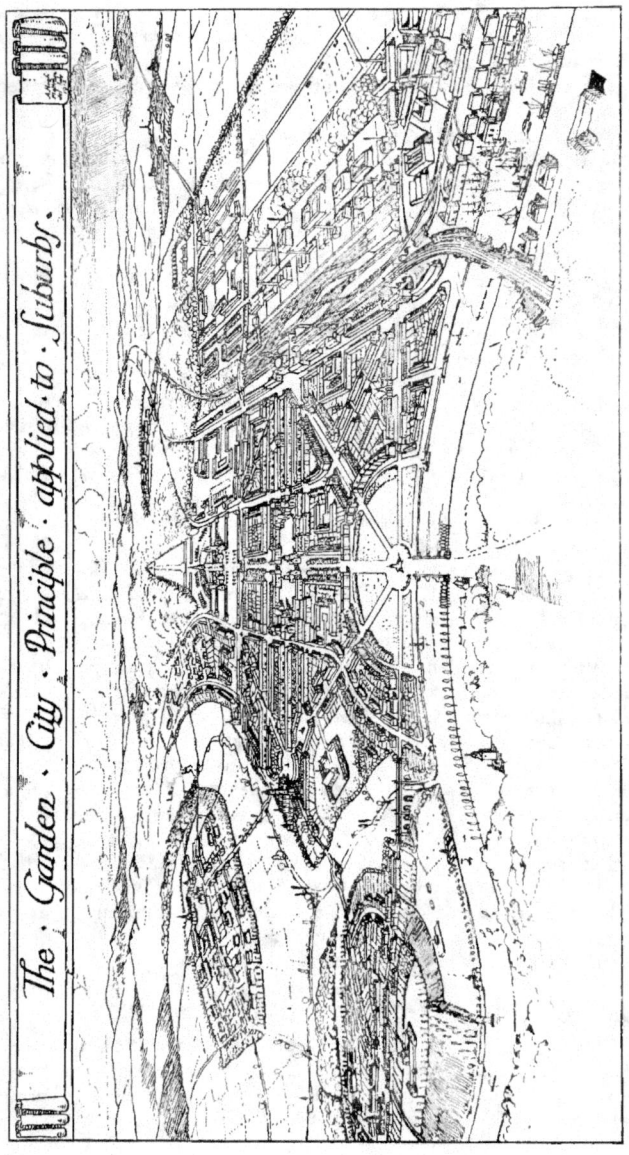

The · Garden · City · Principle · applied · to · Suburbs.

Mr. Raymond Unwin here illustrates the application of the Garden City principle of a belt of green encircling the whole community to the extension of new Suburbs. The Suburbs are seen separated from the city by belts of land, which will remain open for all time.

requirements of the site, and hindered oftentimes by the lack of sufficient capital ; but yet being pressed onwards by men with an ample faith in the soundness of the project and in the ultimate realisation of triumphant success. That success has now been achieved. What a few years ago was arable and pasture land with a scattered population of a few score people is now a thriving industrial and residential centre with a population of some seven thousand people, which is being added to day by day, as the requirements of those desiring to live there are met by the provision of additional cottages.

It was not long before it was seen that this movement had in it a much wider application than the building of new towns. That was the ideal ; that was the solution of the problem. It would keep men on the land, and bring others back to the land. It was grand ; it was heroic ; but it was very hard. And not everywhere were conditions suitable. Our great towns were still growing, and in the nature of things they must continue to grow. Despite the knowledge that this meant the increasing shutting out of nature, and although it would not be possible on the margins of our towns to provide the agricultural belt or the provision for factories and workers, at least the other parts of the scheme were applicable.

Why should our suburbs grow in streets of endless monotony, of absolute lack of beauty? The complete segregation of classes was not good, the absence of local centres destroyed local patriotism, homes become dormitories, and the garden—where it had not become a rubbish heap—was the show ground of weakly exotics, whose too frequent libations were hastening them to an untimely end.

THE GROWTH OF THE GARDEN SUBURB.

With characteristic energy Mrs. Barnett took up the Garden Suburb idea. There was a scheme for the enlargement of Hampstead Heath, and she saw an opportunity of combining this preservation of a beautiful piece of nature's handiwork and an attempt to weave into man's work some threads of nature's. How well she has succeeded need hardly be told. From the opening, in 1907, the original area of 240 acres has already been dealt with, and further extensions have been purchased. The population has increased to 4,500, and, by the exercising of judicious control, a community has been brought into being which is the mecca of the architect all over the world. Many subsidiary experiments are being tried there, and the example so given has encouraged scores of people elsewhere to take similar steps, with a consequence that to-day there are some forty Garden Suburb and Village schemes in existence in this country, all embracing in one degree or another principles which were enunciated by the founder of the Garden City movement.

So far, the second Garden City has yet to be built. The Garden Suburb has not to create new conditions, but simply to direct an existing flow, and, therefore, since we as a people are inclined to take the line of least resistance, the Garden Suburb succeeds the more quickly. The child has outstripped the parent, and in some degree the great truth has been in danger of becoming overshadowed by the lesser truth.

The Garden Cities and Town Planning Association does not for one moment discourage Garden Suburbs. It has helped in the formation of several, and hopes to continue that work, being engaged week in and week out in preaching the advantages of the principle. But that does not mean that we have lost sight of the fact that the true solution is in the Garden City. For the extension of that principle we shall continue to work, side by side with encouraging the growth of the Suburbs. The big landowners are coming to our aid ; in all parts of the country tracts of land are being properly planned by men who have had their training in our Association's work, and areas which might have been covered with unlovely dwellings are being laid out with every regard to decency and order.

Finally, the municipalities are now awaking and joining in the march onward. The Housing, Town Planning, etc., Act of 1909 gives them powers to do what the Garden City has already done, and in this connection it is interesting to read the prophetic words of one of our leading newspapers. In speaking of the growth of the movement some six or eight years ago, it said : " The Garden City pioneers have shown the way. Private enterprise, as it usually does in this country, has given an example to the State." The State has followed the example ; and although no voice of statesmen has been uplifted to sing his praises, there is no man more responsible for the acceptation of town planning principles in this country than was Mr. Ebenezer Howard. When many of to-day's advocates of town planning were dumb and ignorant, he preached its merits. More, he secured its application ; and if a future England sees its towns grow up more healthily, more beautiful, more convenient, more than to any other one man will they owe that fact to the humble pioneer of Garden City principles.

The following details of schemes have been collected with a view to including eventually all housing schemes which have a claim to notice, and therefore others than those on Garden City lines have been inserted. In the table which follows will be found full particulars of the character of these, as far as they can be obtained. Even after months of endeavour many details are lacking, but it is hoped that the attempt to include for the first time some account of the chief English housing experiments in one booklet will find its reward in producing something which shall be of service to all studying the movement.

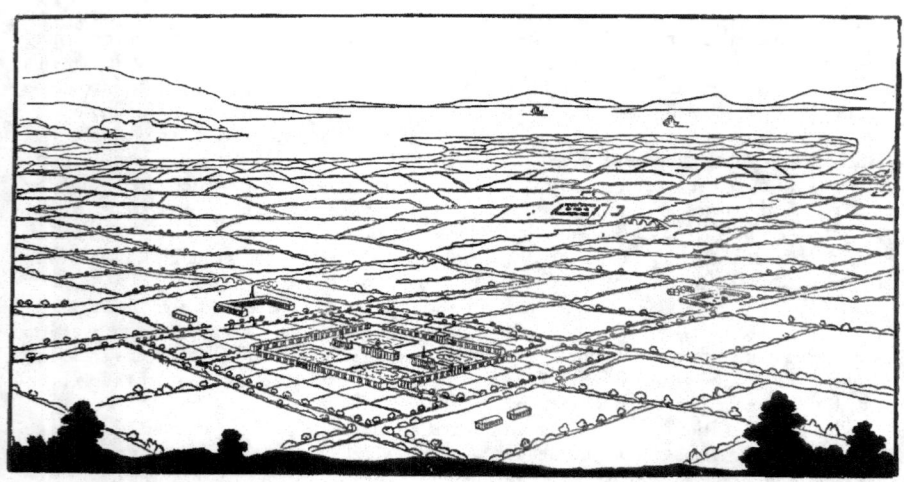

Robert Owen's scheme for a model town " Harmony," from his own
description published in 1817.

8

SUMMARY OF THE PRESENT POSITION OF THOSE ESTATES

Name of Estate.	Total area (in acres).	Now developed.	How Controlled.	Dividend limited to.	Share Capital Authorised.	Share Capital Issued.
Alkrington	700	10	D	—	—	—
Anchor Tenants (Leicester)	48	15	E	5 %	—	£2,387
Blackley	243	9	(Municipal)	—	—	—
Bournville	609	138	C	(see particulars)		
Bournville Tenants	20	20	E	5 %	£10,664	£10,664
Bristol	26	7	A	5 %	£10,000	£5,781
Caerphilly	10	—	E	5 %	—	—
Coventry	14	2	E	5 %	—	£1,660
Cuffley	550	—	B	—	—	—
Datchet	30	30	E	5 %	—	—
Derwentwater Tenants	2½	2½	E	5 %	—	£1,054
Didsbury	2	2	E	5 %	£1,300	—
Ealing	63	40	E	5 %	—	£27,498
Fairfield Tenants	23	—	E	5 %	—	—
Fallings Park	400	8½	D & E	—	—	—
Garden City Tenants ...F	39	39	E	5 %	—	£20,588
Gidea Park	500	108	D	—	£80,000	—
Glasgow	200	5	A	5 %	£25,000	£3,970
Guildford	20	3½	D	—	—	—
Hadleigh	7	—	E	5 %	—	—
Hampden Park	9	9	E	5 %	—	—
Hampstead Garden Suburb	652	180	A	5 %	£75,000	£54,111
Hampstead Heath Extension Tenants	—	—	E	5 %	—	£10,700
Hampstead Tenants ...F	27	27	E	5 %	—	£26,500
Harborne	54	54	E	5 %	—	£8,461
Haslemere	5.09	2	E	5 %	—	—
Hereford	8.75	8.75	(see particulars)			
Hull	94	70	C	3 %	—	—
Ilford	40	20	A	5 %	—	—
Knebworth	800	—	D	—	—	—
Llanidloes	9	—	A & E	5 %	—	—
Letchworth (Garden City)	4,566	800	A	5 %	£300,000	£176,921
Liverpool	180	25½	E	5 %	—	£39,500
Machynlleth	15	—	A & E	5 %	—	—
Manchester (Burnage)	11	11	E	5 %	—	£6,722
Merthyr	17½	—	E	5 %	—	—
New Earswick	120	39	C	(see particulars)		
New Eltham	27	—	E	5 %	—	—
Oakwood Tenants	—	—	E	5 %	—	£6,450
Oldham Garden Suburb	52½	17½	E	5 %	—	£11,271
Otford	160	—	E	5 %	—	—
Petersfield	32	—	E	5 %	—	—
Port Sunlight (a)	223	135	D	(see particulars)		
Rothley	1,000	150	D	—	—	—
Rhubina	110	—	E	5 %	—	—
Ruislip Manor	1,300	100	A	5 %	£75,000	£30,000
Sealand	47	10	E	5 %	—	£5,150
Second Hampstead Tenants ...F	39	39	E	5 %	—	£59,970
Sevenoaks	6½	6½	E	5 %	£40,000	£2,555
Somersham	17¼	—	E	5 %	£20,000	£475
Stirling Homesteads	40	1½	E	5 %	—	£415
Stoke-on-Trent	38½	13	E	5 %	—	£4,890
Sutton (Surrey)	25½	—	E	5 %	—	£1,584
Warrington (Great Sankey)	20	—}	A	5 %	£20,000	{ —
,, (Grappenhall)	22	—				
Woking	9	3	E	—	—	—
Woodlands	127	127	(owned by Colliery Co.)			
Wrexham	200	—	A & E	5 %	—	—

A. Public company, limited dividend.   B. Public company, unlimited dividend.   C. Trust.   D. Owned privately.
E. Society of Public Utility under Provident Societies Act.   (a) Not including works area.
F. Not separate estates. Area included in parent schemes.

AND SOCIETIES OF WHICH PARTICULARS ARE AVAILABLE.

Total Rates.	Operations began.		Present Number of Houses.	Present Population.	Houses per acre (maximum).	Ultimate Houses expected.	Ultimate Population.	Minimum Rents.	Maximum Rents.
—		1911	40	170	12	8,400	30,000	6/6	£50
4/8	Sept.,	1907	84	360	10	250	1,250	6/-†	10/9†
8/1		1901	150	600	17	2,810	11,240	6/4†	7/-
7/4		1879	920	4,390	6	3,654	15,000	5/-	11/6
—	Aug.,	1906	146	750	11	146	750	6/-†	£35/10/-
—		1909	44	178	14	280	1,400	6/6†	£35
—		1913	24	120	10	100	500	5/6	£39
8/5	Oct.,	1912	12	40	14	189	945	6/6†	£35
5/6		1913	—	—	5	2,750	10,000	7/6	£150
—		1913	—	—	10	—	—	10/6	£100
6/-	Oct.,	1909	25	83	12	27	135	5/6	8/6
8/2	Mar.,	1907	30	102	15*	30	102	7/6	8/6
6/8	April,	1901	510	2,000	12	700	3,500	6/6	£57/12/-
—	Dec.,	1912	—	—	12	270	1,080	5/-	10/-
9/4	June,	1907	75	310	12	1,000	1,750	4/6†	10/-†
4/9	April,	1905	322	1,600	12*	322	1,600	4/6	£61
8/-	May,	1910	188	700	8	4,000	16,000	11/6	£100
—	Oct.,	1912	40	140	12	2,600	10,000	6/11	£35
—	Oct.,	1910	32	—	—	160	650	7/6†	9/-
—		1913	—	—	—	—	—	4/3†	—
—		1909	73	—	11	98	450	8/6†	12/6†
5/6	May,	1907	1,550	5,000	8*	2,000	—	5/9	£110
5/6	July,	1912	—	—	—	—	—	—	—
5/6	May,	1907	271§	1,200	10*	277	1,200	6/-	£55
8/2	Sept.,	1907	499	1,600	9.25	499	1,600	4/-†	£40
7/8	Mar.,	1912	20	80	10	60	200	6/4†	10/-†
—		1909	86	430	10	86	430	4/9†	7/9†
10/1	Nov.,	1907	560	2,000	12	700	3,500	4/9†	£35
8/6	Dec.,	1909	70	200	8*	150	750	£30	£100
4/6		1909	250	1,250	8	6,400	19,000	5/6	£120
7/6	June,	1913	—	—	12	60	250	4/-	£30
5/0	Sept.,	1903	1,876	8,200	12*	7,000	35,000	4/3†	£120
8/6	July,	1910	260	1,000	12	1,800	7,000	7/-†	£40
8/2	June,	1913	—	—	12	150	600	4/-	£30
8/4		1908	136	500	12	136	500	5/3	11/6
—		1913	32	—	—	175	875	6/6†	10/-†
—	Dec.,	1904	150	750	10	1,200	6,000	4/6	£60
—	May,	1913	—	—	11	—	1,400	7/6	10/6
5/6	Jan.,	1913	100	420	—	—	—	7/-	£55
8/8		1907	156	750	14	700	3,500	5/11	£30
—		1913	13	—	—	—	—	—	—
—		1913	—	—	—	28	—	—	—
—		1895	823	3,600	10	1,200	5,000	5/3†	—
5/9		1909	69	240	—	—	—	4/6†	£160
—	July,	1913	34	—	12	1,200	6,000	5/-	12/-
7/4	April,	1911	100	300	12	5,000	20,000	5/-	£150
1/10	July,	1910	108	550	10	470	2,500	4/9	8/6
5/6	Aug.,	1909	377	1,900	10*	377	1,900	5/9	£130
6/2		1904	80	250	13	80	250	4/9	12/6
—		1913	6	—	—	20	—	4/-†	7/-
2/6	May,	1910	11	39	6	40	200	4/-	£26
10/-	April,	1910	95	300	12	412	2,000	5/-	£60
6/5	Feb.,	1913	31	18	10	226	1,130	7/-	£60
—	July,	1907	24	100	12	243	1,200 }	6/-†	£30
—	July,	1907	12	55	12	260	1,300 }		
—		1912	21	—	8	72	350	4/-†	10/6†
—	June,	1907	653	3,600	5.2	653	3,600	5/3†	6/9†
6/-	May,	1913	—	—	12	2,000	10,000	4/9	£60

* Excluding roads, etc.   † Including rates.

§ Blocks of shops and residential flats have also been erected.   ¶ A number of estates recently started have not yet made sufficient progress to warrant inclusion here. Reference to most of these will be found on other pages.

INTRODUCTION TO SECOND EDITION

PHENOMENAL GROWTH IN 1913.

THE first issue of the record of a great movement was almost necessarily incomplete in many details. It was found difficult to obtain particulars of some estates, owing to the apathy of those in charge, and there are still omissions from the present edition.

Even in the few months that have elapsed since the first issue was printed there is great progress to record, and information is given of no less than fifty additional ventures. As well as mentioning schemes not previously brought within the book, an attempt is made to give more adequate information regarding the pioneer schemes. A new element is introduced by the application of co-partnership methods to rural housing, and details are given of what has been already done in this direction. A further section deals with the progress of Town Planning under the Act of 1909.

In the past nine months the Garden City movement seems more than ever to have come into its own. The activity in every branch is remarkable, despite adverse conditions in regard to the building trade and an increasing tightness of money. Large additions have been made to the number of new schemes now on foot. Many of the schemes that are called Garden City schemes have nothing in common with the Garden City movement but the name, which they have dishonestly appropriated. Schemes of the wildest speculation, land-sweating, and jerry-building, have all been promoted in the hope that the good name would carry them through, but through the activity of the Association and through the growing knowledge of what Garden City development really means, as a rule these schemes have been countered, and their attempt to exploit the movement has sometimes been attended with financial disaster to themselves.

The educative work which has been done by the Garden Cities and Town Planning Association has spread far beyond what was at first thought to be its borders. Lectures are being given everywhere ; literature is being supplied by thousands of copies ; the monthly magazine, *Garden Cities and Town Planning*, is acquiring a firmer hold and obtaining a wider circulation, being recognised as the chief educative factor in civic improvement published in this country. Scores of landowners have consulted the Association in regard to land which they are developing, and although the Garden City scheme may not be followed out in its entirety, there is the satisfaction of knowing that thousands of acres are being developed upon better lines than there was a probability of securing beforehand, and instead of the countryside being defaced by a repetition of the abominations that have been perpetrated around many of our large towns—and indeed in many of the small ones

9

—decent, comfortable cottages have been erected at a reasonable rental, serving not only to house the people who live in them but providing an example for the whole neighbourhood.

A WORLD-WIDE RECOGNITION.

There is not a portion of the civilised world to which the Garden City message is not now being sent regularly. A return has just been made of correspondence dealt with in a period of two months, and this shows that the following countries have applied for information and particulars regarding the growth of the Garden City movement in England : The United States, Austria, France, Holland, Russia, Germany. South Africa, Poland, Belgium, Canada, New Zealand, India, Hungary, Roumania, New South Wales, Queensland, South Australia, West Australia, Victoria, Tasmania, Turkey, Norway, Sweden, Spain, Italy, Nova Scotia, Argentina, South Africa, Switzerland, Crete, Trinidad, Burma, Denmark, Japan, Ceylon, Uruguay, Greece, Fiji Islands, West Africa, Newfoundland, Egypt. The names are taken haphazard from the list, and with no idea of order. In each of these countries are members of the Association, and the monthly magazine goes there regularly.

In many cases definite results have been accomplished in the formation of allied bodies in different parts of the world ; elsewhere Town Planning schemes have been forwarded ; or, again, model villages have been founded on co-partnership lines. Everywhere this message of the Garden City has been hailed with acclamation by men and women by whom the existing state of affairs is seen to be not only ugliness and inconvenience, but degradation —the loss of the love of the beautiful things of earth, the obsession of the human mind with the things that are really of little value, and the neglect of the great and overwhelming problems of existence.

A FORECAST.

There is much yet to be done before the Garden City movement can really be said to enter into full recognition. Garden Suburbs we can get in abundance ; in five years' time the town that has not got a Garden Suburb will be an exception, and there will grow the tendency of surrounding the great centres of population with belts of houses built in reasonable surroundings ; but still there will remain the great problem of the housing of the man in the middle of the town and the man at the bottom of the ladder.

Improved sanitation will lessen the evils of the old centres, and the progress of humanitarianism in legislation will probably relieve some of the hardships of the very poorest, but after all that has been done and said, it does not seem feasible, under present conditions, to house the lowest-paid workers in decent houses at an economic price which they can afford to pay.

It is hinted that great legislative changes are about to be proposed which will cheapen the cost of providing houses. Cheap money and cheap land are promised, and these together may do something to bring down costs, and Town Planning will probably result in the establishment of many settlements having much the same physical appearance as have our Garden Suburbs. But greater good would come to a greater number of people if there were only available funds to establish new Garden Cities, where the worker and his work can be out of the crowded centres and yet have all the advantages of the town in common with the delights of his garden.

LOST OPPORTUNITIES.

An opportunity of providing a world example is, alas ! being lost through the Admiralty's attitude in regard to the proposal to create a model town at the new naval

Base at Rosyth, and the extraordinary improvidence of the Port of London Authority as to its responsibilities for the people who will have to live in the neighbourhood of the new Docks is not encouraging for those who look in high quarters for help in these matters.

THE HOPE OF THE FUTURE—GARDEN CITIES.

It is in the working out of the complete scheme proposed by Mr. Howard that real progress seems to lie. At present about fifteen thousand acres are included in the area of the proposals of one sort and another enumerated in the following pages, and practically one-third of this area is at Letchworth. If all this land were built upon to the modest extent expected, a population of some nine hundred thousand people would be housed on garden city lines, but at the present time about forty-five thousand are so housed, or a thousandth part of the population.

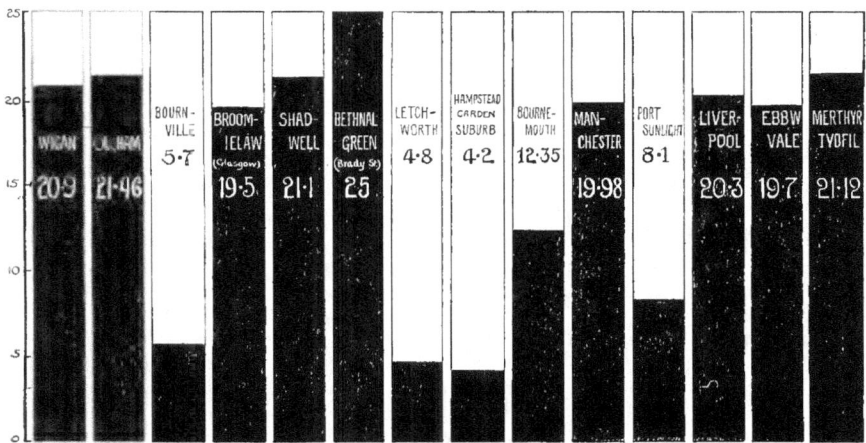

LIFE AND DEATH – THE TRIUMPH OF THE GARDEN CITY AND SUBURBS.

With the enormous improvement in traffic facilities, and the growing tendency to remove factories from town to country, the organised decentralisation of industry becomes less difficult, and as the experience of the pioneers becomes more widely known, the demand for real Garden Cities is likely to spread rapidly. The fact that better conditions of work mean better work, and that better conditions of life mean healthier and happier families, must have its influence, and the multiplication of Garden Cities will afford the best opportunity for clearing out the old slums and recreating that type of man which books and songs tell us of, but which modern town life has gone so far to destroy.

THE INTERNATIONAL ASSOCIATION.

No survey of the movement would be complete unless it included an account of the work in other countries. A summary is therefore given of what has been done abroad. It will be seen that by far the most active progress has been made by the German Garden City Association. The steady and persistent work of its official leaders has resulted in a knowledge of Garden City principles being spread throughout the whole empire, and the amount of useful instructive literature which has been issued by the German Association is equal in bulk and variety to that of the parent organisation.

Shortly it should be possible to record the progress in America and Canada. The three months I have recently spent in the United States and Canada convinces me that there is a great future there for the Garden City movement. The people are ready for such a movement, which attempts to solve problems that are pressing upon them more and more heavily as time goes on. Where land speculation is threatening to ruin the whole community, the Garden City movement would come in with a message of hope for those who are striving to provide decent housing accommodation at a reasonable rent.

These world-wide recognitions of the value of Mr. Howard's proposals have accumulated in an extraordinary manner of late, and there has been evidenced a general desire that the various bodies which are striving towards the improvement of the civic ideal should be linked up with one another. To this end an International Garden Cities and Town Planning Association has been formed with every prospect of a useful career. Already some twenty nationalities are represented and the first congress, to be held next year in England, will give some idea of the extent to which the Garden City ideal has permeated the mind of man. The new Association has done itself the honour of electing Mr. Ebenezer Howard as its first President.

THE CITY OF THE FUTURE.

At home and abroad, therefore, we find every encouragement for progress in Garden City work. The labour of the propagandist is not always requited, and it is given to few to see of the travail of their soul and be satisfied; but to those who labour in this field there is an ever-increasing pleasure in the honour so generously bestowed upon Mr. Howard, and the success of his work, even in the partial and fragmentary manner in which it has so far been attempted, is an incentive to secure wider and fuller recognition. We see now only dim outlines of what the future town will be. We know it will not be like that death-trap which civilisation has created in the last fifty years, and it is just as unlikely to attain to the state of Arcadian bliss as pictured in *News from Nowhere*. We are awaiting still the dawning of that new earth which Isaiah foresaw many years ago, and the woes and horrors of the dark side of town life are apt to make us forget, as we ponder over the problems which confront us, that there is a way out. Years of educational work will have still to be spent, and the folly of tinkering with the evil must be taught to governments and peoples until they are prepared to do as was done at Letchworth—make a clean start. The city of the future will have a new meaning, for it will be a city of homes, and if the garden city idea—improved and perfected as newer conceptions arise—is kept in the forefront of men's vision, and not allowed to be hidden by easier methods of palliation which are not remedies, then they who work to-day will have laid well and truly a foundation upon which shall be reared a City of Hope, worthy of the dreams and hopes of prophets and reformers of all ages, —" and they shall bring the glory and honour of the nations into it."

THE STAGES OF PROGRESS.

The Garden City movement may be described as a modern miracle, and a direct contradiction of the dictum, " A prophet is not without honour, save in his own country." Whereas in many fields of social reform men have toiled and died without recognition, in less than a generation the Garden City movement has attained to a place of supreme importance throughout the world, and its founder has been hailed as one of the greatest men of his generation.   Glancing through the pages which follow, it is difficult to realise that it was only in the year 1898 that Mr. Ebenezer Howard gave to the world his book entitled *To-morrow—a Peaceful Path to Real Reform*, afterwards isssued as *Garden Cities of To-morrow*, which has practically changed the method of development in this and other countries, and which was the beginning here of the new science of town building which led to the passing of the Housing, Town Planning, etc., Act of 1909.

This was not the first that had been heard of the idea.   For years Mr. Howard had occupied all the spare time he could snatch from his busy life as an official shorthand writer in lecturing and writing upon the subject which was nearest his heart.   After the book had been published a number of sympathisers gathered around him, and on June 10th, 1899, formed the Garden City Association for the purpose of studying his proposals and considering their practical application.

IN 1899.

As illustrating the growth of the movement and the many ways in which Mr. Howard's ideas have been adapted, it is of interest to chronicle the changes in the " Objects " of this Association as shown in its rules.   The first statement ran as follows :   " Objects :   To promote the discussion of the project suggested by Mr. Ebenezer Howard in *To-Morrow*, and ultimately to formulate a practical scheme on the lines of that project, with such modifications as may appear desirable."

IN 1902.

In January, 1902, the objects appeared thus :—

" (*a*) To promote discussion of the project suggested by Mr. Ebenezer Howard in his book *To-morrow*."

" (*b*) To take the initial step towards the formation in Great Britain, either by public company or otherwise, of Garden Cities, wherein shall be found the maximum attainable of comfort and convenience to the inhabitants, who shall themselves become, in a corporate capacity, the owners of the site, subject to the fullest recognition of individual as well as mutual and public interests."

In the Fourth Annual Report, for the year ending October 31st, 1902, these Objects are extended into a statement headed " Our Objects " and signed by the Chairman of the Council, Mr. Ralph Neville, K.C., now the President, the Hon. Sir Ralph Neville.   This statement reads as follows :—

" The exodus of the people from the country and the consequent overcrowding in the towns, with its attendant physical and moral evils, occupies the attention of all who are interested in social welfare.

" This Association has been formed to give practical effect to a scheme which attempts to deal with the question of ' How to get the people back to the land ?'

" The idea is to bring the town to the country by the establishment of Industrial Centres in rural districts.   Successful experiments in this direction have already been carried out by Messrs. Cadbury at Bournville, near Birmingham, and Messrs. Lever at Port Sunlight, near Liverpool.

" The outlines of the scheme are as follows :—

" The purchase of land at agricultural prices ;   the laying-out of a town, section by section, upon the central portion of the estate, the remainder to be permanently retained for agricultural purposes. The necessary capital would receive a fixed return, and the balance of the increment in value would be applied for the benefit of the community in affording means of transit, etc.

" It is calculated that upon an estate of 6,000 acres one-sixth would suffice for the accommodation of a population of 33,000 people, and that the ground rents would provide for interest at the rate of £4 per cent. per annum on the capital, and leave a large surplus.

" We claim for our proposals :—

1. That they recognise the impossibility of diverting labour by artificial means from the industries to which it flows by the natural operation of economic law.

2. That they bring the producer and consumer of agricultural produce into contact.

3. That the scheme has a sound financial basis resting upon the increase in the value of land caused by an influx of population.

4. That the economies in regard to construction, supply of power, transit, etc., resulting from the construction of a town in conformity with a predetermined plan, are great.

5. That no economic law is infringed, and no industry interfered with. If the scheme can be carried out, the ultimate benefit to the population of this country would be great. If it fails, the loss will be measured by the difference between the purchase and sale price of the estate and the cost of partly laying out a single section of the proposed town.

" The immediate object of the Association is to secure the attention of the public to their proposals, with the view of putting them to a practical test. The first practical step has been taken, and the Garden City Pioneer Company Limited, with a subscribed capital of £20,000, has been formed to investigate and negotiate with manufacturers.

" It is hoped that those who view with concern the shifting of our population from country to town will give the scheme of the Association their attention, and, if they approve, their countenance and support."

IN 1903.

At a special general meeting held at Essex Hall on July 9th, 1903, the objects were approved as follows :—

" To promote the relief of overcrowded and congested areas, to secure a wider distribution of the population over the land, and to advance the moral, intellectual, and physical development of the people by—

" (a) Taking initial steps to establish Garden Cities in which the inhabitants shall become in a corporate capacity the owners of the sites, subject to the fullest recognition of individual as well as public interest ;

" (b) Encouraging the tendency of manufacturers and others to move from crowded centres to rural districts, co-operating with such manufacturers and with public bodies in securing healthy housing accommodation for the workpeople in proximity to their places of employment ;

" (c) Co-operating with other organisations in promoting legislation to enlarge the powers of public authorities with a view to securing a solution of the housing problem and improved systems of communication ;

" (d) Stimulating interest in and promoting the scientific development of towns so that the evils arising from haphazard growth may in future be avoided ;

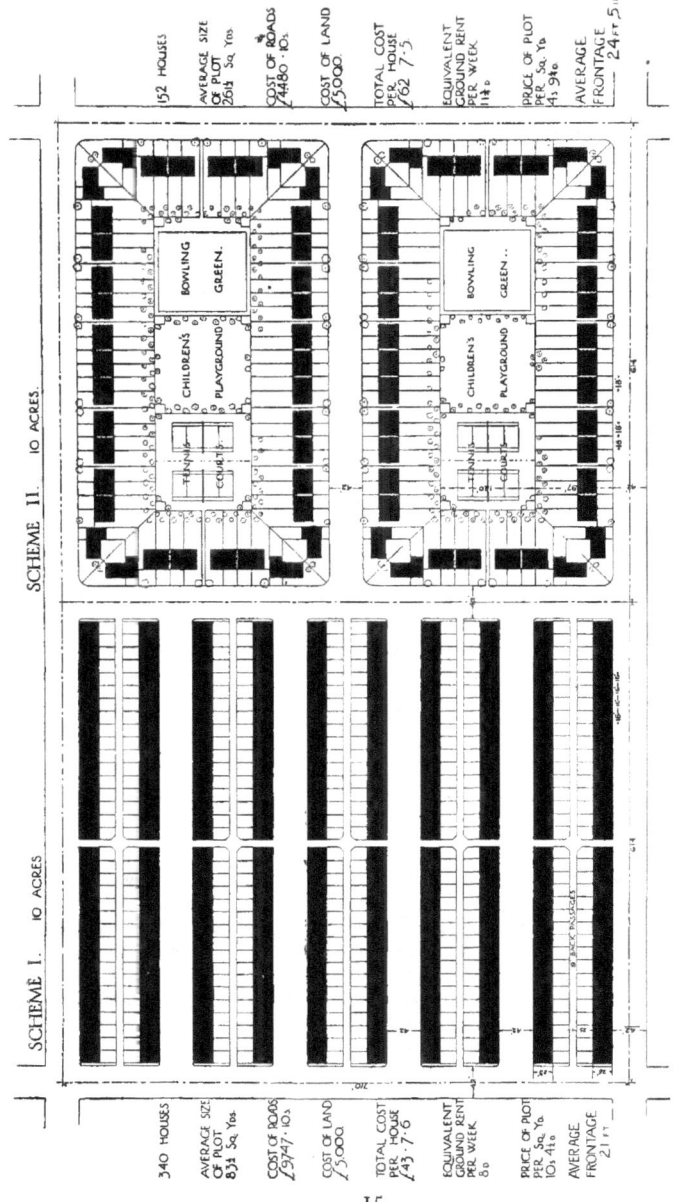

Mr. Raymond Unwin's diagram showing the actual financial results of "Garden City" development as compared with the ordinary town development,

" (e) Promoting the erection of sanitary and beautiful dwellings with adequate space for gardens and recreation.

" Of the above clauses (a) shall be considered the primary work of the Association and the remainder secondary."

The following note was issued with the new rules :—

" It will be seen that this widening of the scope of the Association's work tends greatly to increase its usefulness. It is now possible for us not only to advocate the importance and effectiveness of our specific remedy for overcrowding, but to encourage movements of a related character, and to assist other organisations having similar objects in view."

This was, indeed, the first pronouncement of any society or body in England in favour of municipal Town-planning, although that name does not appear yet in the rules.

IN 1905.

With the publication of the first official handbook of the Association in 1905 (*The Garden City Movement*, by G. Montagu Harris) the rules contained the following objects :—

" To promote the relief of overcrowded areas and to secure a wider distribution of the population over the land.

" PRIMARILY, by advocating and assisting in the establishment of Garden Cities (on the principle suggested in Howard's *Garden Cities of To-morrow*) designed from the outset to secure healthful and adequate housing for the whole population, and in which the inhabitants shall become in a collective capacity the owners of the sites, subject to full recognition of public as well as individual interests.

" SECONDARILY, by encouraging the tendency of manufacturers to remove their works from congested centres to the country ; by co-operating or advising with such firms, public bodies, and other associations to secure better housing accommodation for workpeople near to their places of employment ; by taking steps to promote effective legislation with this end in view ; and by generally advocating the ordered design and development of towns."

IN 1906.

In 1906 the increasing activities of the Association and the growth of that part relating to the establishment of Garden Suburbs resulted in a further definition of its work, and the Objects then appeared as follows :—

" (I) *The building of new towns in country districts on well-thought-out principles, such as the Garden City at Letchworth,* designed from the outset to secure the healthful and adequate housing of its whole population, so that the land shall never become overcrowded with houses, and the town, when built, shall be permanently surrounded by a wide belt of agricultural and park lands.

" (II) *The creation of Garden Suburbs,* such as the Hampstead Garden Suburb, on similar principles for the immediate relief of existing towns.

" (III) *The building of Garden Villages,* as exemplified by Port Sunlight and Bournville, for properly housing the working classes near their work.

" (IV) *The acquisition of open spaces,* and the improvement of existing towns and villages on Garden City principles.

" (V) *The removal of factories* from congested areas to country districts.

" (VI) *The provision of small holdings* in proximity to towns, together with measures for the disposal of agricultural produce to the advantage of the home producer and consumer."

A point of great importance to be noted here is the dropping of definitions such as appeared in earlier rules, an indication of the fact that by now the meaning of the terms had become well enough understood to make it unnecessary to repeat them even in the rules. In view of the shocking misuse of the title term " Garden City " in later days, it will probably be found necessary to formulate some short statement which shall express adequately in what way a true garden city or garden suburb differs from an ordinary building estate or a town planning scheme.

The success of Letchworth and the growing necessity for securing legislation enabling towns to control their extensions is shown in further expansion of the Objects, and in the alteration of the title of the Association. The name Garden Cities and Town Planning Association was decided upon by the Council in the year 1907 and in February, 1908, the name of the monthly official organ (started in 1904) was changed from *The Garden City* to *Garden Cities and Town Planning*. In that issue it was stated, " In using the plural ' Garden Cities,' instead of ' Garden City,' too, we hope still further to emphasise the fact that we are not concerned solely with Letchworth, but that our work is much wider, and, we hope, of more far-reaching effect even than that scheme. Nothwithstanding this, Letchworth has our first claim to notice, as it is in the success of First Garden City Limited that our hope rests for future endeavour upon the same lines."

IN 1909.

In July, 1909, again in order to meet changing circumstances, the Objects were adopted in the following form :—

(*a*) To promote Town Planning.

(*b*) To advise on, draw up schemes for, and establish Garden Cities, Garden Suburbs, and Garden Villages.

(*c*) Housing and the improvement of its sanitation.

(*d*) The collection and publication of information as to the above.

(*e*) The education of public opinion by lantern lectures, cheap literature, conferences, etc.

(*f*) The influencing and promotion of legislation.

(*g*) The improvement of local by-laws.

The question of small holdings, although an integral part of Garden City promotion, was dropped from the rules in consequence of an agreement come to between various bodies concerned with small holdings to amalgamate into one central body. At the same time the rules were changed in other respects to allow the Association to take up what has become an important part of its work, namely, the arrangement of educational tours in Great Britain and abroad.

IN 1913.

Perhaps the next development of importance was in January, 1913, when I was despatched as the representative of the Association on a missionary lecture tour throughout the United States and Canada. That tour lasted over three months, in the course of which I travelled about thirty thousand miles and gave seventy-five lectures and addresses in the principal cities. The result of that experiment is an enormous interest in our publications and work from all parts of the Continent, and the establishment of several societies in affiliation with the parent body.

The growth of interest in the over-seas empire prompted the suggestion as far back as 1911 that a lecturer be sent to Australasia, and in 1912 this was definitely decided upon, a special colonial department being organised and arrangements being made, now, happily, almost concluded, for a systematic visit by a competent lecturer.

These activities, combined with the interchange of visits with other nationalities led up to the formation of the International Garden Cities and Town Planning Association, for the purpose of linking up existing organisations and of extending still farther the knowledge of garden city principles.

October, 1913.   EWART G. CULPIN.

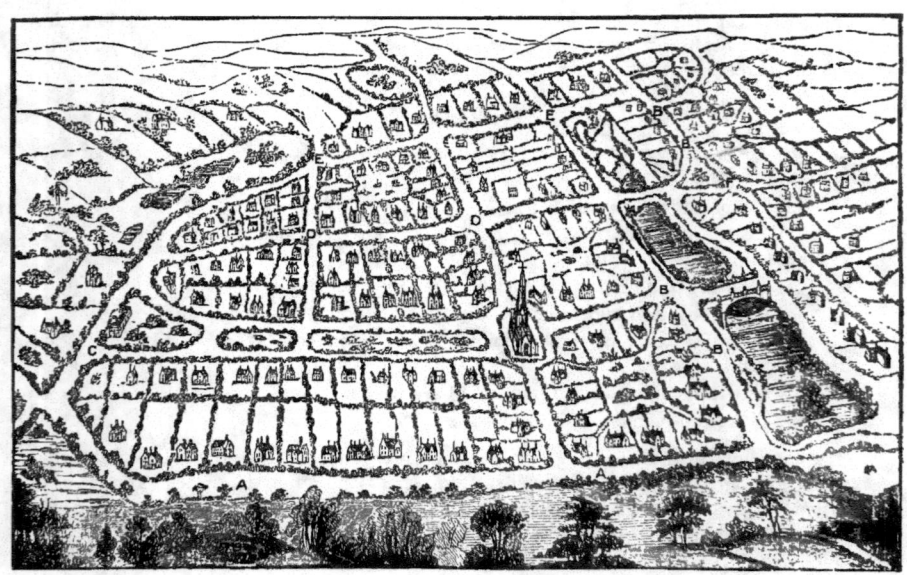

A PROPOSAL FOR A GARDEN VILLAGE AT ILFORD IN 1845.
The present suburb occupies part of the site.

Meadow Way, Letchworth.

Westholm, Letchworth (Garden City Tenants).

Norton Common, Letchworth, showing cottages in the distance. This beautiful open space of over 70 acres is situated in the centre of the Garden City, only a few minutes' walk from the factory and shopping areas, and adjoining the cottage quarter.

Meadow Way and Lytton Avenue, Letchworth.

PARTICULARS OF ESTATES.

In addition to those estates described in alphabetical order here, the societies connected with Co-partnership Tenants Ltd., Rural Co-partnership, and Co-operative Housing are dealt with under those headings.

LETCHWORTH.

Letchworth, the first and only proper Garden City, rightly comes first under consideration here, both chronologically and because of its size and importance from the historical and economic aspects. The estate, of now 4,566 acres, is the property of First Garden City Ltd., a company with a dividend limited to 5 per cent. cumulative, whose memoranda and articles embody the root principles of the movement. The town is situated thirty-four miles from London on the Great Northern Railway, just beyond the old market town of Hitchin. It is served also by the Midland Railway from Hitchin, and being bounded by the Great North Road traffic facilities are excellent.

Letchworth was the first child of the Garden City Movement, and is still the only town where an attempt is being made to put into practice Mr. Ebenezer Howard's suggestions in his book "Garden Cities of To-morrow." The Garden Cities Association promoted a "Pioneer Company" for the purpose of finding a suitable site for the new town, and £5,000 was subscribed for investigating the available estates. The very best advice in the country was drawn upon, and as a consequence Letchworth was selected and the "Pioneer Company" obtained options over the land, which was held by fourteen different owners. First Garden City Ltd. was then formed to take over the options and develop the estate. The authorised capital was £300,000, but less than a quarter of this was subscribed at the outset; the whole idea being new, and the limited dividend appealing only to a limited investing public. Confidence in the movement has grown with every stage of progress at Letchworth, and although a dividend has not been declared, net profits are being made, and the capital value of the estate has almost been doubled, so that the financial success of the scheme is abundantly proved.

Despite all, Letchworth is an astounding success. To its example, more than to anything else, is due, without doubt, the present interest in Town Planning and Housing in this country, and it has also resulted in influencing development in practically the whole civilised world.

First Garden City Ltd., being the owners of what was practically virgin land, have had themselves to provide the necessary equipment of the town, which, in the case of the garden suburbs, is derived from neighbouring towns. Thus the company own the gas, water, and electric light undertakings; they have made the roads; they provide and maintain the sewers and the sewage disposal works; and they have organised such facilities as an omnibus service, swimming bath, etc., to encourage the growth and amenities of the town.

Besides the by-laws of the Hitchin Rural District Council, under whose jurisdiction

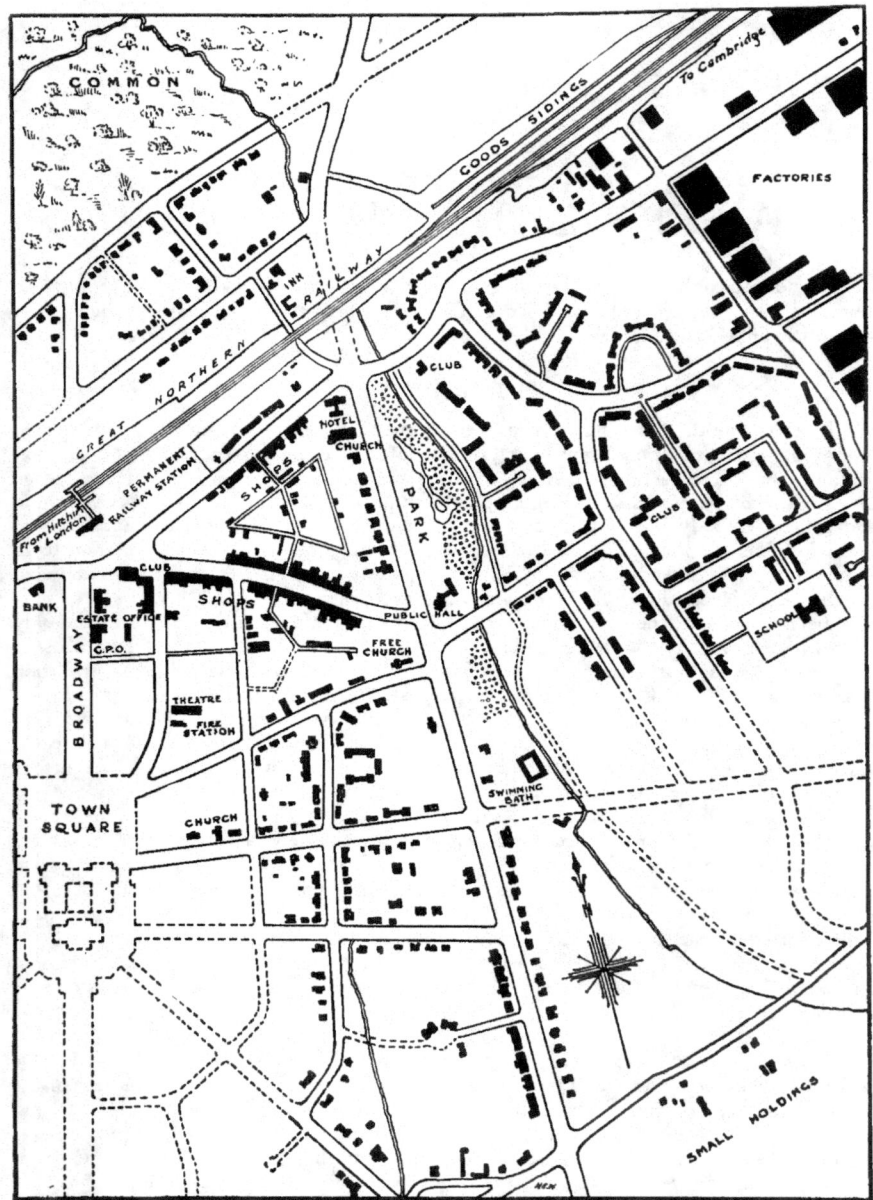

PART OF LETCHWORTH GARDEN CITY,
Showing details of lay-out, workmen's cottages adjoining the factory area,
and the central Town Square.

Letchworth is, the company has its own building regulations and its surveyor exercises some supervision over designs and specifications to ensure proper conditions being observed. The maximum of houses allowed to the acre is twelve, but as the size of the house increases so does the area of the plot, so that all over the building area (which is 1,200 acres only, the remainder being agricultural and park land) there will probably be an average of not more than half that number. An ultimate population of 30,000 people is provided for on the town area, or 35,000 including the agricultural belt, dealt with in the introductory article. Thus, over the whole of the seven square miles of Garden City, there will be an average of only nine people to the acre, compared with the two or three hundred still allowed by the by-laws of many towns.

The agricultural belt of 3,000 acres marks a fundamental difference between Letchworth and every other experiment on garden city lines and, indeed, distinguishes it from every other town in the world. Many places have belts or girdles of green, but none has a definite provision such as this; and as in the town the way is pointed for a new tradition of development, so it is hoped that the agricultural belt will help in the solution of some of the rural problems. A good deal of attention has been given to small holdings, especially in the direction of milk production, and recently an exhaustive inquiry has been made with a view to assisting in this development.

To secure the proper carrying out of the objects of the company leasehold tenure is in vogue, on easy terms, and for either 99 or 999 years. Freehold is granted only for such purposes as churches, etc., or where land is acquired by local authorities.

The estate has been the scene of two cottage exhibitions and has always shown interesting examples of both cottage and other styles of architecture, while cottages recently erected are probably the most satisfactory yet provided in this country. The cheapest rent is 4s. 3d., including rates, which stand at 5s., but these were built before the recent serious advance in building costs.

In addition to the county roads already existing the company have made about ten miles of new roads, and provided nearly twenty miles of water main, fifteen miles of gas mains and fourteen miles of sewers. The roads vary from 10 feet to 100 feet, at costs varying from 15s. to £5 per yard run, and exhibit every style of treatment known to modern advocates of town planning. Grass margins and trees are usual, and the practice has obtained of planting fruit trees and borders of herbaceous plants, while in the business quarters flowering shrubs have been planted. Five miles of roads have so far been taken over by the Hertfordshire County Council.

The past year was an important one in the history of the estate, as it was the first year in which a *substantial* profit was made. The net profit, after paying all expenses and interest on borrowed capital, amounted to £3,086 12s. 2d. This improvement is on the increase, and it may confidently be asserted that the enterprise is within sight of the dividend-paying period. During the year 197 inhabited houses and factories and workshops were added, making a total of 1,761. The number is now nearly 1,900. The ground rents created up to September 30th, 1912, amounted to £5,922.

An important side of the Letchworth experiment, and indeed the crucial test, is the development of its factory area. If Mr. Howard's theory had not been sound, manufacturers would not have gone to Letchworth and the place would never have developed. There are now some thirty industries established in the town, and several of these have been very considerably extended. The trades represented include engineering, printing, embroidery, bookbinding, photographic utensils, joinery works, pottery, weaving, commercial motor engineers, motor car makers, metal works, organ builders, seed and implement factories,

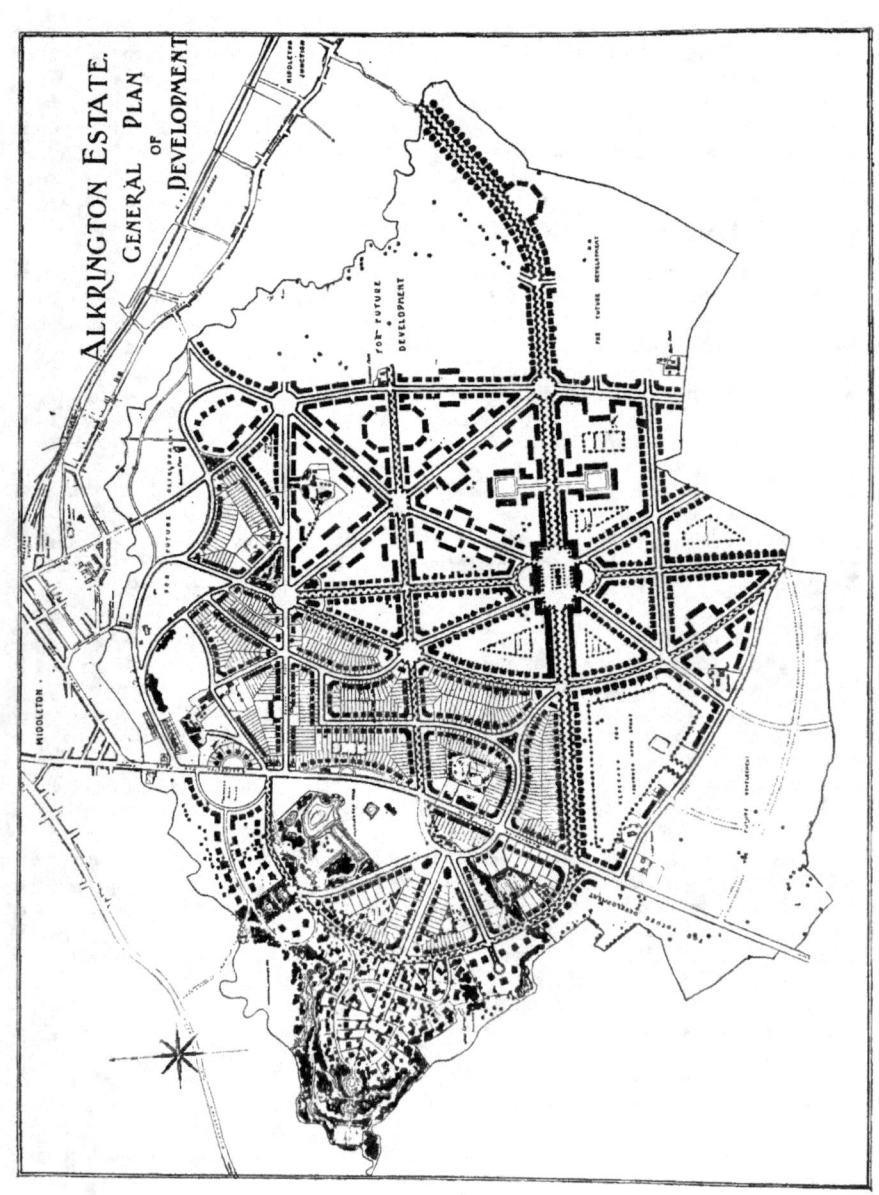

scientific instrument makers, colour printers, corset makers, etc.   There are five building companies working on the estate.   An interesting feature is the co-operative house "Homesgarth."

The town is complete with every facility for commerce, trade and social life.   Its residential facilities are excellent, and as a place of residence alone it is being much sought after. The industrial population have here advantages which have been possessed by no other town in the country.   Its housing is good, the gardens are ample, and there are many opportunities for recreation and social life.   Church life and education are well provided for.   There are several public halls, and the arrangements for water, lighting and sanitation are as near perfect as they can be.   Its scope is infinitely greater and presents the solution of more serious problems than any suburb of a town can possibly do.

Letchworth has been described as England's healthiest town.   Both with regard to the general death-rate and infantile mortality the figures are far below any other place in the country.

ALEXANDRIA.

A society, known as the Vale of Leven Tenants Ltd., has been formed at Alexandria for the development on Co-partnership lines of about 6 acres of land within a mile of Loch Lomond.   The society is registered under the Industrial and Provident Societies Act, and the capital has been raised by shares and loan stock.   The land on which the cottages are built has been granted by the Argyll Motor Company—whose workers have formed the Society—free of feu-duty for five years and at the modified rate of £15 per acre thereafter.   Good progress is being made.   Sixteen houses are now being built.

ALKRINGTON.

It is announced that the Alkrington Hall Estate, Manchester, is to be developed as a Garden Suburb, and it is expected that a large portion of the development will be on Co-partnership lines.   The Estate, which consists of about 700 acres and adjoins the Borough of Middleton, possesses many attractive features.   Some three or four years ago a strong attempt was made by the Garden City Association to form a Company to acquire this land for Garden City purposes.   The Prospecting and Development Committee had surveys made, and local meetings were held, but there was not sufficient response to justify the formation of a Company.   Although unsuccessful in that respect, the Association had the pleasure of knowing that the Estate was to be laid out on proper lines, and Mr. Thomas Adams, who as Hon. Secretary of the Association, had taken much interest in the project, was called in by the owners, the Lees Trustees, as expert adviser.   The Estate is now being developed by Messrs. Pepler and Allen on the basis of twelve houses to the acre, with ample provision for recreation grounds and other open space.   Good progress has been made already.   The first house was opened by Mr. T. C. Horsfall on July 29th, 1911, and building has since progressed steadily.   This scheme was one of the first to be submitted to a local authority as a Town Planning Scheme under the Act, and it is interesting to know that Messrs. Pepler and Allen have been able to come to a mutually satisfactory give-and-take arrangement with the Middleton Corporation.

A Co-partnership Housing Society known as "The Alkrington Housing Society Ltd.," has recently undertaken the erection of thirty houses.

ALTON PARK.

An attempt at the proper Town Planning of a seaside resort, a much neglected art, has been begun at Clacton-on-Sea, and the Alton Park Estate of about 100 acres has been laid out on ample Town Planning lines. The Estate will be purely residential, and the houses will be mostly of the seaside bungalow type, on plots averaging 40 feet wide by 150 feet deep, and numbering about eight to the acre. Several of the roads are 50 feet wide with 24 feet carriage way, two 6 feet paths, and two 7 feet grass margins planted with trees. Sundry spaces and greens are provided, and the general arrangement is intended to produce good facilities of communication, pleasant aspects and vistas, and satisfactory terminal features. The Estate adjoins the Golf Links. The design for the development has been prepared by Messrs. Pepler and Allen.

BLACKLEY.

The Blackley estate of the Manchester Corporation was started in 1901, before the limitations now generally imposed in Garden Cities and Suburbs came in for wide acceptance. It covers a total area of 243 acres, about $2\frac{1}{2}$ miles from Crumpsall (L. and Y.), and situated about four miles from Manchester itself. It is owned and controlled by the Manchester Corporation. About nine acres have been developed with 150 houses thereon. In addition some thirteen acres have been set aside for open spaces, and fifty for small holdings and allotments. Excluding the open spaces, the density allowed is seventeen houses per acre. Ultimately the estate is designed to carry 2,810 houses, with a total population of about 11,240. At the present time there are 600 people resident there. The minimum size of plots allowed is 300 square yards. The death-rate is : general, 13.70 ; infantile, 102. The cheapest house costs £223, and lets at 6s. 4d. per week including rates, which total 8s. 1d. in the £. The maximum rent is 7s. (rates included).

The main roads are laid out sixty feet wide and tree-planted, whilst the minor roads are not less than forty-two feet in width.

BOURNVILLE.

Mr. Ebenezer Howard has often remarked that it was the inspiration of Bournville which largely affected his vision of the Garden City. Situated close outside Birmingham, the village was originated by Mr. George Cadbury as an experiment in the solving of the housing question. The main part of the village dates from the year 1895. It is not primarily for the employees of Messrs. Cadbury Bros., and there is no private gain, the whole of the estate having been vested in the Bournville Village Trust. The revenue is to be spent on the estate, and when this is developed is to be employed elsewhere in building manufacturing villages where not more than one-fifteenth of the total area shall be occupied by factories and one-tenth shall be open spaces. It may also be employed in furthering the interests of good housing generally, and in pursuance of this the funds for the Town Planning Lectureship, recently established at Birmingham University, are supplied by the Trust.

An important recent addition to the public buildings has been made, in the erection of a new Infants' School, which has been presented to the estate by Mr. and Mrs. George Cadbury. The following statistics for Bournville may be of interest :— Total area, 609 acres; density, 25 persons per acre; population, 4,390. Death-rate, 4.9 ; infant mortality, 49.6. Land developed 153 acres, open spaces 18 acres. Total houses 925 (inclusive of 38 the property of the Almshouse Trust) ; houses per acre 6. Cheapest house cost £171 ; maximum rent, 11s. 6d. (rates extra). The cheapest cottage, containing two bedrooms, living-room and scullery, with garden attached, is let at 4/9 per week (rates not included). Cost of development about £250 per acre.

The Trustees are arranging for the development of a further portion of their land by means of a Public Utility Society.

BOURNVILLE TENANTS LIMITED.

The Bournville Village Trust in 1906 leased twenty acres of its holding to the Co-partnership Society known as Bournville Tenants Limited. The maximum dividend is limited to 5 per cent., the last paid being 4 per cent. For every nine acres of land which the Society takes from the Trust one acre is allowed for open spaces, and for every £3,000 subscribed by the Society the Trust advances a loan of £1,000, until the total by this means has reached £28,000. The amount of share capital issued to date is £9,690, and the loan stock £22,043. At present 142 houses are built at a maximum density of eleven per acre. The minimum rent (rates and taxes excluded) is 6s. per week. Tree-planted roads, 42 feet wide, are general to the estate, and cost £4 5s. per yard run. The total area is twenty acres, and only four more houses have to be built to reach the ultimate number expected, viz., 146, which will provide for a population of 750.

BRISTOL GARDEN SUBURB.

Bristol Garden Suburb Ltd. was formed in 1909 to acquire and develop an estate at Shirehampton on Garden City lines, on the principles advocated by the Garden City Association, and the dividend is limited to 5 per cent. The present area of 26 acres can be extended very considerably should the scheme prove attractive. The share capital is ten thousand £1 shares. A number of attractive houses have already been built by the Company. In 1910 twenty-three houses were erected and the roads required for the first area of 7½ acres were completed, since which date twenty-one houses have been added, making forty-four in all. It is expected that the ultimate number of houses on the present area will be 280, the maximum allowed being fourteen to the acre.

It is hoped to form a Co-partnership Society, the initial expenses of which have already been guaranteed by a member of the Board, to undertake further building operations.

CAERPHILLY CO-OPERATIVE GARDEN VILLAGE.

The Caerphilly Co-operative Garden Village Society, which is the most advanced in South Wales, owns ten acres of land on the main road between Caerphilly and Llanbradach. Eight semi-detached houses have been erected and are letting at 5s. 6d. a week exclusive of rates, and a further sixteen are being proceeded with as the next instalment of 100 houses. The land is situated at a point of great strategic importance in respect of the future developments of this district, the population of which will almost certainly double or treble during the next ten years through the development of the existing collieries, and the sinking of three other pits which are now projected. Alderman J. E. Evans (president), and Mr. Joseph Howells (chairman), both members of the Glamorgan County Council, and Mr. Hubert Jenkins, Miners' agent and member of the Caerphilly Council, were amongst the founders of the Society.

CARDIFF WORKERS' GARDEN VILLAGE SOCIETY.

The Cardiff Workers Garden Village Society has been established for the purpose of building the first real garden suburb in Wales for both middle-class and working-class inhabitants. Eighteen acres of land have been purchased situated close to Rhubina Halt on the new Cardiff Railway. The architectural scheme has been most carefully considered by Mr. A. H. Mottram, Architect of the Housing Reform Company Limited, who are Managers for the Society. A striking plan for the site, including altogether 110 acres over which the Society has an option, was prepared by Mr. Raymond Unwin. The vistas, closes, and other features are similar to the best characters of the Hampstead Garden Suburb, but there is rather more spaciousness, and a feature is being made of enclosed children's playgrounds at the backs of gardens in each block of houses. The charm of the beautiful wooded hills bordering the site is a great asset. The character of the architecture is roughcast and stone with grey or green slate roofs, red brick and tiles being excluded altogether from the estate as not suitable to the character of the country, which lies in a district where stone is the natural material.

The fact that this Society's land is reached in ten minutes by train from the centre of Cardiff, is making it popular, and the applications for houses considerably exceed in number the thirty-four houses now being erected. The Society is building by direct labour under the management of Mr. J. O. West, late manager for the Hampstead Tenants.

CARLISLE.

A Co-partnership Society, called Newby West Tenants Limited, has been formed for developing 20 acres to the west of the City. There is a great demand for cottages locally and the undertaking starts with every prospect of support.

CAXTON GARDENS COTTAGE CLUB.

The Caxton Gardens Cottage Club, founded in 1906, is a small industrial concern promoted by Messrs. Billing & Sons Ltd., Printers, Guildford. It is solely a co-operative venture, which has erected twenty-four houses for the employees alone at a cost of £5,688, the land costing £1,250 in addition. The occupants pay 8s. 2d. per week for house and garden, with rates extra. In twenty years they will have repaid capital outlay and interest on the scheme, and the houses become their own property. The houses are well built in pairs on allotments restricted to 21¼ feet frontage and 120 feet depth. In front, separated by a 9 feet gravelled pathway, is a large triangular piece of ground laid out as a lawn, with a shrubbery on the side nearest the road. Each occupier owns a twenty-fourth part. There is little in the scheme which illustrates or has reference to the principles of Garden Cities and Suburbs, but it has proved a successful venture in co-operation, and represents a notable improvement in ordinary housing conditions.

CLYDEBANK GARDEN SUBURB.

The difficulty of raising capital is preventing very rapid advance with the Clydebank Co-partnership Society, which was initiated three years ago. The first few houses, are, however, being proceeded with, and it is hoped that as knowledge of the movement and of co-partnership principles makes headway among the local manufacturers there may be more response to the appeal for capital for the housing of their workpeople.

COVENTRY.

Coventry Garden Suburb is one of the most interesting of the recent schemes with which the Garden Cities and Town Planning Association have been connected. Through the public-spirited interest of Mr. T. A. Cash a start is being made on fourteen acres of land in the only unspoiled district of this beautiful old city, which is desecrated by acres of 12-feet fronted houses. Coventry Garden Suburbs Ltd. is to be conducted on Co-partnership lines, with a 5 per cent. dividend. An option over the adjoining land, which belongs to charity trustees, is being secured, and development promises to be rapid. The first roads taken in hand have been completed and all the houses occupied. The Society suffers from the oppression of the local by-laws, and representation has been made to the Local Government Board and the local Council with the idea of obtaining modifications of the clauses relating to widths of roads and heights of rooms. Nowhere in the country is an example of good lay-out more wanted, and it is hoped that the facilities asked for will be granted.

The land is held on lease for ninety-nine years, renewable for further similar terms at option, at a low progressive rent, which will not exceed £22 an acre. These terms are exceptionally favourable and may be commended to owners desirous of advancing housing.

CUFFLEY GARDEN VILLAGE.

This scheme is another tribute to the work of the Garden Cities and Town Planning Association, the Secretary having induced the owner to arrange the development of his land on Garden City lines. The estate consists of nearly 550 acres, in a most beautiful part of Hertfordshire, and including scenery probably superior to that of any other " garden city " scheme in existence. Cuffley is the last station on the Great Northern Railway Enfield to Stevenage loop line, as at present constructed. The estate is beautifully wooded, and rises to an altitude of over 350 feet. A preliminary plan has been prepared by Messrs. Pepler & Allen. Development is now proceeding and gas, water and main drainage have all been provided, some large houses are being built, and a Tenants Society has commenced operations. A golf links occupying 123 acres has been laid out, so that quite a quarter of the whole estate will be kept as open space.

DARLINGTON GROVE GARDEN SUBURB.

Although differing in its inception from other schemes, this is of interest as being a practical attempt by working builders, on ordinary commercial lines, to provide houses designed and planned on Garden City principles—with a limited number of houses to the acre. The cottages, of which twenty-six are completed, are situated near Thorne, in the South Yorkshire coalfield. They occupy a splendid site, fronting the main highway from Sheffield to Hull, and are intended for the employees of the Moor End Colliery of Messrs. Pease & Partners Limited. The weekly rents have been fixed at 6s., including rates. Mr. A. W. Shelton, F.C.I., Estate Agent, of Nottingham, who is well known as an active member of the Advisory Committee of the National Housing and Town Planning Council, is responsible for having prevailed on the builders, Messrs. J. Tilley & Co., of Nottingham, to depart from their original intention of building about forty houses to the acre—a system which has most lamentably been followed in most of the newly erected colliery districts near Doncaster. The scheme is intended to give about 120 houses on 8½ acres of land.

DIDSBURY GARDEN SUBURB.

This small scheme, which is being carried out by the Didsbury Garden Suburb Provident Co-operative Society Limited, owes its origin to the local members of the Garden City Association. It is situated five miles from Manchester, and the local station adjoins the estate. During 1909 an additional plot of land was purchased. The area of this suburb is just over two acres, and the number of houses allowed per acre is fifteen. Twenty houses have been completed and tenanted, and there are applications for others as soon as they are completed. The plot of ground used as a playground has been secured upon a trust deed for ever. The promoters believe that societies such as this should be possible in every village, if the question of capital is solved. Homes cost from £230 to £250, and rentals are from 7s. 9d. to 9s. rates included. Each tenant is a share-holder, and receives 5 per cent. on his investment.

The Second Didsbury Garden Suburb Ltd. (1911), comprises fourteen houses, with large gardens, at rentals varying from 7s. 9d. to 9s. per week. The tenants are the share-holders, and five of them form the management committee. The sum of £120 has already been cleared off the mortgagee's account, after paying the sum of £44 18s. 0d. to tenant shareholders as bonus on rent, at two shillings in the pound, a very satisfactory result for a new society.

FAIRFIELD TENANTS.

This Society owns twenty-two acres situated half way between Manchester and Ashton, in a district containing large industries, where there is a great demand for houses. There are good gardens provided and reservations are made for recreational purposes. The streets are tree-planted, with grass margins. The majority of the houses will be for working men. Baths, hot and cold water, and electric light are included in all houses, which will be let at from 5s. to 10s. a week.

FALLINGS PARK.

Fallings Park is an estate of 400 acres, situate about one mile and a half from the London and North-Western Railway station at Wolverhampton, on the property of Sir Richard Paget, Bart. The site is in touch with the city by tramway and motor bus. Development began in 1907, when the Fallings Park Garden Suburb Tenants came into existence. The Society has now about eight acres under its control, and some 75 houses built. It is intended to extend this type of development indefinitely, so that the greater part of the 400 acres may be held by one or more co-partnership tenant societies. Large works on a site of ten acres adjoining the estate have been erected by Messrs. Chubb and Sons, and other factories are arriving on the estate.

The original scheme was under the control of Mr. Thos. Adams. The advent of a new railway has necessitated an entirely fresh scheme which is being prepared by Prof. Adshead and Messrs. Pepler & Allen, who will have charge of future development.

FALLSIDE.

Messrs. Brown & Polson have started a small scheme for the accommodation of the employees in their Paisley works. Six blocks of four houses each have been erected on a site about a mile from the town, and another six blocks are now being built. Forty-eight families are being provided for. Previously these were living under the prevailing Scottish conditions of " a room and a kitchen," and the new homes provide two rooms, with kitchen, scullery, etc., so that the sexes may be decently provided for. The houses are well designed and have tasteful elevations. The rent charged is £12 and £12 10s. a year, including rates, but this is not an economic return, producing about 2½ per cent. only on the outlay.

FFORESTFACH.

One of the first attempts at a Garden Suburb in South Wales was that at Fforestfach, a small mining village near Swansea. The first scheme of eight acres was initiated by Messrs. Pepler and Allen early in 1910. Many difficulties were met with, but there is now every sign of good progress. The cottages are being built with 18 in. local stone walls,

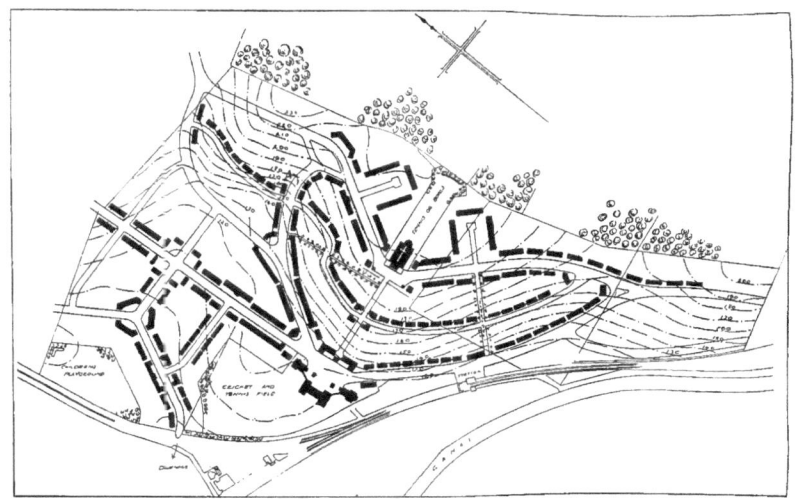

PLAN OF GLASGOW GARDEN SUBURB.

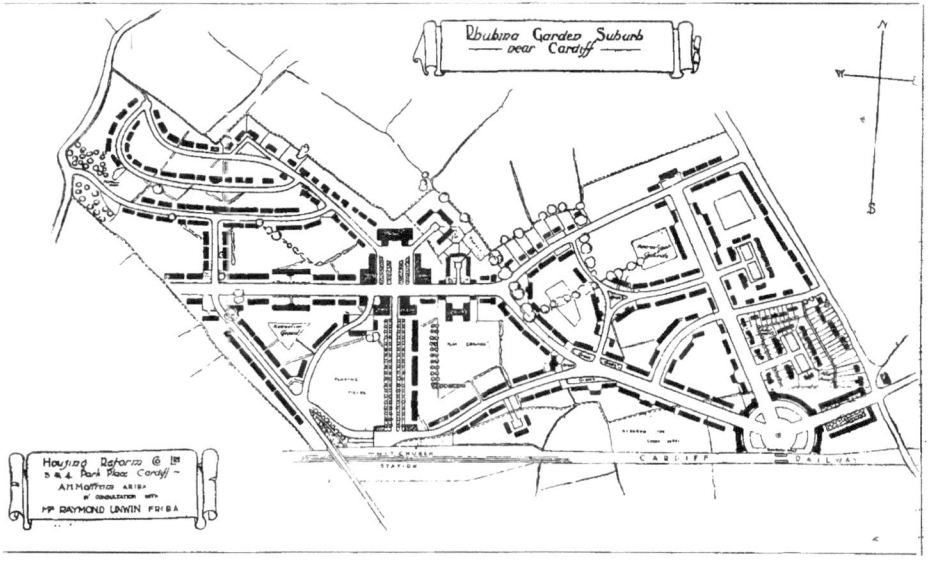

and are therefore extremely solid and fit in well with the old tradition of the place. One hundred houses are provided for, and there is a curved 60 ft. main tree-planted avenue down to the centre designed for continuation when the adjoining lands are developed. Space has been left for allotments, bowling-green, and playground.

A Co-partnership Housing Society has recently commenced operations.

GIDEA PARK.

The Gidea Park Estate, " Romford Garden Suburb," first came into prominence in May, 1910, when development on modified garden city lines was begun. It is openly a commercial venture, with no limitation of dividend, but it has been embarked upon with wide application of good principles. The present plan was the result of a competition held in conjunction with the Cottage Exhibition at the Suburb.

The total area of the estate is about 500 acres, of which 108 have been developed. London is distant 13½ miles by rail, the nearest station being Squirrels Heath and Gidea Park. Already 188 houses have been built, and the estate has a present population of 700 persons. The houses are built eight to ten to the acre, and rents range from £100 to £30 per annum (rates extra). The ultimate number of houses expected is 4,000, with provision for a population of 16,000. Some five acres has been set aside and developed as open spaces, and, in addition, the estate has an 18-hole golf course over ninety acres. Small holdings or allotments are not yet provided for. The average width of the roads is forty feet, and all have turf margins and are tree planted. Some three miles of roads are now completed with water, sewerage, and gas mains.

GLASGOW GARDEN SUBURB TENANTS.

The Glasgow Garden Suburb Tenants Ltd. has now passed the initial stages, and contracts have been placed for sixty houses, of which over forty are nearing completion. The demand for the houses has been most encouraging. An option has been secured over several hundred acres comprising undulating land, with hedgerows and woods, and commanding extensive views of the country on the outskirts of Glasgow at Garscube. The estate adjoins an extensive golf course, and is abundantly sheltered by trees. The proposal to lay out this Suburb on the most approved lines urgently requires realisation in order that the concrete example can be brought to the doors of the great Scotish Metropolis, and act as an incentive to other similar schemes, which are proposed in the Vale of Leven, Greenock, Renfrew, etc. The capital of the Society is £50,000 and the Committee of management includes Sir John Stirling Maxwell, Bart., Sir Samuel Chisholm, Bart., Bailie W. F. Russell, Ex-Bailie Wm. Martin, etc. The Secretary is Mr. M. Boyd Auld.

GLYN CORY.

The garden village of Glyn Cory is situated seven miles from Cardiff and is close to Peterston Station on the Great Western Railway. The site rises from 90 to 350 feet above sea level, with a gentle slope in the form of an amphitheatre. The area of the estate is 300 acres, of which 160 will be built on, 80 for golf course, and 60 for allotments and small holdings. Provision is made for 1,400 houses, with an ultimate population of 5,000 and 6,000. The estate is private property, and the land is let out on leases of 99 and 999 years. The rent is charged from ¾d. to 2d. per yard, or about one-fourth the rental of similar land in Cardiff. A scheme is also in operation whereby residents can obtain 75 per cent. of the money required for building purposes at 4 per cent. interest, repayable in ten to twenty years. Mr. John Cory initiated the enterprise, and since his death it has been looked after by Mr. Reginald Cory.

GOUROCK AND GREENOCK TENANTS.

This, the first co-partnership Society registered in Scotland, has opened its first blocks of houses. As is the case elsewhere in Scotland, loan stock is difficult to secure, and this is illustrated by the fact that the amount of share capital is three times as large as that of the loan stock. The shareholders are principally artisans in the Royal Naval Torpedo factory, who since their transfer from Woolwich have had great difficulty in obtaining suitable housing, the tenement system of the district not meeting with the southern ideas. It is proposed to build 500 houses.

HAMPDEN PARK ESTATE.

Hampden Park Estate, on the outskirts of Eastbourne, is not a garden city, nor a co-partnership suburb, in their true sense. It is due to a venture dating back to 1888, which is now the Eastbourne Artisans and Labourers' Improved Dwellings Company Limited. The housing settlement, known as Hampden Park Estate, was opened in 1909, when 60 houses, nine to twelve to the acre, were taken up. The houses face 50 feet tree-planted roads, and are set back with 100 feet between the building lines. The rents vary from 8s. 6d. to 12s. 6d. per week, including rates and taxes. The success of the venture decided the Directors to acquire another four acres in 1910, making nine in all. Some 73 houses have now been built on the Company's land, the ultimate provision being 98 houses on nine acres. The Company has paid a dividend of 5 per cent. on capital for some years past.

HAMPSTEAD GARDEN SUBURB.

The second of the great schemes inaugurated on Garden City lines owes it origin to the work of Mrs. S. A. Barnett, the wife of the late Canon Barnett, who, after a lifetime spent in the closest touch with the physical and spiritual needs of the people in the East End of London, saw in Mr. Howard's scheme an opening for the improvement of the deadly, soul-killing monotony and hideousness of the average London suburb. Coupled with the scheme was the idea to save a portion of land to be added to Hampstead Heath as an open space for ever, and this was successfully accomplished.

The estate, which is owned by the Hampstead Garden Suburb Trust Ltd., was laid out by Mr. Raymond Unwin, already famous for his work at Letchworth, and in the last three years it has become the best example in the world of modern town planning. Artists and architects from every country under the sun have been to see the work which an unfettered control has been able to effect on the heights of Golder's Green. The growth of the Estate has been phenomenal. Since the first sod was cut on May 2nd, 1907, 1,550 houses have been built and occupied, with an estimated population of 5,000 people.

The value of the houses and public buildings on the Estate is estimated at £800,000, representing, with the land and roads, a capital value of over £1,000,000, while the ground rent secured amounts to no less than £11,330 out of a total estimated rental of £15,000. Dividends at the rate of 5 per cent. per annum on the ordinary shares have been paid during the past four years.

The end of the first portion of the Estate (240 acres) being in sight, the Directors have acquired another 112 acres of land from the Ecclesiastical Commissioners, while the Co-partnership Tenants Limited, who have been responsible for the development of a large portion of the original area, have taken up 80 acres of the added portion and have also taken 300 acres direct from the same authorities, making a total of one square mile of land, the whole of which will be planned by the Hampstead Garden Suburb Trust Ltd.

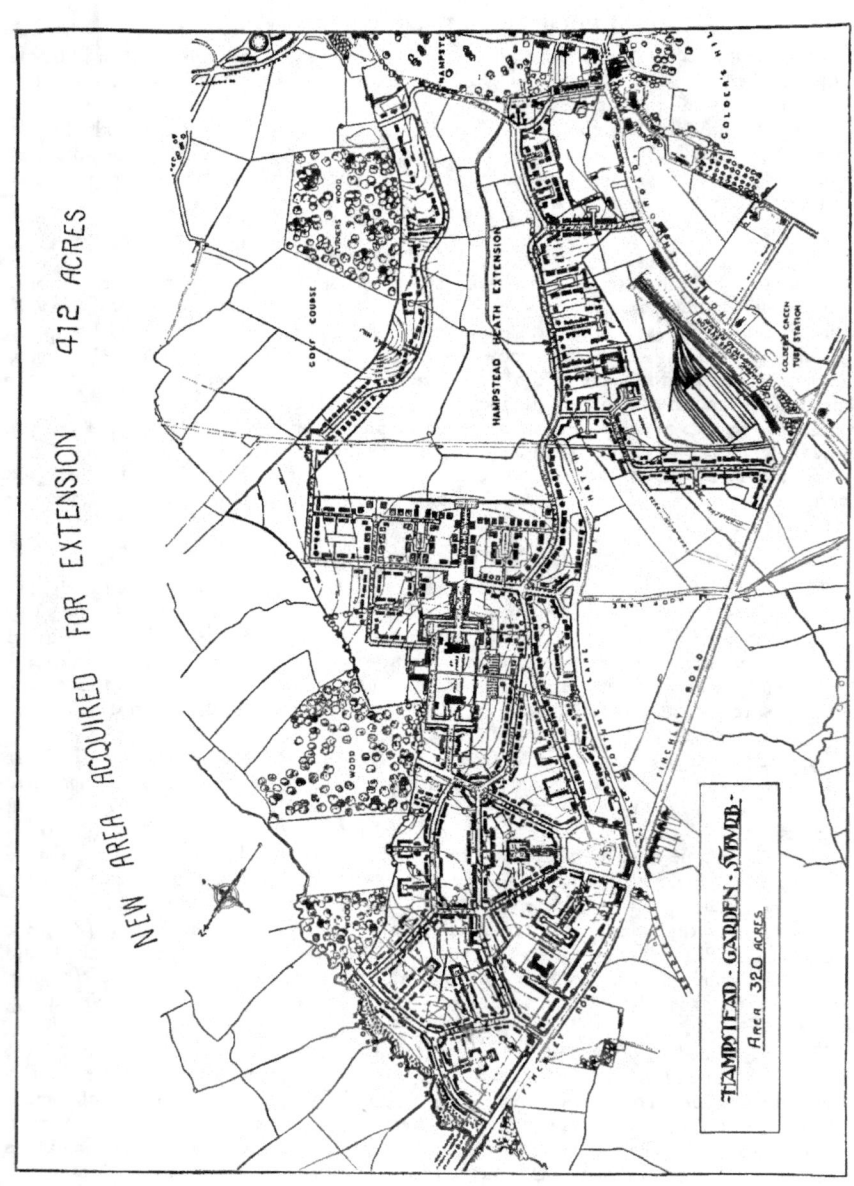

Building operations in the Suburb have been carried out by a variety of enterprise. The Trust has confined itself to erecting housing for its workers, the Institute, and a home for poor children. The Co-partnership Societies have built the larger number of houses, cottages, etc., renting from 5s. 9d. per week to £110 per year ; also the Club House at Willifield Green, and homes for elderly people. The Improved Industrial Dwellings Company have built a number of cottages and houses let at weekly rents from 7s. 6d. to 14s. 6d. Other companies and builders have built and are building houses to sell from £425 to £3,500.

The following figures of the Garden Suburb are available :—Share capital authorised £75,000, issued £54,000. Authorised debentures £150,000, issued £131,000. Total rates, 5s. 6d. in the £. Houses limited twelve to the acre, with an average of 8 over the whole Estate. Maximum rent £110 per year, minimum 6s. 6d. (rates not included). Average cost of cheapest house £300. Roads made 7 miles. Principal roads 40 feet, and others less. Roads are tree-planted and grass margins laid.

HASLEMERE TENANTS LIMITED.

Haslemere Tenants Limited owes its existence to the energies of Mr. Aneurin Williams, so well known in connection with Garden City work generally, and particularly as Chairman of First Garden City Limited. A start has been made with an area of about six acres, which is being dealt with carefully, in order to preserve open spaces and to provide economical houses. Land in the neighbourhood of Haslemere is very expensive, and building is very dear, but the success attending the first endeavours of the Company in putting up twenty houses on the first developed parts leads to the hope that other extensions will follow. The ultimate number of houses expected is sixty, and the density per acre will be ten, with a population of approximately 200. The dividend is limited to 5 per cent. The main sewer is available for drainage, and the Haslemere Urban District Council supply water from their works at Blackdown. Gas and electric current are available.

HEREFORD CO-OPERATIVE HOUSING LIMITED.

Hereford possesses a great distinction over most Garden Village schemes, in that it is the first community of its kind in England to be called into being through the assistance of a municipality. In 1909, as the result of consistent effort on the part of several disinterested citizens, an agreement was entered into between the corporation and the above co-operative body for the creation of a Garden Village on a block of eight acres thirty poles, in the city of Hereford. The City secured the land and leased it for a period of eighty years to the Company. The maximum rent payable till 1932 is not to exceed £133, and after that date for the remainder of the term £62 per annum. The actual rent is taken at the cost per year to the City by way of principal, interest and expenses in connection with the loan raised for the purchase and laying out of the land. The terms are such as to ensure the Corporation recovering the whole of the expenditure involved upon the municipality. The cost of the land is repayable in eighty years, but the cost of laying out has to be refunded in twenty-two years. An advantage to the Company was that the Corporation secured the money for the purchase of the land at the Government rate of interest. At the end of the term, when all repayments have been made, it is further provided that the Corporation shall hand over the land, other than roads, etc., to the Company without further charge.

Under the agreement the Company pays taxes, and had to provide not less than thirty nor more than 100 separate self-contained houses in two years from the date of signing, and this has been done. Safeguards are provided ensuring that none of the land shall, during the eighty years of lease, be used for advertisement hoardings, music halls, or theatres, noxious trades or a publichouse.

The land cost £1,500. The rents of the houses range from 4s. 9d. to 7s. 9d. (including rates). The roads are laid out in picturesque curves, and there is a total width of 70 feet between the houses.

The estate has now been completed and eighty-six houses have been erected.

HULL GARDEN VILLAGE.

Situated a mile and a half from Hull Paragon Station, this picturesque Garden Village is an example of a Village within a City. It was begun in 1907. The estate, for which Sir James Reckitt, Bart., is mainly responsible, is right in the centre of the town. It covers an area of ninety-four acres, of which seventy have been developed, at a density of twelve houses per acre. Some 560 houses have been built, and it is anticipated that eventually from 640 to 700 homes will be provided. The cheapest house costs £180, and is let at 4s. 9d. per week, including rates. The maximum rent is £35 and rates. The land tenure is free-hold, but the houses are let only, all the building being undertaken by the proprietors. The present population is about 2,000. The village is controlled by a private company, with a dividend limited to 3 per cent. Special by-laws enable economies to be made in regard to road construction, but the grass lined thoroughfare characteristic of most of the schemes has not yet been found possible. The widths of road in use are thirty feet, forty feet, and fifty feet, and all are planted with trees.

ILFORD GARDEN SUBURB.

This is a direct result of the work of the Garden City and Town Planning Association, and possesses features of exceptional interest, inasmuch as the acquisition of the land was the result of a desire to preserve from the ravages of the ordinary builder, which are only too painfully evident in this suburb, a charming piece of park land, contiguous with the existing park, which was coming into the market. No profit is being taken by the pro-moting Company (Town Planning and Garden Cities Company Ltd.), and the whole profits beyond the payment of fees and expenses are to be devoted to public objects in the district. The area of the land is forty acres, and the number of houses will be about seven to the acre. An area of twenty acres of park land, together with the mansion house, stables, con-servatories and gardens, was reserved for the extension of the Valentines Park belonging to the Ilford Urban District Council. The Company were enabled to offer the proposed ex-tension to the Council at £528 per acre, which the Council accepted, and have recently completed the purchase of the proposed extension, which now forms one of the most attractive features of the Valentines Park. The price of £528 per acre compares very favour-ably with the £800 per acre paid by the Council for the adjoining fields.

This is one of the many examples of the good work being done by the Association.

JESMOND PARK.

Jesmond Park Estate is situated near Rochdale. It is the property of Mr. S. Smethurst, J.P., President of the National Federation of Building Trade Employers. An area of 50 acres is available, of which it is intended to develop 30 acres on the following lines : Houses to average 16 to the acre, roads at least 40 feet wide, with grass margins and trees. The houses are to be built mainly in pairs, with an occasional group of three or four, the minimum cost per house being £200 ; and it is intended that tenants shall buy their own houses at a weekly charge of 5s. 6d. for the cheapest. The scheme was hung up

Hull Garden Village.

Wordsworth Walk, Hampstead Garden Suburb.

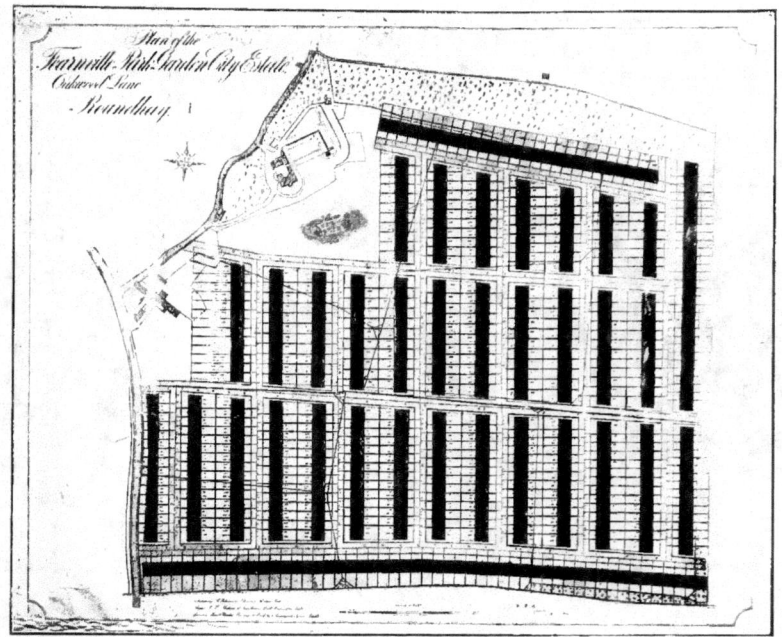

A so-called "Garden City" whose promoters have gone so far as to use the words "Garden City Association" in connection with it. A glance will show the ruthless way in which the plan has been made in entire disregard of all Garden City principles, the rigid straight line having been preserved at the expense of many natural beauties.

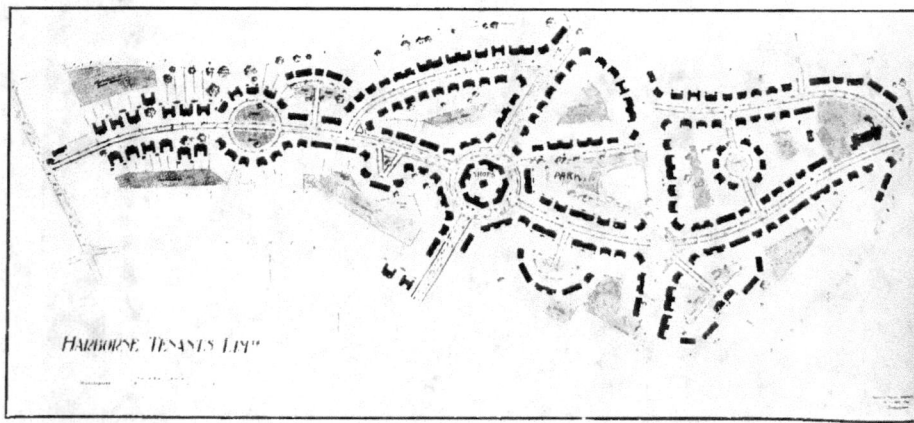

Harborne Garden Suburb, providing picturesque and convenient thoroughfares, main arterial streets for heavy traffic open spaces, garden plots, sites for public buildings, recreation ground, etc.

A PLAN OF PART OF THE CO-PARTNERSHIP ESTATE AT HAMPSTEAD.
(Showing the care taken in the lay out of the land, and the grouping of the houses under
Garden City principles.)

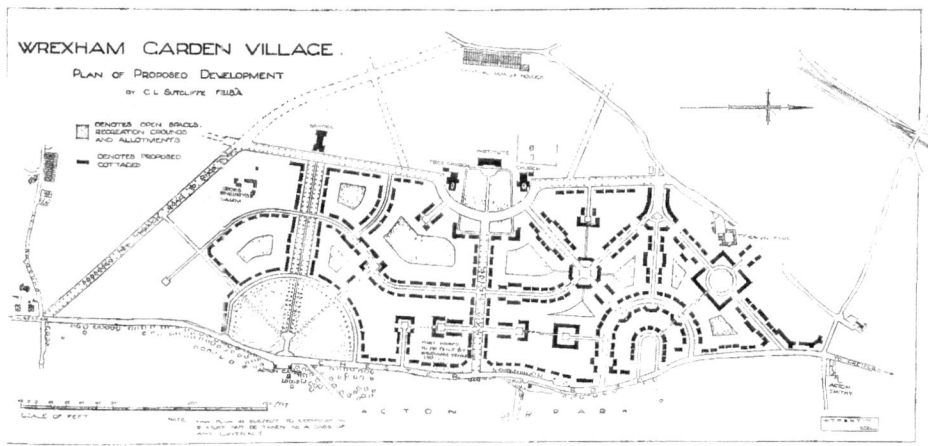

Corner treatment at Hampstead.

Sutton Garden Suburb Woodend & Woodend West

owing to the proposals in regard to roads coming into conflict with the Town Council's by-laws, and the subject, according to latest information, is now before the Local Government Board.

KNEBWORTH GARDEN VILLAGE.

This scheme owes its origin to the interest of the Earl of Lytton in Garden City work. A considerable part of his estate adjoining the railway station has already been planned and work is progressing. The first beginnings of the village were on the old lines, but now that Lord Lytton, who owns all the land, has had a proper scheme prepared, a happy future is assured, and is being helped greatly by the operations of a development company, Garden Villages Ltd. A Co-partnership Society has also been formed and its first houses are all taken by tenant members and new houses are bespoken before erection. The area of this garden village is about 800 acres, with about eight houses to the acre. The total number of houses to be built will thus work out at about 6,400, of which 250 are already erected.

Knebworth is on the Great Northern Railway, thirty-five minutes' run from King's Cross, the estate itself being pierced by the line, down to which the country slopes on either side. The ceremony of cutting the first sod for the Tenant Society was performed on April 20th, 1912, by Mrs. Cecil Harmsworth, the speakers being Lord Robert Cecil, Sir Sydney Lea, and Mr. Cecil Harmsworth, M.P.

LLANIDLOES.

An estate of nine acres near the little Montgomeryshire Borough of Llanidloes has been acquired privately and will be made over to the Welsh Town Planning and Housing Trust. The Town Recreation Ground is included in the area, and it is intended to build some forty houses as a small adjunct to the town, adjoining the Recreation Ground. A co-operative housing society has been formed to do the building, and it is expected that a start will be made in the summer of 1913. The plans have been prepared by Mr. Alwyn Lloyd.

LIVERPOOL'S MUNICIPAL HOUSING.

In 1864 Liverpool possessed the worst slums in England—places that were the haunts of typhoid fever, immorality, crime, and drunkenness. Rows of houses four and six storeys high, built back to back, only nine feet apart, were inhabited by about one-fifth of the entire population of the city.

The social results of this state of overcrowding were little short of appalling. The death rate averaged sixty per thousand, whilst the homes of the people were never free from infectious disease.

Since that time Liverpool has spent considerably over a million sterling, tearing down these filthy slums and re-housing the people who were displaced in model tenements and cottages. The rents for the new houses are let at a figure within the means of the tenants. The poverty of the tenants generally can be imagined when it is stated that several thousands of them subsist on an average of less than 10s. per week, and the greater number on less than 15s. per week. More than half of them are casual labourers employed at the docks.

The result of re-housing in Liverpool is an extremely satisfactory indication that large cities faced with large slum problems should take a bold and vigorous policy. Liverpool's figures up to December 31st, 1912, are as eloquent as they are simple. They read as follows :—

35

Total number of of sanitary dwellings erected   2,663
Erected prior to 1897   629
Erected since 1911   2,034
(*These are for labouring classes, and they are reserved for the dishoused*).
Death-rate—Declined from 60 to 27 per 1,000.
Typhus Fever—Once never absent ; in 1910, not a case.
Tuberculosis—Declined from 4 to 1.9 per 1,000.
Typhoid—In 1896, 1,300 cases ; in 1911, 200 cases.
Police Prosecutions—Have fallen 50 per cent.

The rents paid do not cover the charges involved by the public expenditure. The deficiency is made by striking a rate of 2½d. in the £. It is estimated that the ratepayers, if re-housing had not been carried out, would be paying a rate of 5d. in the £ in order to cover the cost of increased inspection, police prosecutions, extra Poor Law rate, and all the other charges that fall upon a city which neglects to deal with its slums.

The cash saving to Liverpool under the re-housing policy is estimated at £65,000, or double the cost of providing decent homes for the slum dwellers.

LONDON COUNTY COUNCIL DWELLINGS.

Some idea of the magnitude of the work undertaken by the London County Council in the housing of the working classes is shown by the fact that the accommodation provided on March 31st, 1913 was over nine thousand tenements, and nearly two thousand cubicles, with a population of 55,571 people and bringing in a gross annual rental of nearly £220,000. Besides this, accommodation for a further 11,726 persons is in course of provision. The capital cost is £3,400,000. The yearly receipts amount to £225,000. The return upon the cost varies considerably, the return on some estates being as high as nine per cent. This is all the result of twenty years' work.

The first housing schemes for London were started by the Metropolitan Board of Works, though, owing in some measure to defective legislation, it was some years before anything was done. The first houses to be erected were on the Boundary street area, which, as far beforehand as the year 1839, had been reported upon adversely. In 1890 there was a death-rate of forty per thousand over the area. Accommodation for 5,525 persons was completed in March, 1900, and opened by the late King Edward, then Prince of Wales.

The greater part of the Council's work has been in block buildings, but the more recent ventures have been conceived on better lines and some of the estates provide excellent examples of housing. The Totterdown Estate at Tooting and the White Hart Lane Estate at Tottenham provide welcome change from the ordinary monotonous housing of the district and an architectural effect has been introduced into the grouping with pleasing results while the latest estate of all, the Old Oak Lane, has provided an opportunity for Garden Suburb lay-out as well as for architectural treatment of the houses.

Tooting Estate is 38¾ acres in extent, costing £1,150 an acre. The cottages are two-storey buildings, in terraces of not more than twenty, and there are no back additions. The houses are 31.81 to the acre and the average cost is as follows : Five-roomed cottage, £282 17s. ; four-roomed cottage, £240 14s. ; three rooms and box room, £225 17s. ; three-roomed cottage, £190 13s.

The accommodation provided is as follows :—

37

48 two-room cottage flats at rents 6s. 6d. per week.
625 three-room cottages at rents 6s. 6d. to 9s. per week.
208 three-room and box room cottages at rents 9s. to 10s. per week.
205 four-room cottages at rents 9s. to 11s. per week.
175 five-room cottages at rents 10s. 6d. to 13s. 6d. per week.

1,261 tenements accommodating 8,788 persons.

The White Hart Lane Estate consists of 222 acres, which cost £400 an acre. At present nearly fifty acres are developed, and there is a central feature of over three acres known as Tower Gardens, which was secured by a gift from Lord Swaythling. 781 cottages with accommodation for 6,202 people have been completed and 105 were in March last in course of erection. The majority are fitted with baths. The houses will be about twenty-five to the acre. The average cost is : Five-roomed cottage, £245 ; four-roomed cottage, £225 ; three-roomed cottage, £175.

The rents charged are :—

    Three-roomed houses 6s. 6d. to 8s. per week.
    Four-roomed   ,   8s. 6d. to 8s. 9d. per week.
    Five-roomed   „   9s. 3d. to 13s. per week.

The Old Oak Estate at Hammersmith is one of the most interesting Municipal housing schemes in the country. A small portion only is at present being developed. Fifty-two dwellings have been provided with a population of 345 people, the rents being :—

    Two-roomed tenements 4s. 6d. to 5s. per week.
    Three-roomed tenements 6s. 6d. to 7s. 6d. per week.
    Four-roomed tenements 8s. 6d. to 10s. 6d. per week.
    Five-roomed tenements 12s. per week.

The building has taken the form of squares and crescents surrounding open grass spaces, and on this estate the Council has put into force a scheme for enabling tenants to purchase leases of their houses on the payment of a deposit of £5 and to make equal payments for the first fifteen, twenty or twenty-five years, sufficient to repay the amount expended. It is estimated that the total extra weekly cost to the lessee if he wishes to pay for the building in fifteen years will be from 3s. 3d. to 4s. for a four-roomed cottage rented at 10s. 6d. a week ; and from 4s. 2d. to 4s. 10d. for a five-roomed cottage, rented at 12s. 6d. a week. If the twenty years' period be chosen the increased weekly cost will be from 1s. 9d. to 2s. 4d. for a four-roomed cottage, and 2s. 3d. to 2s. 10d. for a five-roomed cottage. If the lessee chooses the twenty-five years' period, he will purchase the cottage for a charge approximately equal to the ordinary rent.

MACHYNLLETH GARDEN VILLAGE.

This Garden Village adjoining the old town of Machynlleth, comprises some fifteen acres of delightfully situated land. The estate has been vested in the Welsh Town Planning and Housing Trust, who will hold the freehold—making the roads and supervising development—and lease land to a Co-operative Housing Society (with a Welsh name—" Tregerddi Machynlleth ") which has been formed there to do the building. The dividend on the ordinary shares is limited to 5 per cent. and the loan stock to 4 per cent. This example is interesting, in that it is an attempt to deal with the housing problem in a small country town, the population of which is not increasing but which has a large number of tumble-down, insanitary, and overcrowded houses in the old parts of the town. The Urban

District Council is taking a great interest in the scheme, and is rendering assistance by allowing narrower roads to be constructed than the by-laws formerly allowed where there is no through traffic. The lay-out plans for the estate and plans for the houses have been prepared by Mr. Alwyn Lloyd, Architect to the Trust.

MERTHYR CO-OPERATIVE GARDEN VILLAGE.

At Merthyr a Co-operative Garden Village Society has been formed. Sixteen acres of land have been leased at Penydarren for 999 years, the lessor granting in addition one acre free for a recreation ground. Mr. Raymond Unwin has prepared the plan, which provides for about 170 houses. It is an excellent example of hillside planning, the houses being placed upon the upper side only of narrow roads. The land slopes to the south, and rises to a height of about a thousand feet above sea level. The Garden Village is in close proximity to some of the worst housing in the kingdom, so that its educational value will be very great. The work is being supervised by Professor Jevons. The first contract is for thirty-two houses of nine different types, which will be let at rents varying from 5s. to 8s. 6d. per week exclusive of rates.

NEW EARSWICK.

The Garden Village of New Earswick, near to the city of York, owes its origin to the generosity of Mr. Joseph Rowntree, who was desirous of making a practical contribution to the housing question. With this end in view he founded a Trust, in December, 1904, known as The Joseph Rowntree Village Trust, of which the following clause is vital to the appreciation of the experiment :—

" The object of the said Trust shall be the improvement of the condition of the working classes (which expression shall in these presents include not only artizans and mechanics, but also shop assistants and clerks, and all persons who earn their living wholly or partially, or earn a small income by the work of their hands or their minds, and further include persons having small incomes derived from invested capital, pensions, or other sources) in and around the City of York, and elsewhere in Great Britain and Ireland, by the provision of improved dwellings with open spaces and, where possible, gardens to be enjoyed therewith, and the organisation of village communities, with such facilities for the enjoyment of full and healthy lives as the Trustees shall consider desirable, and by such other means as the Trustees shall, in their uncontrolled discretion, think fit."

The property lies some 2½ miles to the north of York. The rents of the houses vary according to the accommodation provided. Every house contains three bedrooms, a living-room, scullery, larder, coal-house, etc. In this type of house the bath is generally placed in the scullery. It is covered with a hinged lid, and when not being used for bathing purposes forms a useful table. A good garden is attached to every house in the village.

The total area of the estate is 120 acres, of which over twenty-eight have been developed, and 150 houses have been erected ; ten houses per acre is the maximum number allowed. About five acres has been set aside and developed as open spaces, and some two acres has been reserved for allotment gardens and small holdings. Rents range from 4s. 6d. per week to £60 per annum, rates being payable by the tenants to the Flaxton Rural District Council. All roads are tree planted and have grass margins. The estate provides excellent examples of the way in which roads should be laid out both in traffic and non-traffic thoroughfares, and its whole appearance—due to Mr. Unwin's oversight—is perhaps the most pleasing of all the schemes mentioned. The rents are low, the gardens ample, the cottages attractive and the roads economical. As a concrete object lesson of what a local authority could do under the Town Planning Act it would be hard to beat.

NEW ELTHAM.

New Eltham Garden Suburb is one of the schemes in a district of London which is greatly in need of good building examples. Clare College has followed the example of some of the other seats of learning and has offered an estate of 27 acres for development on co-partnership lines. A society has been formed by old members of the College, who have placed the development in the hands of Mr. George L. Pepler. On the area named 282 houses will be built, and the demand is such that in all probability the whole will be taken up in a very short time. Cottages are proposed at rentals of from 5s. 6d. to 7s. a week. A capital of about £70,000 is being raised for building.

NEWTON MOOR.

The Newton Moor Estate is situated in Cheshire, but close to Stockport, and therefore closely connected with the Lancashire manufacturing industries. In this example there are already in existence several mills and considerable cottage property of the usual crowded type. The general lay-out was already determined by the two main roads across the estate before the new plan, prepared by Mr. Thomas Adams, was created. The leading feature is a wide tree-planted avenue, intersected by open spaces in its course, running parallel to one of the main roads already in existence. The estate has not made much progress at present, but when completed it should form an interesting example of what in the future will be characteristic of a large number of suburban schemes—that is, the superimposition of garden suburb planning on a partially developed site.

OLDHAM GARDEN SUBURB.

The Oldham Garden Suburb owes its existence largely to the work of Mrs. Higgs, one of the earliest members of the Garden Cities Association. The " Beautiful Oldham " movement had given an impulse to the desire for a better mode of living and a better style of home, and despite many difficulties substantial progress has been made. Of the 52 acres one-third has been developed by the Oldham Garden Suburb Tenants Ltd. The houses let from 5s. 11d. a week to £30 a year. Houses of a larger type are built for sale as well as for rent. The roads have been made with grass margins and are tree planted, and 3 acres are reserved for open spaces. The infantile mortality for the last year shows the following vital statistics :—*Birth Rate* : 42 per 1,000 population. *Death Rate* : 59 per 1,000 births. The *General Death Rate* is 10 per 1,000.

PARK LANGLEY.

This scheme is somewhat different from most of the Garden City ventures. It is the work of a firm of builder owners who have been working on housing schemes for the last forty odd years. Park Langley is the latest of their ventures, and was started in June, 1909. The houses vary in design considerably, being the work of many different architects. The principal feature of the lay-out plan is found in the converging avenues and roads upon a shopping centre, the idea being to group practically all the shops into one area around a circular winter garden. Above, ample accommodation is provided for those who occupy the shops, with large roof gardens. The following figures in connection with this scheme may be of interest : area, 700 acres ; population, 500 ; number of houses allowed per ac e, 4 ; ultimate number of houses, 2,800. Number of houses now erected, 100. Ultimate population, 14,000.

PORT SUNLIGHT.

Messrs. Lever Brothers' Model Village on Bromborough Pool, a tributary of the Mersey, is well known all over the world. The land first acquired, in 1888, was only 56 acres in extent, and of this area 24 acres were devoted to business and manufacturing purposes. Now the works and village comprise an area of 440 acres, in the proportion of 217 allotted to factories, wharves and sidings, and 223 to houses, gardens, village institutions and recreation grounds and other open spaces. The houses are all picturesque and substantially built by Messrs. Lever Brothers as part of a scheme of Prosperity Sharing, and are let (to employees only) at rents just sufficient to cover upkeep and repair. Sir William Lever holds that his Company gets an ample return for this attention to the housing of the work-people, and for the Co-partnership Scheme more recently launched.

The deep ravines of the Bromborough Pool, most of them now filled up where not needed for navigation, practically decided the original plan of the village, and this has since been the subject of interesting central treatment on lines partly suggested by a prize competition of the students of Liverpool University Department of Civic Design. The village is peculiarly rich in institutional and public buildings, including two large schools, a church, Gladstone Hall, Hulme Hall, the Auditorium, Technical Institute, Co-partners' Club, Girls' Club, the Bridge Inn, Open-air Bath and Gymnasium, and a Cottage Hospital. The total cost of the 223 acres (area of the village itself), to develop and provide all roads, buildings, houses, etc., is £588,000. The annual cost to the firm is £28,608 a year for interest.

ROTHLEY GARDEN SUBURB.

This private scheme has been initiated by a member of the Garden Cities and Town Planning Association, and is providing a good example of development for the district adjoining Rothley station on the main line of the Great Central Railway between Leicester and Loughborough. Some of the Architects most successful at Letchworth and Hampstead have been employed. An 18-hole golf course and club house has been opened with a membership of about 200. Tennis courts are also provided. It is contemplated ultimately to develop an area of about 250 acres. Building plots vary from 400 square yards to two and three acres. Up to the present time sixty-nine houses have been erected and about 1,000 yards of the roads, which are tree planted and have grass margins, have been taken over by the Local Authority. The development of the estate has been delayed by the restrictions of the local by-laws and the want of proper sewerage facilities ; these are now in course of adjustment. The Estate is five miles from Leicester and Loughborough, and the railway station has been put on the Estate.

RUISLIP MANOR.

Development began in January 1912, and there are now 100 houses erected, largely through a cottage company which has been formed for the estate. Houses have varied from four to twelve to the acre, and the average for the whole area will be six. The cost of the cheapest houses so far has been £175 each. The land tenure is both freehold and leasehold, and the houses are both let and sold, the proprietors building where necessary. A mile and a half of new roads has been made, and these have been sewered and gas and water mains laid. The widths of road in use are forty feet and twenty-four feet, the cost being £3 to £8 per yard run, with a further charge for the final making up. The roads are well made and are tree planted, with grass margins.

Under the Town Planning scheme of the Ruislip-Northwood Urban District Council, special by-laws are applicable to the land, and these will assist in economical development.

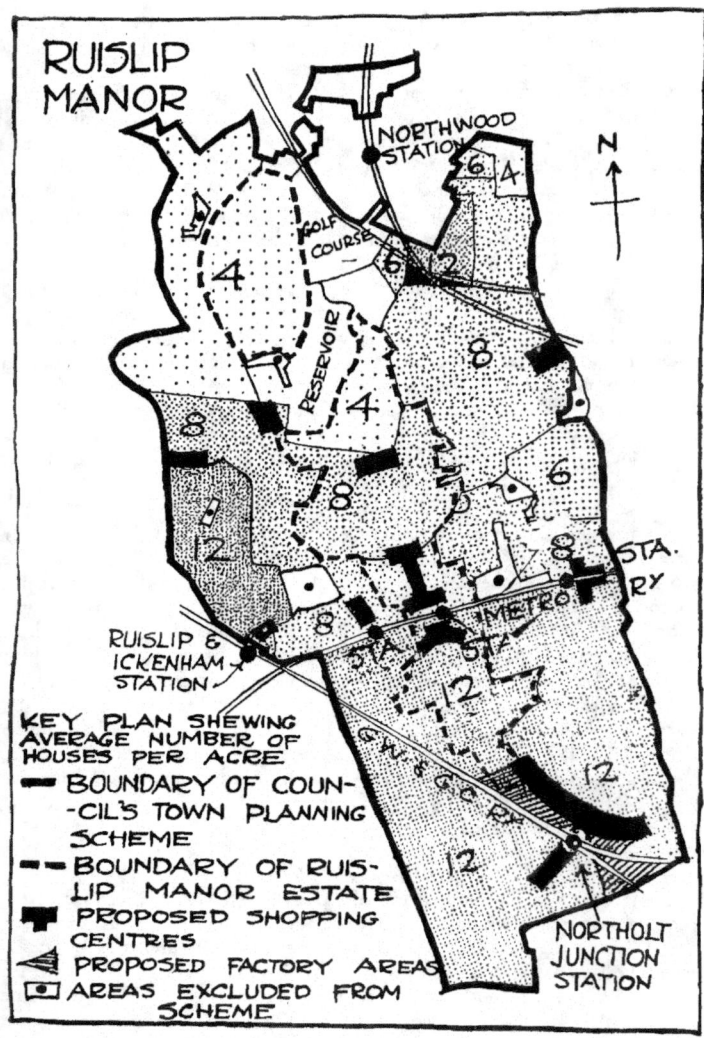

This illustrates both the area of the Ruislip-Norwood Town Planning Scheme, one of the largest in the country, and also the Ruislip Manor Estate situated in the middle. The figures refer to open spaces and unbuilt-on areas.

One-tenth of the total area will be reserved as open space, and provision is made for allotments and small holdings. Under the scheme, five acres constitutes a land unit, and the Company is at liberty to group the houses in one land unit upon one portion, provided not more than twenty are put upon one acre and the remainder of the land is left as open space. This allows of the houses being grouped for architectural effect, and provides for economy in roadmaking, etc.

The cost of development has varied from £200 to £500 per acre. There are six railway stations close to the estate, and, being quite adjacent to London, the prospects of success are very encouraging.

SEALAND TENANTS.

Sealand Tenants Ltd., whose forty-eight acres of land is situated just over six miles from Chester, have developed ten acres, and, since August, 1910, have built 108 houses out of the 470 provided for at the rate of ten to the acre. Five acres have been set aside for recreation purposes and garden allotments. The society has provided its own sewage works, and is making its roads thirty-six feet wide, with eighteen feet carriage ways. Nearly a mile of road is at present under construction, with both trees and grass margins. Rents range from 4s. 9d. to 8s. 6d., the rates, which are extra, being 1s. 10d. in the £.

SOUTHAMPTON GARDEN SUBURB.

The Southampton Garden Suburb, situated just beyond the boundaries of the city, in the area controlled by the Itchen District Council and Bitterne Rural District Council, dates only from August, 1911. It is a commercial project adopting modern Garden Suburb development. The total area available is 136 acres, of which some 5½ have been reserved for open spaces, together with fifteen acres of copse. The size of the minimum plots is restricted to 25 feet by 120 feet. It is hoped in time to provide 522 houses for an ultimate population of about 2,600.

STIRLING HOMESTEADS LIMITED.

Stirling Homesteads Limited is a Co-partnership group. It differs from the ordinary Garden Suburb Scheme principally in this—that the group lease a farm along with the houses and manage this collectively, through a farm committee employing a farm manager, who is also a member of the group.

The object of this is eventually to reduce the cost of the distribution of milk and dairy produce to a minimum and secure the benefits of this to the group. Also to stand as distributing agent for the produce taken off the allotments by the tenants, thus securing Co-operative marketing.

The housing and farm buildings necessary have been erected to meet the Association's requirements by H.M. Office of Woods, and the ground has also been leased on a 31 years' lease to the Association by the same body. The experiment is just in its infancy, and it is too soon to say anything definite about its prospects, but many of the initial difficulties have been passed, and it is hoped to overcome successfully the few remaining ones.

Out of a total area of 40 acres, 1½ has been built on, 5 are being used as gardens, and 35 are being farmed. The estate is situate 1½ mile from Stirling, and provision is made for an ultimate population of 200 persons and 40 homes. The maximum dividend is limited to 4 per cent. on loan and 5 per cent. on share capital. The enterprise dates from the close of 1910. The rents range from £10 10s. to £26, rates 2s. 6d. in the £ extra.

43

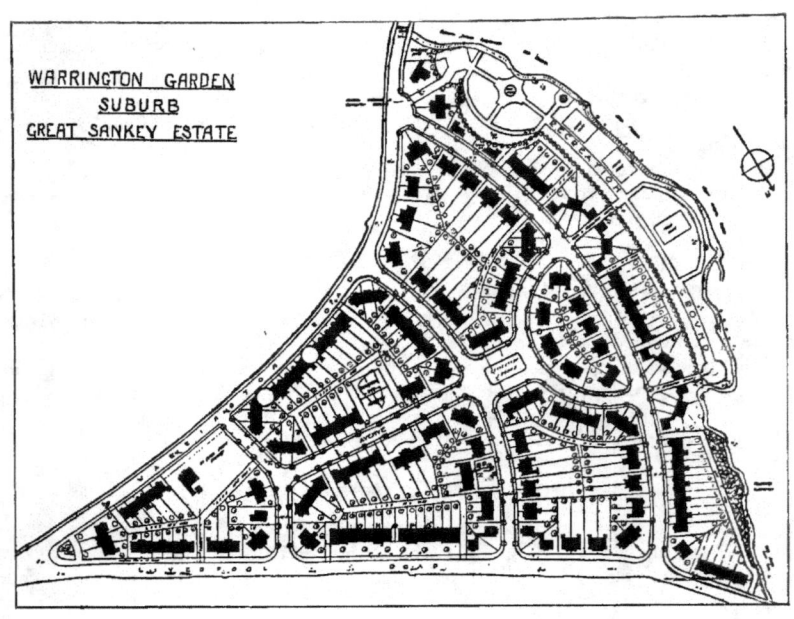

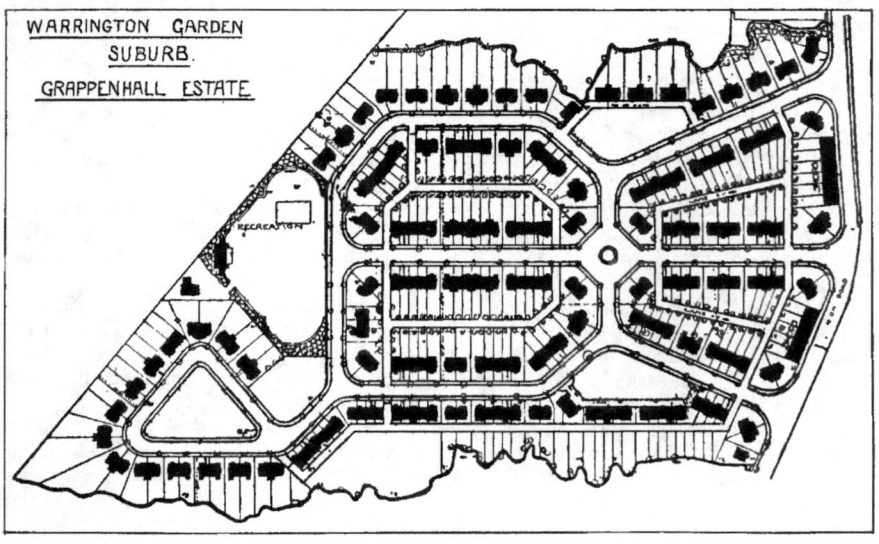

44

SUTTON (SURREY) GARDEN SUBURB.

Sutton Garden Suburb Limited has purchased 25½ acres of the Rose Hill estate, Sutton (Surrey), and has an option over another 74½ acres of well-wooded land on the edge of the Downs. Each tenant must be a co-partner, with a maximum holding of £200, and a minimum of £50, which may either be invested straight away or paid by instalments of not less than 5s. a month. Above the £200 investments may be made in loan stock. Shareholding is restricted to tenants and prospective tenants, but loan stock may be applied for by anyone. As 4½ per cent. will be paid on share capital and loan stock, the loan stock having

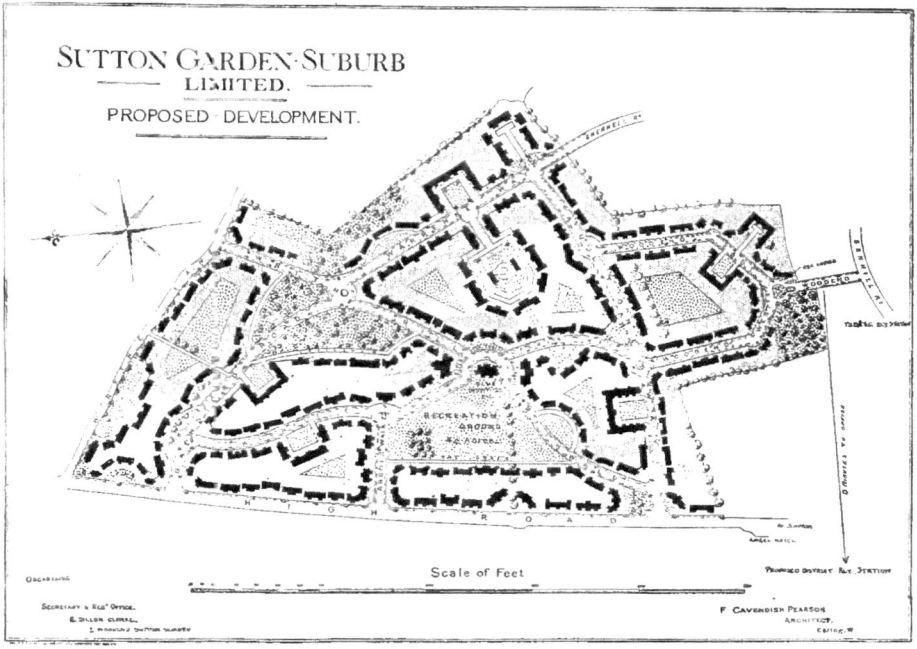

the prior claim but the tenants being more closely associated with management, this should prove an attractive investment. Two loan-stock holders have seats on the Committee. Houses are ten to the acre, and provision is made for extensive recreation grounds and club premises.

WARRINGTON GARDEN SUBURBS LIMITED.

Warrington Garden Suburbs Limited has an outstanding feature of note in that it is the only Company possessing two estates, and which has set out with the definite idea of eventually girdling the town with a ring of Garden Suburbs. It was formed in 1907, and, in the same year, estates were purchased at Great Sankey of about twenty acres, and at Grappenhall of about twenty-two acres. A competition was held with a view to obtaining the best plans for laying them out, and the premiums were won in each case by Messrs. A.

and J. Soutar, of Wandsworth. The Company is based on the same lines as First Garden City Limited. The nominal capital is £20,000, the dividend is restricted to 5 per cent., the number of houses limited to an average of twelve to the acre, and ample open spaces and recreation grounds are carefully provided for. A Society called "Warrington Tenants Limited," was registered in 1908 to assist in the development of the Company's property, and a second Society in 1911, called "Grappenhall Tenants Limited," with similar objects. The progress of the scheme has, hitherto, been somewhat slow; but there are now twenty-four houses on the Great Sankey estate, and twelve at Grappenhall, whilst arrangements for an additional fifteen are practically completed. The cheapest houses on both estates cost about £185; the maximum rent is £30 and the minimum £15 12s. per annum. Rates are usually paid by the owners. Provision is made for an ultimate number of houses thus: At Great Sankey 240, at Grappenhall 265.

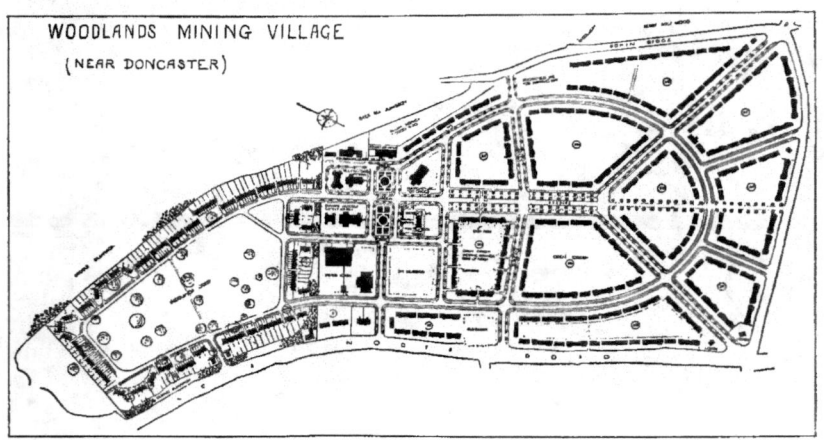

WOODLANDS MINING VILLAGE.

The pretty mining village of Woodlands is one of the most valuable projects which demonstrate the economy and value of town planning. Its total of 653 houses is now complete. The village was commenced in June, 1907, to house the workers of the Brodsworth Main Colliery, largely owing to the determined efforts of Sir A. B. Markham. The capital required was borrowed on debentures at 5 per cent. interest—a high rate for housing purposes—and the basis of the undertaking is that the village shall, at the rentals charged, return 4 per cent. on capital after everything, including ground rent, rates and maintenance, is paid. The plan is the work of Mr. Percy B. Houfton, of Chesterfield. The estate is of great natural beauty, and adjoins the private residence known as "The Woodlands," which is being converted into a Workmen's Club. Its immediate gardens and the Home Park, in all twenty-one acres, are reserved as recreation grounds.

The village is divided into two sections, linked up by the sites for public buildings and institutions. The portion known as "The Park Site" comprises 121 cottages, which were built in one year, and overlook the Home Park, which contains some magnificent forest trees and is surrounded by a belt of shrubberies. The second portion, "The Field Area," contains 532 houses, built and occupied in fifteen months. The rate of speed, which is too high to ensure good workmanship throughout, was necessitated by unforeseen developments in the coal seam. A main avenue, 120 feet wide, and planted with a quadruple row of trees, is the principal feature of the design, together with numerous open spaces, gardens, an artificial lake covering some four acres, and all the advantages of landscape gardening. Churches, baths, an institute, and co-operative stores are features of the village. The rents are as follows : Living-room cottage, 5s. 3d. ; parlour cottage, with bath in scullery, 6s.; parlour cottage, with bathroom, 6s. 6d.; similar house to the last, but larger, 6s. 9d. All rates are included in these figures. The cost of building varied from £156 per house for the smallest to £212 for the largest.

WORCESTER.

A co-partnership society—Worcester Tenants Ltd.—has been formed largely through the energies of the Dean, Dr. Moore Ede, to start work upon eleven acres of land which has been secured. It is hoped to build houses to let at about 5s. a week.

WREXHAM TENANTS.

The Welsh Town Planning and Housing Trust Limited has acquired control of some 200 acres of very desirable and well situated land at Acton, adjoining the town of Wrexham, in North Wales. Wrexham is the centre of a large and rapidly developing Coal and Iron district, and in addition to the normal expansion of the town, a new Colliery has just been started near Acton where it is expected that some 3,000 men will be employed in the next two years. A Co-partnership Housing Society has been formed locally under the name of Wrexham Tenants Limited to do the building, with Lord Kenyon, Mr. David Davies, M.P., and others as Directors, and contracts for the first forty-four houses will be let immediately. The Trust will make the roads and supervise the development of the estate. The lay-out plan for the estate includes provision for a village institute, two places of worship, and school, in addition to a liberal provision for open spaces and recreation grounds. The District Council has agreed to modified by-laws, which will allow of narrower carriage-ways being provided, in exchange for a greater distance between the houses, and ample open spaces.

YNYSYBWL CO-OPERATIVE GARDEN VILLAGE SOCIETY LIMITED.

The Ynysybwl Co-operative Garden Village Society will be building about fifty-five houses on Lord Plymouth's land at Old Ynysybwl, about three minutes' walk from the upper railway station. The site is scarcely three quarters of a mile by road from the Lady Windsor Colliery, where 1,100 men are employed ; and it is close to the Mynachdy level, which now employs about 300 men, whilst extensive developments are anticipated. The demand for houses at Ynysybwl is very great, many families being obliged to reside in apartments who could well afford a house, because there is not one vacant in the town. The conditions of overcrowding prevailing at Ynysybwl, and the many abuses to which the extreme shortage of houses has led, have been described in the publication of the Association. This Society was formed by the Miners' lodges of the locality, who appointed a joint committee. The Chairman and the Secretary of the Lady Windsor Lodge, with six other miners, were the founders of the Society.

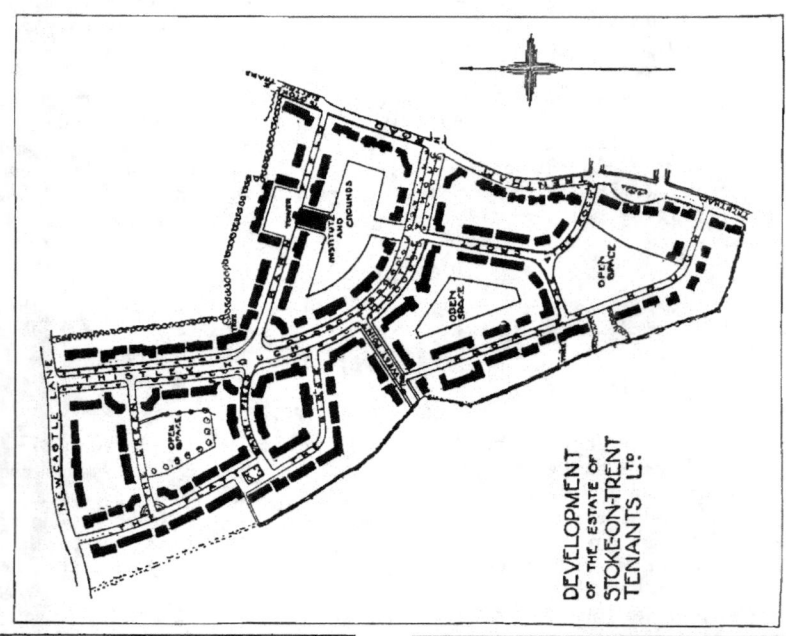

DEVELOPMENT
of the ESTATE of
STOKE-ON-TRENT
TENANTS Lᵗᵈ

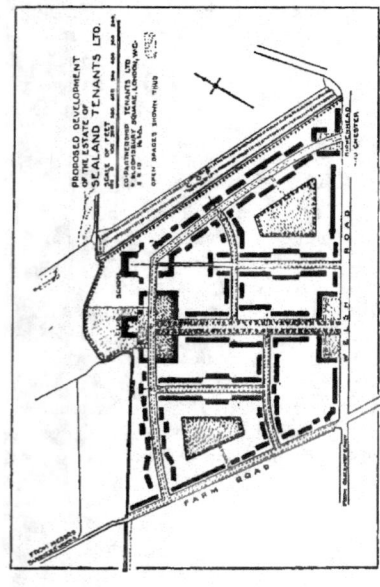

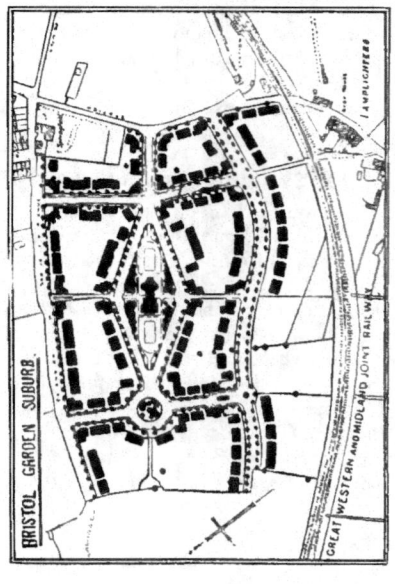

BRISTOL GARDEN SUBURB.

CO-PARTNERSHIP HOUSING

TENANT CO-OPERATORS LIMITED

The forerunner of co-partnership in housing was the Tenant Co-operators Ltd., which is still in existence at Red Lion Square. This organisation was founded in 1888 by Mr. Benjamin Jones, then manager of the London branch of the Co-operative Wholesale Society. The Rules were prepared by a sub-committee of which, among others, Mr. (now Sir) H. J. Vansittart Neale, Mr. J. J. Dent, Mr. Walter Hazell, the late Mr. Francis William Buxton, the Hon. T. A. Brassey, Sir H. Lawrence, Mr. H. W. L. Roscoe, and the Rev. T. G. Gardner were members, and under the guidance of the late Mr. E. V. Neale and the late Mr. J. C. Gray (of the Co-operative Union). The rules and prospectus thus prepared have been in operation without any variation in principle from that time until now, and have formed the basis of all the tenant societies established since. Mr. Howard Hodgkin was the honorary secretary.

The object of the promoters was to demonstrate the possibilities of the principle and to advocate the formation of similar societies throughout the country. Little or no developments, however, took place until the very remarkable public interest and enthusiasm in housing was aroused by Mr. Howard's scheme for Garden Cities, since when the idea of the combination of the tenant ownership system with the Garden City or Garden Suburb policy has made the establishment of societies so attractive and successful.

The Tenant Co-operators Ltd. established, either by purchase or erection, five estates : at Upton Park, Penge, Camberwell, East Ham, and Epsom. The total value of the properties at the present time is £28,670 ; £3,327 has been written off for depreciation. The share and loan stock capital stands at £13,969, in addition to which loans from the Public Works Commissioners and other bodies, amounting to £9,841, have been secured. The fundamental principle of permitting tenants to become shareholders by the holding of one £1 share, such holding entitling them to a vote equally with any other shareholders, irrespective of the amount of value of the capital held, has been continued throughout the existence of the Society. In this respect other societies have made considerable departure. The capital holding of tenants in other societies is usually much larger, and quite recently, in many copartnership societies, the voting power of tenants has been either restricted or removed entirely. The net profits realised by the Tenant Co-operators Ltd., for the whole period of twenty-five years, after payment of all charges, expenses, depreciation, and interest upon loans, deposits, and loan stock, has worked out at 6.7 per cent. upon the amount of share capital. For 1912 it was 8.3 per cent. Interest upon share capital being limited by rule, however, to 4 per cent., the surplus profits have been distributed in dividends to tenants, rising to as much as 2s. 6d. in the £.

CO-PARTNERSHIP TENANTS LIMITED

One of the most striking features of the modern movement for better housing has been the successful application of the co-partnership principle. Beginning as recently as 1901 Co-partnership Housing has already made history. Under the inspiration of Mr. Henry Vivian co-partnership tenants societies have been formed in various parts of the country and are in course of formation in British speaking countries across the seas. Many are now federated in the Co-partnership Tenants Ltd., a society that has secured public confidence in the movement to a degree that would otherwise have been impossible. There are now fourteen societies in membership. In 1904 the cost value of their land and buildings was £17,308 ; already it is a million and a quarter sterling, and the estimated value of the houses when the estates now being developed are completed is £3,450,000. The headquarters are at 6, Bloomsbury Square, London, W.C., where an efficient organisation with trading, architectural, publishing, and other departments has been built up to render substantial assistance to the federated societies.

At present 900 acres are under development by the societies associated with Co-partnership Tenants Ltd., and the following figures concerning the rentals of the property already built are of interest :—

Below 6s. weekly	..	.. 640	Brought forward	..	2,553
From 6s. and below 8s.	..	.. 921	From 12s. and below 15s.	..	168
,, 8s. ,, 10s.	..	.. 558	,, 15s. and up to 20s.	..	79
,, 10s. ,, 12s.	..	.. 434	Over £52 per annum ..	..	155
Carried forward	..	..2553	Grand total	..	2,955

The strong position which the Co-partnership Tenants societies have attained may be gathered from the fact that eight co-partnership societies in federation which have practically completed their building operations and having property to the value of £797,345 have not only no dwelling of any kind to let, but have "waiting lists" of applicants.

The following particulars show the growth of the Society's Capital, and the extent to which the Society has aided the movement in raising Capital.

On December 31st, 1912, the Society's Capital consisted of :—

		£		£
Shares of £10 each	..	.. 68,160	Increase during the year 6,350	
Loan Stock	.. ..	.. 198,368	,, ,, ,,	60,584
Loans ..	.. ..	.. 70,317	,, ,, ,,	30,801
		£336,845		97,735

A typical new street of an industrial town. The houses are built forty or more to the acre, and in this instance the frontages are 12 feet only.

A street at Hampstead Garden Suburb.

Hampstead, showing a Common Green.

Bournville.   The Shopping Centre.

Bristol Garden Suburb Cottages costing £150 each.

A Crescent, showing Common Green.

During the year the Society, as Agent, also raised direct for the various Societies in membership :—

		£	£
Shares	..	1,810	
Loan Stock	..	21,768	
On Mortgage	..	97,575	
			121,153

Total amount raised in 1912 .. .. — 218,888

From June, 1907 (when the Society was registered), to December 31st, 1911, the total sum raised direct in Shares, Loan Stock, and on Mortgage for the various Societies was 651,269

There was invested in Co-partnership Tenants Limited up to the same date 239,110

890,379

Grand Total £1,109,267

Continued progress was made in 1913, the total paid-up capital of Co-partnership Tenants Ltd. on September 1st being :—Shares, £76,960 ; Loan Stock, £224,520 ; a total of £301,480.

In the development of the work the Co-partnership Tenants Housing Council has rendered considerable assistance, and under its guidance much of the educational and social work is fostered on the various estates—the activities being chronicled in *Co-partnership*, the penny monthly magazine of the movement. It also organises the Co-partnership Festival which is held annually on one or other of the co-partnership estates—Ealing, 1912, and at Hampstead, in July, 1913—at which a Flower Show, Choral Contests, a Pageant, displays by children living on the estate, and other features demonstrate the advantages of these co-partnership suburbs both in their effect on the individual and on the general welfare of the community.

Below, particulars are given of the estates affiliated to Co-partnership Tenants Ltd., that fact alone being an assurance of the exercise of forethought and prudence in development. Details which are common to all estates have been omitted for the sake of brevity. In every case, of course, the owners are a society of public utility, the maximum dividends being 5 per cent.

ANCHOR TENANTS LTD. (LEICESTER).

The Anchor Tenants Ltd., Leicester, own forty-eight acres a mile and a half from the boundary of the town ; and since a start was made in 1908 eighty-four houses and three shops have been built, and there is a population of about 360 residents. Ten houses are allowed to the acre. The vital statistics for the estate are very striking ; there was only one death in four years, and the birth-rate is thirty per thousand. Rents range from 6s. to 10s. 9d. including rates, which are at 4s. 8d. in the pound. The streets are tree-planted with grass margins. Roads have been formed and sites plotted for another sixty houses. Provision has been made for a larger playing ground, comprising about three acres, part of which has been levelled and re-turfed for a cricket pitch.

BRENTHAM GARDEN SUBURB (EALING).

  The Brentham Garden Suburb, as the estate of the Ealing Tenants Ltd. is now called, is the oldest of the ventures connected with Co-partnership Tenants Ltd. Various portions of land have been acquired since 1902, and the estate now consists of sixty-three acres. Its easy access to London, the new Brentham Station having been opened close at hand, gives every reason for expectation that the whole area will soon be built upon. The roads

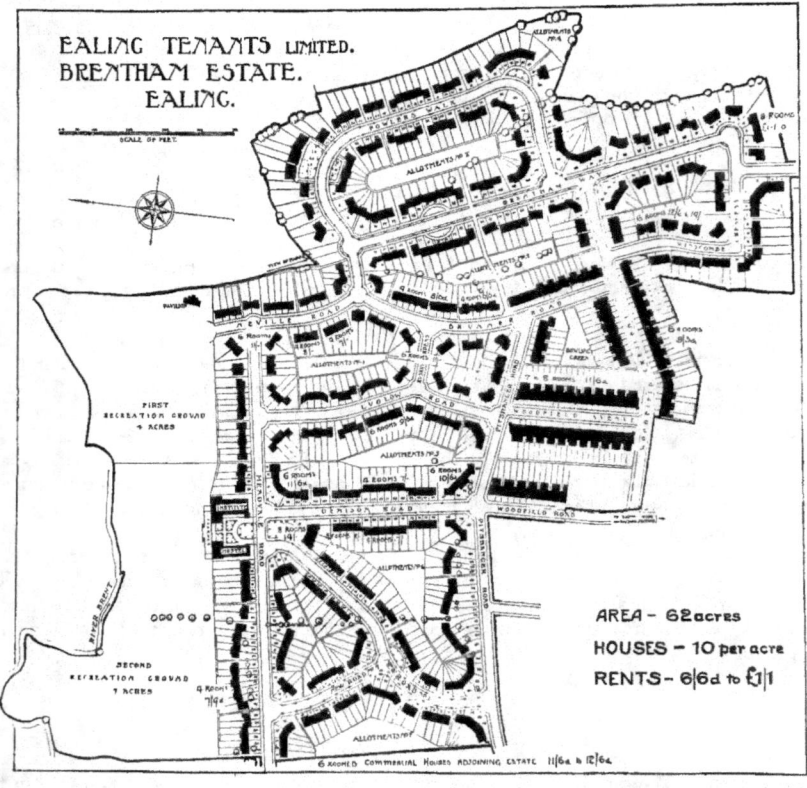

are forty feet wide, and all are tree planted. At present 500 houses are built out of 700 anticipated, and there is a population of about 2,000 out of the three to four thousand expected. The houses are limited to twelve to the acre. The maximum rent is 21s. and the minimum 6s. 6d., the rates, which are extra, being 6s. 8d. in the £. A block of twenty-four small flats has also been completed and tenanted, with rents from 6s. 6d. per week inclusive of rates, taxes, and lighting. The Institute, opened by H.R.H. the Duke of Connaught, provides excellent facilities for social intercourse. It contains a large billiard room, hall for social purposes, reading room and library; and connected with it, the Society has reserved twelve acres of recreation grounds. These facilities are much appreciated by the residents, and full advantage is taken of them. Other open spaces are reserved for additional gardens, etc.

BURNAGE.

Manchester Tenants Ltd. have completed their Burnage estate of eleven acres, their 136 houses giving accommodation to 500 people. Rents vary from 5s. 3d. to 11s. 6d., the rates, which are extra, being 8s. 4d. in the £. The society has made its roads of twenty-two feet and eighteen feet, and has planted the whole of these with trees and provided grass margins. Application is now being made to the local authority for them to take over the roads.

FALLINGS PARK TENANTS.

Fallings Park Garden Suburb Tenants have so far developed 8½ acres of their estate, which is one-and-a-half miles from Wolverhampton. At the rate of twelve houses to the acre, seventy-five have been erected since June, 1907. The rents range from 4s. 6d. to 10s. inclusive. The rates are 9s. 4d. in the £. Thirty-six feet roads are in use, and these are planted with trees.

GARDEN CITY TENANTS.

The Garden City Tenants Ltd. was the society whose inception led to that combination of garden city principles with co-partnership methods which has revolutionised both movements, and has brought into being the enormous structure of Co-partnership Tenants Ltd. Thirty-nine acres have been developed, and 322 houses providing accommodation for 1,600 people. Twelve houses to the acre are allowed ; but the generous garden space provided and the charming open greens, which are such a feature of the estate, reduce the total number of houses to 322. The rents range from 4s. 6d. a week to £61 a year, rates, which are 4s. 9d. in the £, being extra.

GRETA HAMLET.

Greta Hamlet, Keswick, is the property of Derwentwater Tenants Ltd., who started with 2½ acres in 1909, and have practically covered this area. The roads are made twenty-four feet and twelve wide, and are planted with grass and garden margins.

HAMPSTEAD HEATH EXTENSION TENANTS LIMITED.

Hampstead Heath Extension Tenants Ltd. was registered on the 25th March, 1912, and was formed to develop some of the finest sites on the Hampstead Garden Suburb, overlooking and bordering on the eighty acres of the Hampstead Heath Extension. On this area houses of varying rentals are being erected, mostly of the larger type. Some of these houses have frontages to the Heath while overlooking the Hampstead Golf Course and Turners Wood at the rear. The land is situated within a few minutes' walk of the old Spaniard's Inn, and other historical spots associated with the neighbourhood.

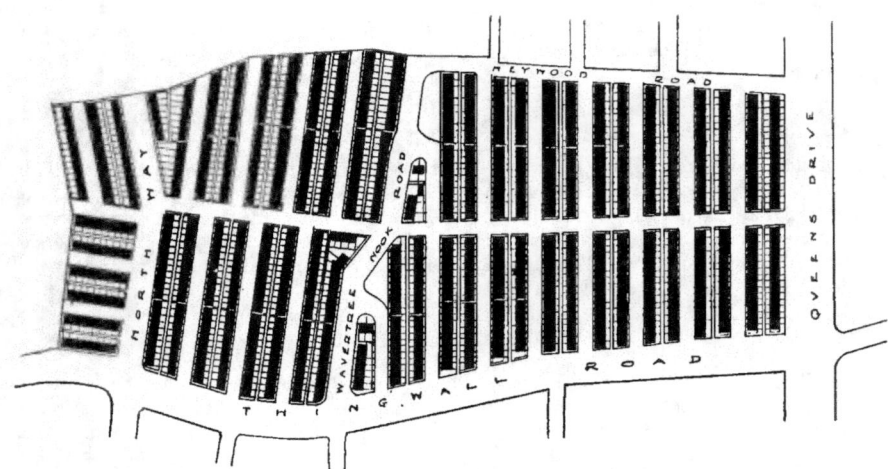

TWENTY-FIVE ACRES OF LIVERPOOL GARDEN SUBURB AS IT MIGHT HAVE BEEN.

The plan shows how the land could have been laid out to comply with the minimum requirements of the Liverpool Corporation's Acts, with 41 houses per acre.

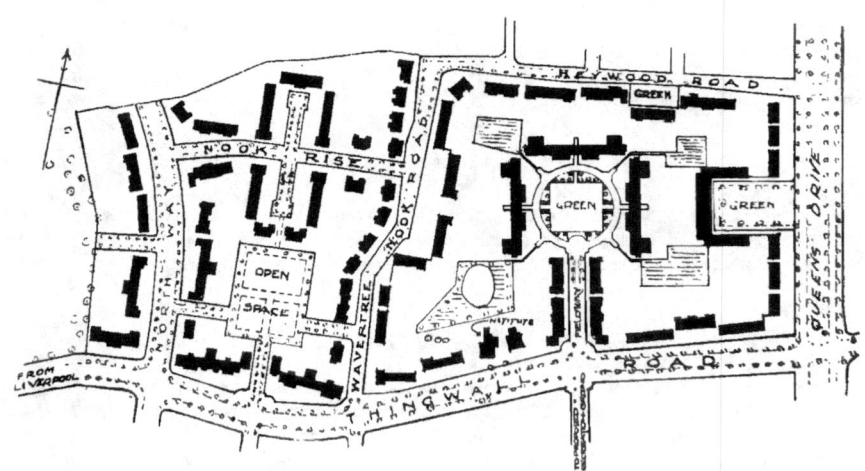

TWENTY-FIVE ACRES OF LIVERPOOL GARDEN SUBURB AS IT IS.

The first part of the Estate, showing eleven houses per acre.

THE HAMPSTEAD TENANTS SOCIETIES.

Hampstead Tenants Ltd. has perhaps had the greatest amount of publicity directed to it owing to the visit of the King and Queen and other members of the Royal Family, as well as statesmen from all parts of the world. The first two Co-partnership Societies formed on the Hampstead Garden Suburb have developed the whole of their area and now an additional 380 acres have been taken for development by kindred societies.

Hampstead Tenants Ltd. started in May, 1907, and its first houses were opened by Sir William Treloar (then Lord Mayor of London) in October of the same year. The buildings comprise 271 houses, a block of shops with flats over, and fifty-four Homes for Old People, the whole population being about 1,200. The rents of the Homes are as low as 3s. 3d. per week, and the houses are let, mostly at weekly rentals, from 6s. upwards.

Second Hampstead Tenants Ltd. has developed its thirty-nine acres (exclusive of roads and common open spaces), having 377 houses, a block of shops with flats, seventy-six work-men's flats, and another block of larger flats, altogether housing about 1,900 people. This Society commenced operations in the autumn of 1909 and, like the Hampstead Tenants Ltd., has the whole of its property fully let. Rents range from 5s. 9d. per week to £130 per annum, exclusive of rates.

HARBORNE TENANTS.

Harborne Tenants, Birmingham, have now developed the whole of their fifty-four acres, which is situated only 2½ miles from the centre of the city. Since September, 1907, 499 houses have been built, with a present population of 1,600. The character of the site presented great difficulties on this estate, and the way they have been overcome proves the soundness of the idea. Nine acres of land have been given up to allotments and playgrounds. The vital statistics show a death-rate of four per thousand, and birth rate of forty, and there has been no infantile mortality from the commencement. With rates at 8s. 2d. in the £, houses with from one-tenth of an acre of garden are let as cheaply as 4s. per week, including rates, and the rentals go to £40 a year without rates. Two and one-eighth miles of roads have been made, and have been planted with trees and have grass margins, while the estate has provided 2¼ miles of gas and water mains. The local authority has so far taken over 694 yards of road.

LIVERPOOL GARDEN SUBURB.

Liverpool Garden Suburb Tenants Ltd. have so far the biggest co-partnership estate, having taken from Lord Salisbury 180 acres of his Childwall estate, of which thirty acres are being proceeded with. Since July, 1910, 260 houses have been built, from ten to twelve to the acre, and it is anticipated that this number will grow to 1,800, housing nearly 7,000 people. One acre in every ten is set aside for open spaces. The rents range from 5s. 7d. a week to £31 a year, the rates, which are extra, being 8s. 5d. in the £. The roads are of varied construction. They are planted with trees and with grass margins, and the widths vary between thirty-six, fifty, sixty and eighty feet. In addition to the buildings a recreation ground containing bowling green and tennis courts has been laid out, and a children's playground has been provided. The estate has appealed strongly to those anxious to see better conditions of housing in Liverpool, and in his annual report the Building Surveyor for the City of Liverpool has testified to the advantages of the Liverpool Garden Suburb and said that " the beneficial effect on the character and well-being of the people who live in such delightful surroundings, in which the provision of sunlight and pure air, and other sanitary necessities of healthful living are so admirably secured, must be incalculable."

OAKWOOD TENANTS LIMITED.

The latest of the Co-partnership Tenant Societies on the Hampstead Garden Suburb is that of the Oakwood Tenants Ltd., registered in January, 1913. This Society has already over 100 houses in hand and will continue the policy of the Hampstead Tenants Ltd. and the Second Hampstead Tenants Ltd., of building houses at rents ranging from 7s. per week to £80 per annum exclusive of rates. The land acquired occupies some of the pleasantest sites on the fringe of the two woods which have recently been included in the Suburb area.

SEVENOAKS TENANTS.

Sevenoaks Tenants Ltd. has its land split up in three different parts of the town ; but on the 6½ acres which it has been able to acquire some excellent housing has been provided. A start was made in 1904 and the area is now developed, eighty houses having been built. About an acre of woodland playground near 34 houses has been set aside, and land is hired close by for small holdings. Rents are from 4s. 9d. to 12s. 6d., rates inclusive. Additional land has been obtained at Kemsing upon which six houses have been erected, and efforts are being made to do something for the neighbouring villages.

STOKE-ON-TRENT TENANTS.

Stoke-on-Trent Tenants Ltd. owns 38 acres, of which ten have been developed. This Potteries Garden Village, close to the newly-formed borough of Stoke-on-Trent, is providing an excellent example of the co-operation of all sections of the community. Since April, 1910, about ninety-five houses have been built at ten to the acre. One-tenth of the estate is set aside for open spaces, and allotments are provided. The rents are from 5s. a week to £60 a year, rates being 10s. The widths of the roads, all of which have trees and grass margins, vary from twenty-four to seventy feet. The estate as already planned has been adopted into and forms part of the proposed town planning scheme prepared for the Borough Council by Mr. A. Burton, A.M.I.C.E., the Borough Surveyor of Stoke-on-Trent, which includes a large area adjoining the estate and extending from Harpfield to Trent Vale. The main avenue through the estate, which is being constructed seventy feet wide between the boundaries and 100 feet between the houses, will be linked up with the main arteries of the scheme.

RURAL CO-PARTNERSHIP.

In order to promote Co-partnership housing in rural districts a Rural Co-partnership Association has been formed with similar objects to the Co-partnership Housing Council. A business department has been formed, known as the Rural Co-partnership Housing Trust Limited, with which are affiliated several societies engaged in building, these being Datchet, Bucks, 30 acres ; Otford (Kent), 160 acres ; Petersfield (Hants), 33 acres ; Somersham (Hunts), 17¼ acres ; Hadleigh (Suffolk), 7½ acres ; Budleigh (Devon), 4 acres. There are other societies in process of formation as far apart as Bridge-of-Weir and St. Mawes, Cornwall.

One of the societies has put up a pair of brick cottages at a total cost of £232, including all extras, pumps, paths, fencing, gates, and fees for plans and supervision. The accommodation consists of a living-room 12 ft. by 12 ft., scullery 8 ft. by 7 ft., pantry 6 ft. by 3 ft., and three bedrooms, one on the ground floor alternately usable as a parlour. The largest bedroom is 12 ft. by 12 ft., and the smallest 10½ ft. by 8½ft. A novel arrangement was made with the contractor, under which his percentage fees, instead of increasing with the amount of the contract, increased according to the extent to which he was legitimately able to lessen the cost.

The Council is following the true method of co-partnership and the tenants take up three £1 shares, paid for by instalments of a penny a week, with a preliminary payment of 1s. a share, and it is interesting to notice that security of tenure is given to the tenant, and this tenancy passes to his family after him so long as the conditions of membership are fulfilled. This meets one of the difficulties often raised in connection with co-partnership tenancy and does away with the fear of a tenant being victimised in consequence of some temporary difference of opinion.

BRIDGE OF WEIR.

At Bridge of Weir, a town of some 2,500 population near Glasgow, having one or two factories, the intention is to afford the industrial employees a much needed opportunity of getting into touch with garden and agricultural environment. The housing conditions of many wage earners in Scotland are of a primitive kind, and it is hoped that once a model society is successfully established in Lanarkshire, the example set will be followed elsewhere.

DATCHET.

This society has now nearly completed its building of twenty-eight cottages, and some of the tenant members are in. All the land is under cultivation. There are some seventy allotment tenants, additionally to the house tenants. The total cost of land and cottages will work out at nearly £8,000. Lord Rothschild is President of the society, which has powers under its rules to form a co-operative trading society and probably at an early date will add this development to the existing organisation.

HADLEIGH.

The society formed for this district has purchased its land and is building its first cottages. The inclusive cost per cottage, counting all extras, will be £140. They will be built in pairs and have not less than a quarter of an acre of land attached. Rents will be 4s. 3d. inclusive of rates, and the accommodation will include five rooms, scullery and pantry. The society has twelve cottages for its first scheme, the estimated cost of land and building being £2,000.

OTFORD.

This society has made much progress and is well forward with its building programme. Various tenant members are already housed and the estate has been subdivided into holdings, and is under varied cultivation. The brook has been utilised for a water supply on the ram system. The services of a Danish agriculturist have been secured to exemplify on the estate Danish expert methods of small farming. Schemes for an agricultural co-operative society and a credit bank are under consideration.

PETERSFIELD.

The society has purchased thirty-three acres of suitable and well situated land, and is about to build for its first scheme eighteen cottages, which are already bespoken by tenant members. Each cottage will have not less than a quarter of an acre of land as garden. The estimated cost of land and cottages totals £6,000. Lord Selborne is President.

ST. MAWES.

The scheme at St. Mawes, Cornwall, is to meet the need of fishermen and others of the labouring classes for better cottages with some land attached. Owing to the increase in the number of visitors to this fishing village there is a danger of the poorer inhabitants having their cottage accommodation curtailed.

SOMERSHAM.

Seventeen and a quarter acres of good fruit land have been purchased, and building begun. The contract price for the cottages in pairs, including all extras, paths, wells, fencing, etc., is £134 5s. Not less than half an acre of land will go with each cottage. All the tenants earn their living by agricultural work. The society will continue building until the demand for cottages and land is met, and if necessary, steps will subsequently be taken to secure further land. The estimated cost of land and houses for the first scheme is £3,300.

THE CO-OPERATIVE MOVEMENT AND HOUSING REFORM

It is somewhat remarkable that the wave of housing enthusiasm that is sweeping throughout the country has to a very large extent left almost entirely untouched a movement supposed to be progressive in character.

The co-operators of the United Kingdom, with their unrivalled and compact organisation, their vast resources of capital, and exceptional facilities for gauging the housing requirements of their 2½ million members, have, comparatively speaking, done very little towards meeting the needs of their members in this respect. The housing that has been undertaken falls very far short of what the Garden City and Garden Suburb movement claims as a standard of working-class housing, and lacks the foresight and comprehensiveness that one might have expected.

The latest statistics published are as follows :—

Co-operative Societies who have building departments	413
Money lent to members for the purchase of their houses	£6,532,000
Number of houses so built	32,000
Money spent by Societies on houses built and afterwards sold to members	£1,232,000
Number of houses so built and sold	5,577
Money spent by Societies on building houses let to members ...	£1,839,000
Number of houses so let	8,530
Total—46,707 houses at a capital cost of	£9,603,000

The Co-operative Garden City Committee, of Halton House, Holborn, E.C., is an organisation of Co-operators formed in 1908 for the purpose of improving the housing conditions in the Co-operative movement, and giving technical advice and assistance in the matter of capital raising, planning of estates, etc., to those societies desirous of setting on foot housing undertakings of an improved character. One of the principal members of the organisation is Mr. Aneurin Williams, Chairman of First Garden City Ltd., while Mr. F. W. Rogers, hon. secretary, has a wide inside knowledge of the movement on both its propagandist and practical sides.

In the first few years of its existence the committee's energies were largely confined to work of a propagandist character, but lately one or two definite garden suburb schemes have been initiated that are a distinct improvement on typical co-operative housing undertakings.

The Co-operative Garden City Committee are hoping that five or six other co-operative societies with whom they are in negotiation, and to whom they have supplied schemes of estate planning, will soon be engaged in the building of co-operative garden suburbs, which will both act as a stimulus to the co-operative movement and help to remove the reproach of bad housing that seems to have fallen upon it.

CHIPPING NORTON.

A scheme of development for a twelve acre Co-operative Housing Scheme at Chipping Norton is also in hand which will involve the erection of houses to let at rentals as low as 4s. 6d. per week inclusive.

WOKING.

The most recent example is an admirable scheme of nine acres that is being evolved in connection with the Woking Co-operative Society Ltd., and known as the Horsell Estate. Only eight houses will be erected to the acre, and these when built will be let to the members of the Woking Society at rentals ranging from 7s. 6d. to 10s. per week.

Mr. H. Clapham Lander, A.R.I.B.A., the hon. advisory architect to the Co-operative Garden City Committee, has been responsible for the plan of development. At the present time one-third of the Estate has been developed, with buildings completed and roads made. The President of the Local Government Board recently inspected the Garden Suburb and expressed himself favourably towards it. When completed, the whole scheme will cost about £20,000, a proportion of the capital required having been obtained from the Co-operative Wholesale Society at 3¾ per cent., and the remainder will either be found by the Woking society itself or obtained from the Public Works Loan Commissioners.

THE GARDEN CITY MOVEMENT ABROAD

GERMANY.

So far as the continent of Europe is concerned, Germany has made by far the most substantial progress, thanks to the devoted enthusiasm of the cousins Kampffmeyer and of Adolf Otto, who between them have borne the chief burden of the organisation.

There are difficulties to contend with in Germany which are unknown in England, and, considering these, the progress which has been made is remarkable, and last year's success was very gratifying. One thing which makes the work more difficult is the fact that many of the banks and institutions which lend money on mortgage for the building of ordinary houses will not do so for cottage property, and it is only provincial labourers' insurance institutes (Landesversicherunganstalten) which will lend any considerable sums, up to 75 or even 90 per cent. of the value of land and houses. These excellent terms are obtained chiefly in the western and southern parts of the country. In some of the eastern parts—Berlin, for example—money cannot be obtained because, the flat system being almost universal, cottage property is not considered sufficient security. The Prussian Government, however, will advance money on second mortgage to co-partnership societies, among the members of which must be a good number of officials.

It will be seen, therefore, that, as was found in England, the progress of the movement depends largely on the question of money, but there is also the difficulty that because of the opposition of many landowners to the improved methods of housing the people, most of the Corporations object to the new plans.   Nevertheless, in both eastern and western Prussia progress is being made, although only one example exists—that of the Garden Suburb Ratshof, near Königsberg. A number of towns in that district have, however, made application for the travelling exhibition of the Association to be shown in their towns, and as a result of this, preliminary work has been started.

Germany suffers perhaps more than England from the unwarranted use of the term Garden City, and there are a number of schemes unconnected with the Association of which it is apparently impossible to obtain particulars. The chief difficulty operating against greater progress is the land difficulty, which often makes it impossible to proceed, and added to this is the road problem. Almost everywhere the municipal authorities insist on wide expensive thoroughfares, even for residential districts, despite the universal testimony of the newer school of Town Planners, who have learnt the lesson of the narrow metalled surfaces adopted at Letchworth and elsewhere. The ideal plans, therefore, have frequently to be abandoned, and for example the requirements at the new Berlin Garden Suburb prevent altogether the erection of labourers' cottages. The Government favours the proposed plan, but can do nothing in face of the corporation, which insists on having the same broad streets as those which carry the traffic of Berlin.

In addition to issuing a monthly magazine (*Gartenstadt*), with a circulation of 5,000 copies, a number of excellent books have been issued, which are among the best literature issued in connection with the whole movement. Each year large parties of municipal representatives, architects, engineers, and educationalists are brought to England to study the movement at first hand.

The biggest and the most important of the German schemes is that of Hellerau, near Dresden, in which, in the past four years, nearly eight million marks have been invested. The second big estate is the Garden Suburb, Stockfeld, near Strassburg, a very interesting scheme, which provides also small homes for poorer families. This scheme was made possible by the assistance of the Corporation of Strassburg, which has sold land to the Association cheaply and has guaranteed a sum of two million marks for building purposes. Further, there is the Garden Suburb of Margaretenhöhe, near Essen, which may be described as the German Bournville, being conducted under a trust similar to that instituted by Mr. George Cadbury. It was founded by the widow of the late Mr. Krupp.

Both Stockfeld and Margaretenhöhe are being built by only one architect each, while in Hellerau a number of the best architects in Germany have been assigned certain quarters to plan and build, in order to secure the best result.

A very interesting community on pure co-partnership lines is the Garden Suburb of Wandsbeck, near Hamburg, where an estate has been bought from the Corporation and where already, in the third year, more than 200 houses are ready. The Corporation of Altona, who in the past year has sent its Lord Mayor and a number of officials to England to study the Garden City question, will lease land to the same association for an estate for 30,000 people, and in order to fulfil its programme for the whole district of Hamburg and its environs, the various co-partnership associations have united into one large organisation. For this work the Prussian Government has advanced a good deal of money.

After some very hard work, the Garden Suburb of Karlsruhe has begun building operations, and forty houses are inhabited. The same applies to Nürnberg. The Mannheim Garden Suburb is being built on municipal land let on lease. The Garden Suburb of Marienbrunn, which is also leasehold on municipal land, will have the first portion completed early in the Spring, when the Leipsig International Building Exhibition will be opened, of which for the summer it will form a part.

During the past year large and small co-partnership associations have been founded, and estates have been secured at Aachen, Bonn, Gera, Hamm, Dortmund, Aschersleben, Liegnitz, Frankfurt-a-O., Halle, Skopau, Thorn, Allenstein, Danzig, etc.

In the case of Munich, where much was hoped for, it has been found impossible to proceed, although a well-wisher gave the Corporation of Munich a sum of 200,000 marks to start. It has been found, however, that the questions of incorporation, traffic, sewerage, etc., were too difficult to surmount.

A much more important scheme is the Garden Suburb near Berlin, founded by the members of the German Association Committee. 150 acres have been secured. Already in Berlin-Britz a Co-partnership Society is building cottages and small tenements on very expensive ground, where usually the huge German tenements would have been built, and have thereby given a very useful example to the community.

Hüttenau, near Essen, is of much interest, inasmuch as the two communes of Blankenstein and Welper have given a guarantee to the Insurance Institute for the whole of the capital required, and this is endorsed by the Rural District of Hüttenau. In this case both the money for the purchase of the land and for the building of the houses has been advanced.

The following tabulates the estates in Germany :—

Altona (Hamburg).—Provision for 30,000 people. Municipal assistance.

Gross-Berlin.—Society three years old. 150 acres secured, and thirty-five houses have been built with the assistance of the Government, which has advanced the necessary money on second mortgage for this first stage. A second sum of M.200,000 has been secured for the second batch of houses.

Güstrow, in Mecklenburg.—Existing town of 18,000 inhabitants, largely agricultural. Started by a manufacturer (Herr Dettmann) on 3 hectars. To be extended and handed over to the community.

Hellerau, near Dresden.—140 hectars purchased in 1908. 200 dwellings completed, as well as factories and institutions.

Hopfengarten (Magdeburg).—65 morgen. After one year 400 inhabitants. System of purchase of freehold by inhabitants, with power of repurchase by society in a number of eventualities.

Hüttenau.—Founded 1909 in consequence of the growth of one large firm. 400 morgen. Supported officially by the two communes concerned, who have agreed to the carrying out of one plan. 166 houses built in 1910-11.

Karlsruhe.—12 hectars. Building begun July, 1911. Forty houses ready.

Marienbrunn (Leipsig).—Land leased by municipality. The first section constitutes part of the Leipsig International Building Exhibition and includes some interesting garden architecture.

Margaretenhöhe.—Started in 1906. An endowment of 1,000,000 marks by Mrs. Krupp. 50 hectars for 15,000 to 18,000 inhabitants. Gardens 70 to 300 qm.

Mannheim.—Society founded 1910. Town granted 40 hectars. First groups now ready.

München-Perlach.—A project to lay out 80-85 hectars for 12,000 to 13,000 inhabitants.

Neumünster.—100 hectars. To provide houses for well-paid artisans, with four or five rooms at 5,000 to 6,000 marks, with good gardens, the average size of plots being 700 qm. By the spring of 1912, 75 houses completed.

Nürnberg.—In 1908 chose 65 hectars of State land. In 1910 began with 4 hectars, having obtained a municipal loan of 20,000 marks ; 74 houses now ready.

Ratshof bei Königsberg.—Society built tenement houses from 1895 to 1906. In 1906 bought 200,000 qm. for single houses, of which 51 have been built.

Stockfeld (Strassburg).—Scheme initiated by Municipality, which handed over 123,930 qm. to a society to develop. 170 detached, 280 semi-detached houses. Many arrangements for self-government and life of community.

Wandsbeck (Hamburg).—Started in 1910. 4½ hectars. 150 houses completed by summer, 1912.

Associations have been formed for co-operative housing at Rostock, Tilsit, Plaüen, Chemnitz, Bonn, Aachen (Aix la Chapelle), Dortmund, Halle, and Erfurt. At Gera a society with a limited dividend is building houses on Garden City lines.

A word should be added as to the most excellent housing work which has been accomplished by the firm of Krupp's for the benefit of their workpeople. Some forty thousand people, all the families of their employees, are housed in the fourteen village settlements provided for them at rents much below those charged in the district and in surroundings superior to anything provided in the German Empire. One of the most attractive of

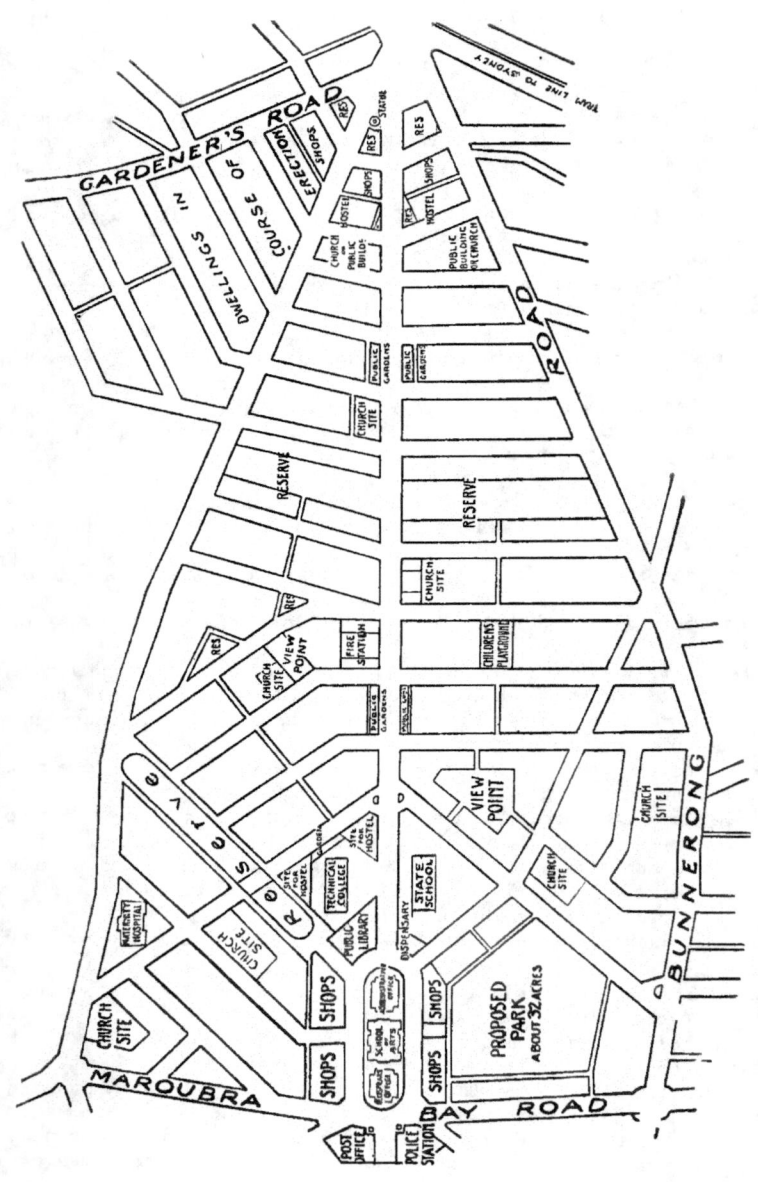

Lay out of the New "Garden Suburb," Daceyville, in Sydney, New South Wales, which is now being developed by the State Housing Board. It will be observed that not only is the lay out open to serious objection, both on the practical and aesthetic sides, but the roads are planned absurdly wide—all 66 feet, in accordance with legislative requirements—and practically the only feature common to Garden Suburbs is that the area is pre-planned!

the villages is Altenhof, designed, as its name suggests, for the old people, pensioners of the firm. There are 600 inhabitants, who live rent free and receive a pension of from £3 to £4 a month. Merely to enumerate the advantages provided for the firm in the way of social and educational advancement, as well as of material benefit, such as savings' banks —where a generous bonus is added to the employees savings—and co-operative societies would occupy more than the whole space devoted to this section. As a social and housing scheme there is nothing in the world in any way comparable to the work at Essen.

Close by, but unconnected with the Krupp colonies, is Margaretenhöhe, the "last word" in artistic development and building. The work of an architect who is an artist to his finger tips, promoted by a generous lady who believes in restoring the love of real beauty to a class long divorced therefrom, it is one of those things which no description will do adequate justice to. It should be seen by everybody who wishes to appreciate the possibilities of development which is unstinted in reasonable resources and uncramped by architectural prejudices.

FRANCE.

The French Garden City Association was the first founded outside England, dating from the year 1904, after a visit to Letchworth and the attendance of some meetings by Monsieur Benoit-Levy, who has from that time been the secretary and treasurer of the Association and responsible for the greater part of its activities. Among the founders were Senateur M. d'Estournelles de Constant and Professor Charles Gide, names of world-wide repute.

Although, so far, the Association has not been able to proceed with the work of building on Garden City or Garden Suburb lines, they have influenced the creation of a model mining village of Dourges and have taken an active part in the scheme for the acquisition and preservation of the fortifications. This project, which was drawn up by Monsieur Dausset, the general reporter for the Budget of Paris, has been accepted by the Paris Municipality, and now awaits the sanction of Parliament. The fortifications, which are of an average of 125 metres wide and are 33 kilometres long, are the property of the State, who have offered them to the City for one hundred million francs. The Association is now organising a campaign in support of purchase.

Largely through Monsieur Levy groups of workers for the Garden City movement have been formed in a number of European cities and assistance has been given in the forming of Associations in other places. In Luxemburg, Italy, Roumania, Bohemia, and Turkey, groups have been formed, and it was only the occurrence of the war which prevented the Turkish Association under Niazi Assim Bey being formed. The objects and methods of these various groups, etc., however, are not on all fours with those elsewhere, and it is not easy to determine to what extent the real garden city ideal is advocated.

An enormous amount of literature has been issued, the Association working not only for Garden City ideas properly, but assisting with many other social schemes such as Industrial Welfare, which in England are the affairs of individual associations. Monsieur Levy has written a large number of well illustrated books dealing with the Garden City movement, and recently has, in three excellent volumes, dealt with the whole movement with detailed information of the principal schemes in England.

AUSTRIA.

Dr. Max Ermers (XIX Springsiedelgasse 21, Vienna), well known as a writer upon artistic and architectural subjects, is organising a Garden City Association for Austria and has already gathered round him a number of enthusiastic adherents, many of whom accompanied him last year on a trip of inspection to England. The difficulties to contend with in the country are numerous, but it is hoped that before long active propaganda will be proceeding throughout the empire.

BELGIUM.

M. Charles Didier, who has for many years carried on the propagandist work in Belgium, acting as secretary to the Belgian Garden City Association, sends the following particulars regarding the movement in his country :—

"The number of people in this country who are interested in Mr. Howard's wonderful conception is infinitely more numerous than one might believe, and that grand social movement, 'The Garden Cities,' is followed intimately and with the greatest sympathy by all those who concern themselves with the great political questions of our day and, above all, of industrial countries like our own.

"Unfortunately, I have to make a confession of our lack of success in Belgium. On several occasions my friends and I have tried to realise that dream of a Garden City, of a simple Garden Village even, and every time we have failed, but I hasten to add that that failure does not apply in any way to the idea, for everybody, without distinction of party, finds it superb.

"In this country we find ourselves face to face with conditions as to land tenure, etc., which really in a measure make the Garden City unrealisable in Belgium. But Mr. Howard's idea has none the less a very sensible echo in Belgium, and it has strengthened very much the sense of the absolute necessity of remedying in a definite manner the overcrowding of the towns."

HOLLAND.

Mr. D. de Clercq, of Bloemendaal, who has succeeded Mr. Bruyn as the secretary of the Dutch Garden City Association, has during the past few years given a large number of lectures on the Garden City movement and has collected a good deal of literature and a number of lantern slides. He has arranged to translate this book into his native language. He reports :—

"I very much regret to say I cannot give very good news of the movement in Holland. We have tried several times to start a society for actual work, but although we have got a few people together, we have not been able to go further. It seems that Holland is not yet ready for the movement, the reason being perhaps that we have here only a few big towns, and hundreds of small towns and thousands of villages, with cheap houses and gardens, while the rich people have their country seats quite close to the great towns. I have lectured a good many times on the subject and a number of people have taken interest in the movement. We intend to continue our lecturing and our propaganda, and by the translation of your books into Dutch, we shall be able to instruct people in the great idea for which you have been responsible."

ITALY.

Several efforts at reformed housing have been made in Italy, but these have been made chiefly upon the old lines of tenement dwellings. Near Milan a trial has been made with cottages, and this is said to be upon Garden City lines. Repeated application, however, has failed to elicit any information as to whether the scheme is on genuine lines, or is another of the pseudo-garden cities which can be found in practically every European country.

Some German Experiments : 1, Nuremberg ; 2, Margaretenhöhe ; 3, Hellerau.

1903-1913.

Nothing could illustrate more vividly the change which the Garden City movement has effected in regard to the question of housing than the above views. The first is a picture of Woodfield Avenue on the estate of the Ealing Tenants Ltd., the first houses erected by the society before it was influenced by the Garden City movement. The second is Fowler's Walk, on the newer portion of the estate.

HUNGARY.

Dr. Elemer Kovats, of VI. Andrassy-ut 60, Budapest, has been responsible for the initiation of a Garden City Association for Hungary, which has decided to issue a periodical dealing with the subject. The organisation has only just come into being, but it has considerable promises of support.

POLAND.

The Polish Garden City Association was founded by Dr. Dobrzynski in 1909, at Warsaw, and in connection with this a further society was formed, called " The Society for Permanent Dwellings," with the object of preventing speculative building. This body has obtained the sanction and approval of the Emperor of Russia. In 1910 an important exhibition was held with the idea of securing support for the movement, and at the end of that year an estate of 210 acres on the Vistula was acquired for the establishment of a Garden Suburb. The estate was planned by Mr. Bernouilli, an active member of the German Garden City Association, whose work as an architect has won much praise, and architects are now at work on the houses, which will be both detached and in blocks. The cheapest house, which will be a two-storey one with four rooms and a garden, will cost 2,600 roubles (about £270). The Association has issued a number of publications and given many lectures. A translation has been made of Mr. Ebenezer Howard's book *Garden Cities of To-morrow*, and this has had a good circulation in the Russian language. In 1912 a further society was formed called " New Warsaw," with the object of permanently continuing the propaganda. The office of the Association is at Faubourg de Cracovie, 66, Warsaw.

The garden suburb of New Warsaw has been approved by the authorities, and a new electric tram service has been provided to connect the new suburb with the old town. A great deal of good is expected to come from the establishment of this garden suburb, which is primarily due to the devoted labours of Dr. Dobrzynski, one of the founders of the new International Association, and a sincere exponent of Garden City principles. The necessity for the work may be judged from the fact that with a population of 900,000 people, Warsaw possesses only 7,000 houses—one to each 130 people.

RUSSIA.

With M. Dimitri von Protopopoff and M. Alex Bloch as correspondents, a group of workers has been got together in St. Petersburg, and it is hoped that practical steps will shortly be taken for the establishment of a Garden Suburb.

SPAIN.

A Spanish Garden Cities Association was founded in 1912 by Mr. C. Montoliu, who now acts as Secretary. It bears the name Sociedad Civica La Cuidad Jardin, and has a similar scope to those of other countries. In addition to giving many lectures, the Association has taken part in preliminary steps towards the establishment of a Garden Suburb at Barcelona, and has issued many publications, Mr. Montoliu having been very active in disseminating information. The registered office of the society is in Barcelona, Calle de Urgel, 187.

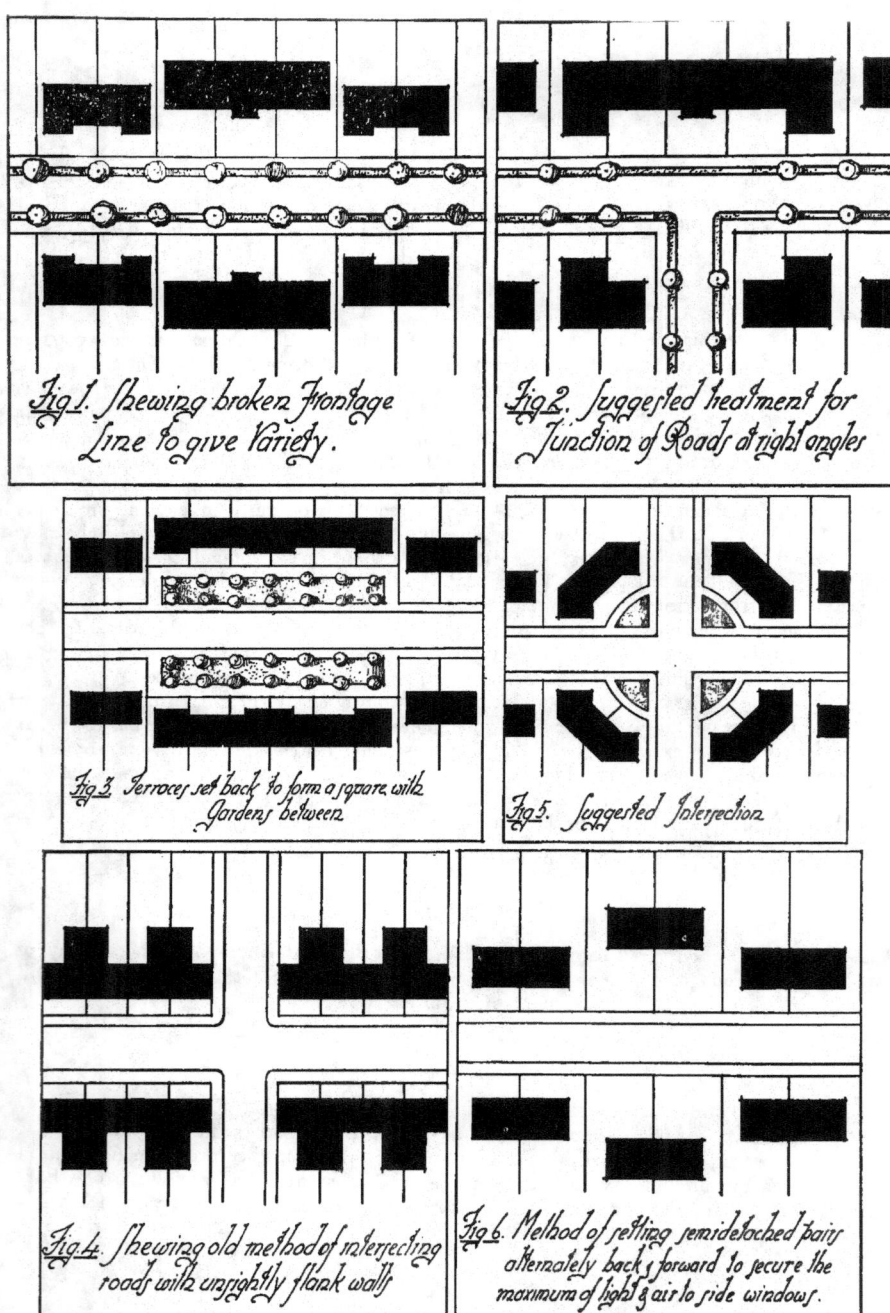

Fig. 1. Shewing broken Frontage Line to give Variety.

Fig. 2. Suggested treatment for Junction of Roads at right angles

Fig. 3. Terraces set back to form a square with Gardens between

Fig. 5. Suggested Intersection

Fig. 4. Shewing old method of intersecting roads with unsightly flank walls

Fig. 6. Method of setting semidetached pairs alternately back & forward to secure the maximum of light & air to side windows.

These illustrations, prepared by Mr. H. Clapham Lander, demonstrate some of the principles of Town Planning in Garden Cities and Suburbs.

THE INTERNATIONAL GARDEN CITIES AND TOWN PLANNING ASSOCIATION

The International Garden Cities and Town Planning Association was formed on August 22nd, 1913, in order to strengthen the international movement for the extension of the knowledge of the principles laid down by Mr. Ebenezer Howard in his book *Garden Cities of To-morrow.*

President—Mr. EBENEZER HOWARD.

Chairman—Mr. G. MONTAGU HARRIS.

Hon. Secretary—Mr. EWART G. CULPIN.

Offices—3, Gray's Inn Place, Gray's Inn, London, W.C.

Committee—The Committee consists of representatives of affiliated Societies in the following countries :—

Great Britain	Norway	Hungary
France	Holland	The United States
Germany	Belgium	Canada
Austria	Spain	Australia
Russia	Italy	New Zealand
Poland	Roumania	Japan

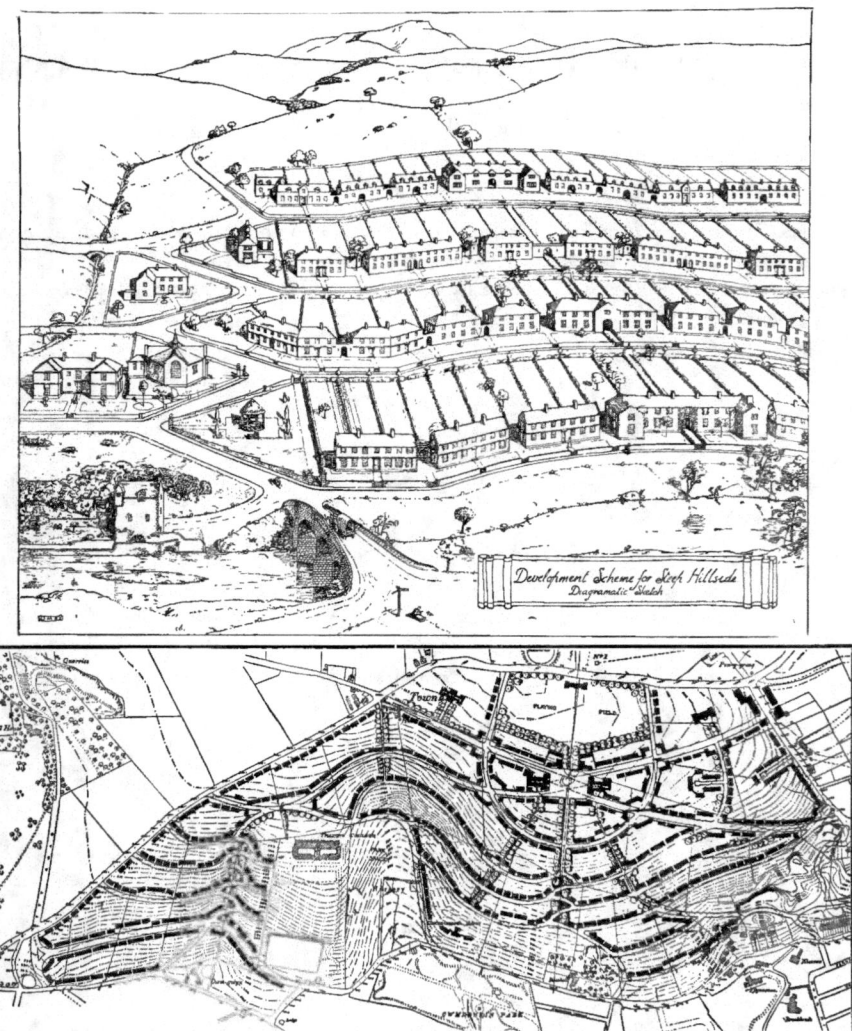

A REMARKABLE EXAMPLE OF TOWN PLANNING ON A HILLSIDE.
This estate has been laid out on Town Planning lines by Mr. Raymond Unwin, F.R.I.B.A., and Mr. George Bell, A.M.I.C.E., Borough Surveyor of Swansea. The contours are shown at 5 feet distances. The top plan shows how this would work out in actual development.

THE GARDEN CITIES AND TOWN PLANNING ASSOCIATION

President—THE HON. MR. JUSTICE NEVILLE.

Chairman of Council—CECIL HARMSWORTH, M.P.

Chairman of Executive—GEORGE L. PEPLER, F.S.I.

Hon. Treasurer—FRANCIS E. FREMANTLE, F.R.C S.

Hon. Solicitor—HERBERT WARREN.

Hon. Auditors—W. B. PEAT & CO.

COUNCIL.

*E. R. ABBOTT.
THOMAS ADAMS.
PROFESSOR S. D. ADSHEAD (Liverpool).
H. COLIN ALLEN.
†J. H. BARLOW (Bournville).
MRS. S. A. BARNETT.
*J. STANWELL BIRKETT, M.A.
†EDGAR L. CHAPPELL (Cardiff).
RT. HON. LORD CHARNWOOD (Lichfield).
*†HAROLD CRASKE (First Garden City Ltd.).
*†C. M. CRICKMER, F.R.I.B.A.
†WM. DALZIEL (Glasgow).
DAVID DAVIES, M P.
GEORGE M. LL. DAVIES.
DR. WALTER E. LL. DAVIES.
*W. R. DAVIDGE, F.S.I.
*WARWICK H. DRAPER, M.A.
†A. E. FRANKLIN (Social Welfare Association.)
*FRANCIS E. FREMANTLE, F.R.C.S.
*†BERNARD GIBSON (M.P.G. Assn.)
G. P. GOOCH, M.A.
H. D. HARBEN.
*G. MONTAGU HARRIS, M.A.
*EBENEZER HOWARD.
PROFESSOR H. S. JEVONS.

PHILIP T. KENWAY.
*H. CLAPHAM LANDER, A.R.I.B.A.
†H. J. LEANING (London Society).
BRYCE LEICESTER (Liverpool).
†F. LITCHFIELD (Co-partnership Tenants Ltd.).
T. ALWYN LLOYD.
*R. O. MOON, M.D.
REV. C. MOOR, D.D.
J. S. NETTLEFOLD (Birmingham).
MISS E. M. NICKOLL.
*G. L. PEPLER, F.S.I.
ASSHETON POWNALL.
MISS J. RECKITT.
†GEORGE ROSE (Liverpool).
†G. W. ROUSHAM (Hampstead Garden Suburb Trust Ltd.).
F. ROWNTREE, F.R.I.B.A.
†J. F. ROXBURGH (Edinburgh).
A. S. SOUTAR, L.R.I.B.A.
RAYMOND UNWIN, F.R.I.B.A.
*F. CHILDE WARREN.
*HERBERT WARREN.
ANEURIN WILLIAMS, M.A.
*GLYNNE WILLIAMS.
J. FISCHER WILLIAMS.
R. A. YERBURGH, M.P.

* Executive Committee.   *† Representative Member.*

Secretary and Offices—

EWART G. CULPIN.

3, Gray's Inn Place, London, W.C.

BRANCH AND AFFILIATED ASSOCIATIONS.

Bolton—W. M. FARRINGTON, Borough Hall, Bolton.

East London—J. THREADKELL, 17, Clarissa Road, Chadwell Heath.

Edinburgh—GEO. DEAS COWAN, 31, Charlotte Square, Edinburgh.

Glasgow—J. M. BIGGAR, 180, West George Street, Glasgow.

Letchworth—R. W. TABOR, Letchworth.

Liverpool—F. GRAY WALLIS, 16, Cook Street, Liverpool.

Newcastle-on-Tyne—F. W. SHIELDS, Newcastle.

South Wales—EDGAR L. CHAPPELL, 3, Pembroke Terrace, Cardiff.

Foreign Correspondents.

Austria—DR. MAX ERMERS, Glatzgasse 5, Vienna, XIX.

Belgium—CHARLES DIDIER, rue Armand Campenhout, Brussels.

Canada (Halifax)—R. M. HATTIE, 27, Coburg Road, Halifax.

Canada (Montreal)—W. H. ATHERTON, PH.D., City Improvement League, 62, Beaver Hall Hill.

Canada (Regina)—R. E. A. LUCK, Secretary, City Planning Association.

France—G. BENOIT-LEVY, 11, rue Malebranche, Paris.

Germany—ADOLF OTTO, Schlachtensee, bei Berlin.

Holland—D. DE CLERQ, Bloomendaal.

Hungary—DR. ELEMER KOVATS, vi, Andrassy-ut 60, Budapest.

Japan—MR. MASAO ITO, Osaka Higher Commercial School, Japan.

Norway—T. SCHLYTTER, Christiania.

Poland—DR. DOBRZYNSKI, Faubourg de Cracovie 79, Warsaw.

Roumania—EMIL GUIRGEA, Strade Lueger, 10, Bucharest.

Russia—DIMITRI VON PROTOPOPOFF, 14, Kabinetskaja, St. Petersburg.

Spain—M. MONTOLIU, Musee Social, Calle de Urgel, num. 187, Barcelona.

United States—DR. E. E. PRATT, 192, Claremont Avenue, New York City.

The Garden Cities and Town Planning Association.

CONSTITUTION AND RULES.

I.—Title.

The name of the Association shall be " THE GARDEN CITIES AND TOWN PLANNING ASSOCIATION."

II.—Objects.

The objects of the Association are :—

(a) To promote Town Planning.

(b) To advise on, draw up schemes for, and promote Garden Cities, Garden Suburbs, and Garden Villages.

(c) Housing and the improvement of its sanitation.

(d) The collection and dissemination of information as to the above.

(e) The education of public opinion in these matters.

(f) The influencing and promotion of legislation.

(g) The improvement of local bye-laws.

III.—Membership.

The Association shall consist of a Central Society and Branches. The Central Society shall comprise : (a) Honorary Fellows ; (b) Members ; and (c) Delegate Members.

Honorary Fellows shall be elected at General Meetings on the nomination of the Council, for services rendered to the ideals of the Association.

Members shall pay a minimum subscription of 5s. per annum.

Delegate Members shall be the representatives of Societies approved by the Council, in respect of whose membership such Society shall pay a minimum subscription of 10s. 6d., and such members shall be Members of the Council, and shall otherwise have the same powers and rights as ordinary members. Each such Society may send one Delegate Member.

IV.—Management.

1. COUNCIL.

(a) Composition.—The management of the Association shall be vested in a Council of not more than fifty members, of whom thirty shall be elected annually. The remaining twenty Members shall include ex-officio Members, representatives of Branches and Delegate Members, and the Council may at any time fill up any vacancies by co-option.

(b) Election.—Fourteen days before the Annual General Meeting the Secretary shall send by post to each Member a form inviting nominations for the Council and Officials of the Association. The names so nominated shall be submitted to the Annual General

73

Meeting for its selection. The Council shall elect its own Chairman at its first meeting after the Annual General Meeting.

(c) *Meetings.*—The Council shall meet quarterly. Special meetings may be called by the Secretary with the authority of the Chairman or on the application of not less than ten Members of the Council. Seven shall form a quorum.

2. EXECUTIVE.

(a) *Appointment.*—At its first meeting after the Annual General Meeting the Council shall elect from its members an Executive Committee of not more than fifteen members.

(b) *Powers.*—Subject to the authority of the Council, the Executive Committee shall exercise all powers necessary for the management of the Association, and shall appoint a Finance Committee, and may at its discretion appoint sub-committees, composed either of its own members or other members of the Association, with or without other persons, for the advancement of the purposes enumerated in Rule II., and for any other purposes such as Prospecting and Planning, Legal and Parliamentary, Housing and Public Health, Architecture and Building, Agriculture (including Small Holdings and Allotments), Engineering (Roads, etc.), General Purposes and Finance, Women's Organisation Committee, Joint Committees with First Garden City Limited, and similar companies, Foreign Tours, Lectures, and otherwise as it may think fit. Casual vacancies shall be filled by co-option.

3. SPECIAL COMMITTEES.

The Council shall have power to appoint such other Committees as it thinks fit, and to co-opt on such Committees persons who are not Members of the Association.

V.—Officials.

The Association shall have a President, Vice-Presidents and Treasurer, who shall be elected at the Annual General Meeting, or in default thereof, by the Council. The Chairman of the Executive shall be appointed by the Executive. The Executive shall be empowered to appoint a Secretary and such other officials as may be necessary.

The President and the Honorary Treasurer shall be *ex-officio* Members both of the Council and of the Executive. The Chairman of the Council and Executive and the Honorary Treasurer shall be *ex-officio* Members of all Committees.

VI.—Branches.

Whenever the Executive thinks fit, and upon the application of residents in any locality, the Association shall recognise a Branch for such locality, if not within the area of any Society already constituted, which should be affiliated to the Association upon the following terms :—

1. That the Branch will subscribe to the principles of the Association as set out in the official handbook, and will undertake to conform to those principles.

2. That each Branch shall pay an annual sum to the Association amounting to 20 per cent. of the gross subscriptions, this to entitle the Branch to the following benefits :—

(a) A copy of the journal free for each subscriber of 5s., and other literature at trade prices. Journals to be supplied in bulk.

(b) Services of a Lecturer, if required, on the payment of out-of-pocket expenses, and the help and advice of the central organisation.

(c) Each Branch shall be entitled to send one representative to act on the Council of the Association, and one Delegate to the General Meeting for any number of members up to 50, two up to 100, and one for each additional 100.

3. The Central Association is not to be debarred from receiving subscriptions direct from any person in the district of the Branch, whether a Member of the Branch or not, and such person subscribing direct to the funds of the Association shall have direct representation, according to General Rules 3 and 4.

4. That the Association will not accept any financial responsibility in respect of any Branch.

5. That GARDEN CITIES AND TOWN PLANNING shall be recognised by each Branch as its official organ, to which local information should be supplied.

6. No Branch shall be recognised as such until it has received the Certificate of Membership from the Council.

7. A copy of the audited accounts, and list of local subscriptions for the previous twelve months shall be sent to the Central Office not later than January 14th each year.

VII.—Accounts.

No accounts shall be paid unless and until they have been authorised or passed by the Finance Committee.

VIII.—Annual General Meeting.

An Annual General Meeting shall be held at such date, hour and place as the Executive may appoint, after giving not less than fourteen days' notice by post to each Member.

IX.—Special General Meeting.

The Council may, at any time, and shall, upon a written requisition sent to the Secretary by Twenty Members, call a Special General Meeting of the Members, giving not less than seven days' notice by post, stating the purposes]of the Meeting. At such Meeting fifteen shall form a quorum.

X.—Annual Report.

At the Annual General Meeting a report by the Council on the transactions of the Association and an audited statement of accounts shall be presented for adoption. The report and accounts shall apply to the year ending December 31st.

XI.—Alteration of Rules.

These Rules may be altered at the Annual General Meeting or at any Special General Meeting convened in due form for that purpose. At least fourteen days' notice of any proposed alteration must be given to the Secretary, and such proposed alterations must be set out in the notice convening the meeting.

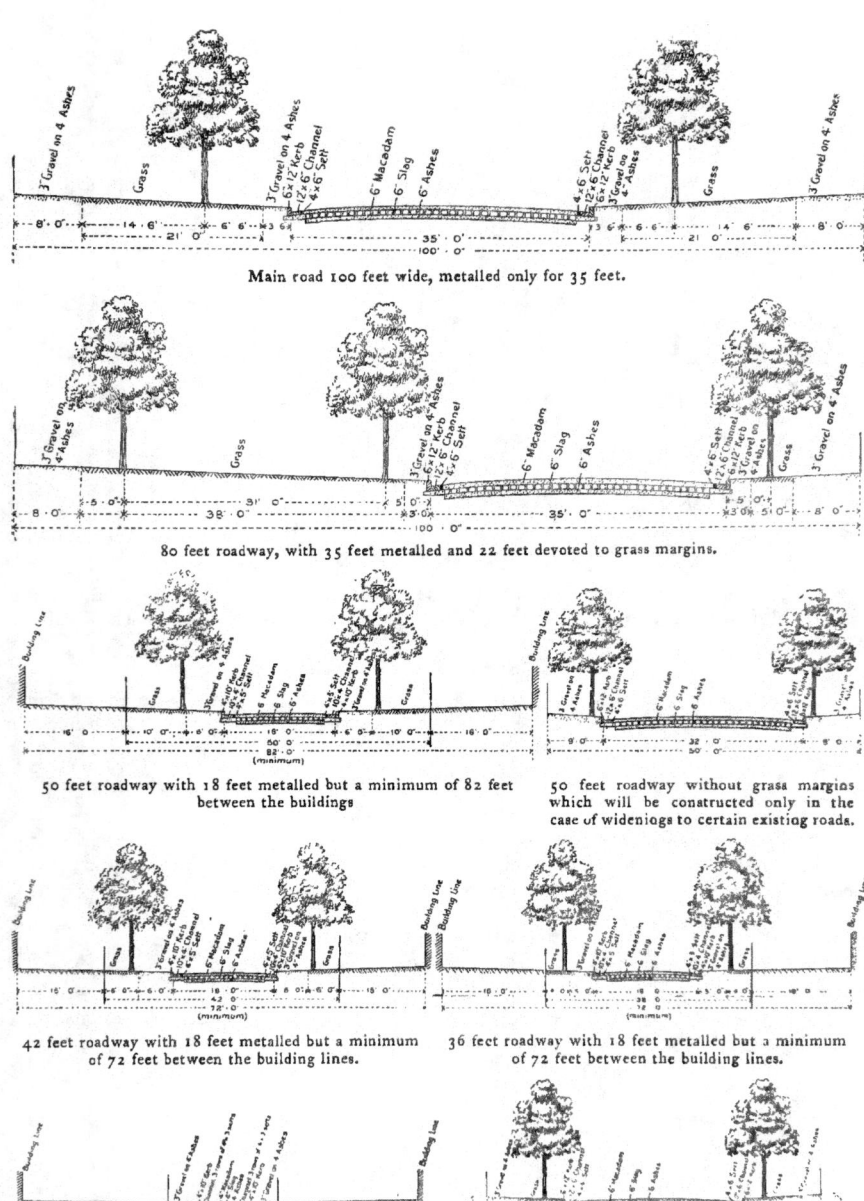

Main road 100 feet wide, metalled only for 35 feet.

80 feet roadway, with 35 feet metalled and 22 feet devoted to grass margins.

50 feet roadway with 18 feet metalled but a minimum of 82 feet between the buildings

50 feet roadway without grass margins which will be constructed only in the case of widenings to certain existing roads.

42 feet roadway with 18 feet metalled but a minimum of 72 feet between the building lines.

36 feet roadway with 18 feet metalled but a minimum of 72 feet between the building lines.

20 feet roadway with 8 feet metalled but a minimum of 72 feet between the building lines.

60 feet roadway on an embankment showing 2 ft. 6 ins. allowance on either side beyond the boundary lines.

TYPES OF ROADS ADOPTED FOR THE HARBORNE-QUINTON TOWN PLANNING SCHEME.

The Town Planning Act.

It has been announced that schemes have been prepared by local authorities and submitted to the Local Government Board for approval in the following cases:—

Birmingham Corporation.—The Quinton, Harborne and Edgbaston Town Planning Schemes relating to an area of about 2,320 acres in the city. (Now finally approved.)

Birmingham Corporation.—The East Birmingham Town Planning Scheme relating to an area of about 1,442 acres in Aston, in the eastern part of the city.

Rochdale Corporation.—The Rochdale Town Planning Scheme (Marland) relating to an area of about 43 acres in the borough.

Ruislip-Northwood Urban District Council.—An area of about 5,906 acres in the urban district and in the parish of Rickmansworth (rural) in the rural district of Watford.

In the following additional cases the Board are stated to have given authority for the preparation of schemes by local authorities:—

Bournemouth Corporation.—An area of about 202 acres in the Boscombe East and Southbourne Wards of the borough.

Bournemouth Corporation.—An area of about 223 acres in the Southbourne Ward of the borough.

Blackburn Corporation.—An area of about 887 acres in the borough and in the rural district of Blackburn.

Carshalton Urban District Council.

Cheadle and Gatley Urban District Council.—471 acres.

Chesterfield Corporation.—A small area of about 64 acres in the borough.

Ellesmere Port and Whitby Urban District Council.—An area of about 3,539 acres in the urban district and in the rural district of Chester.

Finchley Urban District Council.—An area of about 1,044 acres in the urban district.

Halifax Corporation.—An area of about 877 acres in the Ovenden and Illingworth Wards of the borough.

Halifax Corporation.—An area of about 749 acres in the Warley, Copley, Illingworth, Ovenden and Pellon Wards of the borough.

Hanwell Urban District Council.—An area of about 198 acres in the urban district.

Leeds Corporation.—Six acres.

Liverpool Corporation.—An area of about 88 acres near the eastern boundary of the city.

Liverpool Corporation.—An area of about 1,220 acres in the city and in the urban district of Allerton.

Luton Corporation.—An area of about 4,266 acres in the borough and in the rural district of Luton.

Much Woolton Urban District Council.—An area of about 993 acres in the urban districts of Much Woolton, Little Woolton, and Allerton, and in the rural district of Whiston.

Newcastle-upon-Tyne Corporation.—A small area of about 53 acres in the city and in the urban district of Gosforth.

North Bromsgrove Urban District Council.—An area of about 554 acres in the urban district.

Oldbury Urban District Council.—An area of about 1,763 acres in the Warley portion of the urban district.

Prestwich Urban District Council.—1,900 acres.

Richmond (Surrey) Corporation.

Scarborough Corporation.—A small area of about 40 acres in the borough.

Sheffield Corporation.—An area of about 488 acres at Greystones and Bannerdale in the city.

Sheffield Corporation.—An area of about 97 acres at Sandygate in the city.

Sheffield Corporation.—An area of about 624 acres at Firth Park, Wincobank and Shire Green in the city.

Southport Corporation.—An area of about 2,848 acres in the borough.

Stockport Corporation.

Stoke on-Trent Corporation.—An area of about 83 acres in the borough.

Sutton Coldfield Corporation.—An area of about 6,378 acres in the borough.

Twickenham Urban District Council.—An area of about 1,860 acres in the urban districts of Twickenham, Heston and Isleworth.

Walthamstow Urban District Council.—An area of about 1,530 acres in the urban district.

Warrington Corporation.—An area of about 1,456 acres in the borough.

Wirral Rural District Council.—An area of about 5,742 acres, consisting of the parishes of Great Sutton, Little Sutton, Childer Thornton, Hooton, and Eastham.

Wirral Rural District Council.—An area of about 3,431 acres, consisting of the parishes of Heswell-cum-Oldfield, Gayton, Pensby, and Barston.

Wirral Rural District Council.—Two areas of 4,526 acres and 3,013 acres.

Applications for authority to prepare schemes have been made by:—

Hazel Grove and Bramhall Urban District Council.

Hunslet Rural District Council.

Halifax No. 3 Scheme.

Ham Urban District Council.

Newton-in-Makerfield Urban District Council.

Sheffield Corporation No. 6 Scheme.

Bridlington Corporation.

Doncaster Rural District Council.—Over 5,000 acres.

In the following case the Local Government Board have given authority to a Corporation to adopt with modifications a scheme proposed by owners of land:—

Middleton Corporation.—An area of about 300 acres in the borough.

In one case, that of an application from the Corporation of Rochester relating to a very small area, the Board were unable to give the authority asked for as the land was for the most part held by the Secretary of State for War, and being Crown lands could not be included in a town planning scheme.

Preliminary notices have been given under the regulations by the following local authorities with a view to application being made to the Board for authority to prepare schemes, viz.:—

Acton Urban District Council.
Barnet Valley Urban District Council.
Barrow-in-Furness Corporation.
Bristol Corporation.
Chesterfield Corporation.
Doncaster Rural District Council (No. 2).
Finchley Urban District Council.
Hull Corporation.
Middlesbrough Corporation.
Nelson Corporation.
Shrewsbury Corporation.
Willesden Urban District Council.

It is probable that notices have been given in many other cases.

Other cases in which proposals for schemes are under consideration.—In 31 other cases the Local Government Board reported in November last that information in their possession would seem to indicate that the consideration of the matter by the local authority has reached a stage practically equivalent to a decision to proceed with a scheme. Since then other authorities have been reported in the press as taking preliminary steps. The following is a list of authorities reported to have proposals for schemes under consideration:—

Allerton Urban District Council.
Barnes Urban District Council.
Bath Corporation.
Beckenham Urban District Council.
Bentley Urban District Council.
Birmingham Corporation.—Three areas.
Bolton-upon-Dearne Urban District Council.
Bredbury and Romiley Urban District Council
Caerphilly Urban District Council.
Cheadle and Gatley Urban District Council.
Cleckheaton Urban District Council.
Colne Corporation.
Coventry Corporation.
Croydon Corporation.
Croydon Rural District Council.
Denton Urban District Council.
Doncaster Corporation.
Greenford Urban District Council.
Grimsby Rural District Council.
Hailsham Rural District Council.
Hendon Urban District Council.
Heston Isleworth Urban District Council.
Huddersfield Corporation.

Kingston-upon-Hull Corporation.
Lincoln Corporation.
Little Bebington Urban District Council.
Little Woolton Urban District Council.
Maldens (The) and Coombe Urban District Council.
Manchester Corporation.
Mansfield Corporation.
Merton Urban District Council.
Mexborough Urban District Council.
Middleton Corporation.
Newcastle-upon-Tyne Corporation.
Otley Urban District Council.
Portsmouth Corporation.
Ripon Corporation.
Rotherham Rural District Council.
Scarborough Corporation.
Sedgley Urban District Council.
Sheffield Corporation.
Shoreham-by-Sea Urban District Council.
Smethwick Corporation.
Southall-Norwood Urban District Council.
Southgate Urban District Council.
Stockport Corporation.
Stoke-on-Trent Corporation.
Surbiton Urban District Council.
Sutton (Surrey) Urban District Council.
Tynemouth Corporation.
Wallasey Corporation.
Wallsend Corporation.
Warrington Rural District Council.
Yeovil Corporation.
York Corporation.

In numerous other cases the question of preparing a scheme is under consideration without any definite steps being decided upon, and in this connection the
following cases may be mentioned:—

Birkenhead Corporation.
Bispham with Norbreck Urban District Council.
Bognor Urban District Council.
Bolton Corporation.
Brixham Urban District Council.
Buckhurst Hill Urban District Council.
Burnley Corporation.
Bushey Urban District Council.
Christchurch Corporation.

Darfield Urban District Council.
Eastry Rural District Council.
Enfield Urban District Council.
Epsom Rural District Council.
Epsom Urban District Council.
Esher and the Dittons Urban District Council.
Exeter Corporation.
Gosport and Alverstoke Urban District Council.
Hale Urban District Council.
Harrogate Corporation.
Herne Bay Urban District Council.
Hessle Urban District Council.
Irlam Urban District Council.
Leek Urban District Council.
Little Crosby Urban District Council.
Margate Corporation.
Newport (Mon.) Corporation.
Northwich Urban District Council.
Ormesby Urban District Council.
Ossett Corporation.
Rotherham Corporation.
Sidmouth Urban District Council.
Stanley Urban District Council.
Stourbridge Urban District Council.
Stratton and Bude Urban District Council.
Stretford Urban District Council.
Thornton Urban District Council.
Thurnscoe Urban District Council.
Wath-upon-Dearne Urban District Council.
Wakefield Corporation.
Wembley Urban District Council.
Wetherby Rural District Council.
Weymouth Corporation.
Wrexham Corporation.

It will be seen that the names of several local authorities occur in more than one of the foregoing lists, and in these cases the entries refer to different schemes.

There can be little doubt that many other authorities are contemplating town planning schemes. The City of Sheffield alone has ten schemes under consideration.

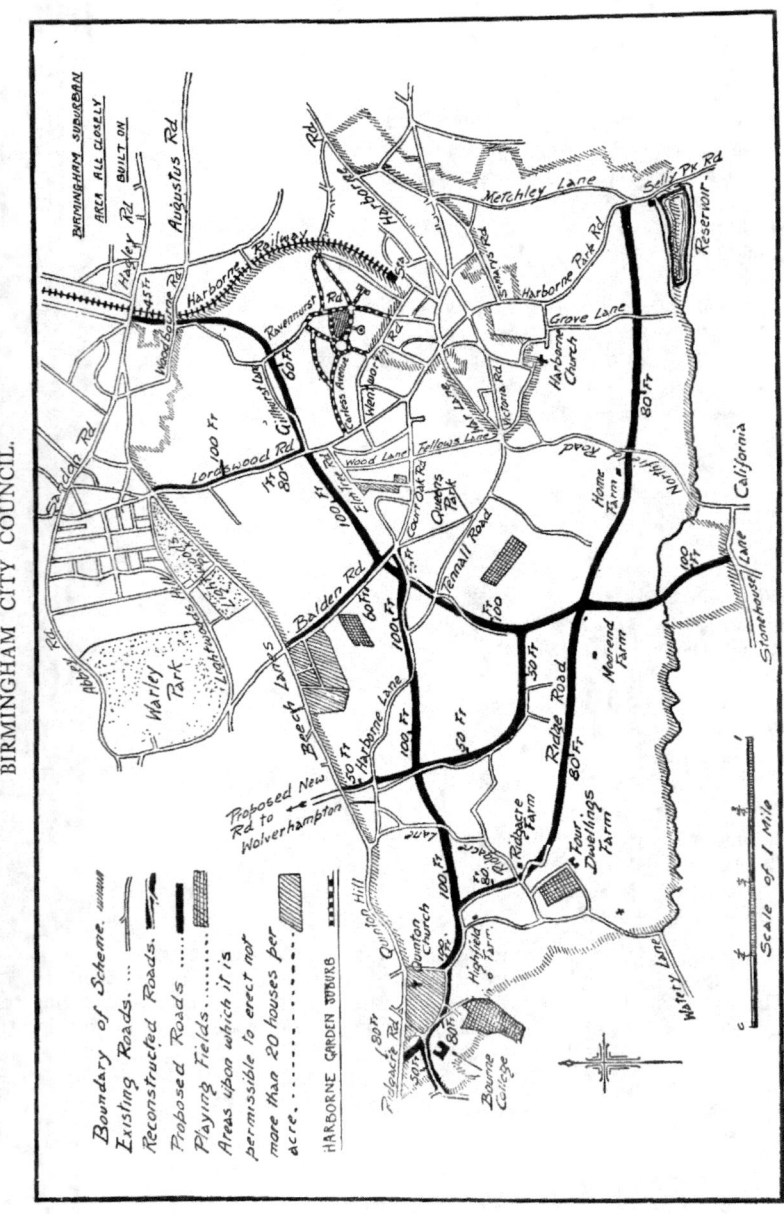

PLAN OF THE HARBORNE-QUINTON TOWN PLANNING SCHEME AS ADOPTED BY THE BIRMINGHAM CITY COUNCIL.

This is the first scheme adopted under the Town Planning Act of 1909. The Harborne Garden Suburb is included in the area.

The Pioneer Garden Suburb
(EALING TENANTS LTD.).

GARDEN CITY PRESS LIMITED, PRINTERS, LETCHWORTH.